VINTAGE YOUNGMAN:

* Frank Sinatra once told me that money isn't everything, and I said, "Quite right, but you can't be rich without it."

* My wife said it wasn't a fit night out for man or beast, so we both stayed home.

* I went to see a Beverly Hills analyst. He said, "Lie down and tell me everything." I did. And now he's doing my act.

* I really wanted to be in show business. Then I met Milton Berle. Even that didn't make me change my mind.

* As soon as things got good, my wife said she wanted a mink. I got her a mink. Then she wanted a sable. I got her a sable. Then she wanted a chinchilla. I bought her a chinchilla. The house was full of animals.

The King of the One-Liners proves that his own life is his best act yet!

TAKE MY WIFE... PLEASE!

The Autobiography of
Henny Youngman

as told to Carroll Carroll

A BERKLEY MEDALLION BOOK
published by
BERKLEY PUBLISHING CORPORATION

To

Yonkel Jungman

Contents

Illustrations will be found
following page 201.

TAKE MY WIFE...PLEASE!

People who keep talking to you on airplanes make you want to sit next to the window . . . on the outside!

1

Air Pollution

SO many people have asked me what made me decide to write this book, I thought I'd better explain.

But first let me ask, what made you decide to read it?

Take your time and get a good excuse.

While you're thinking, I'll answer the question.

I was on a plane going to Los Angeles. The man next to me was finishing his second drink. He turned, gave me a look, stuck out his hand, and said, "I'm Marvin Reiter."

I said, "Hello. I'm Henny Youngman."

He said, "Who's he?"

It made me wonder. It's a good question. Who *is* he? It made me think. And it made me think, oddly enough, about the kids today.

I've got children, but they're grown-up. I have friends with kids. They don't know where they are. They ran away from home to find out *who* they are. When I was a kid, all you had to do was ask the mailman. The kids say they're trying to get themselves together.

I couldn't do that. If I got myself together there'd be four or five different Henny Youngmans and that's bad. I work alone.

1

I'm sitting there asking myself: Why do I have to be upset because some half-drunk heckler says something that makes me think? Thinking is very upsetting. It tells you things you'd rather not know.

Suddenly my seatmate turns to me again and says, "You going to Los Angeles?"

I said, "Yes. Unless I decide to jump out over Des Moines."

"So am I," he said.

"In that case," I said, "you're lucky you're on this plane. A lot of them don't go there."

He said, "I don't want to go there."

I said, "Then *you* jump out over Des Moines."

"It's my kid," he said. "I'm going to look for him."

"What's he doing in Los Angeles?"

"I don't know. He ran away to find himself."

"How does he know to look in Los Angeles?"

"He liked the weather there."

It reminded me of the guy who lost his wallet one night in the middle of the block and went to look for it on the corner because the light was better.

So it goes. Life copies jokes. Jokes reflect life.

People make fun of me because my monologues don't follow any definite line.

Neither does life. Think of the jokes it's played on you.

Some people object to the fact that my jokes are just jokes. That's all I mean them to be. Am I a philosopher?

They say I ought to get some satire into my material. George Kaufman once said, "Satire is something that closes on Saturday."

Other people say there's no message in my gags.

When Louis B. Mayer was running MGM at the height of its success, he only wanted "entertainment" pictures. He used to tell his producers, "If you've got a message, call Western Union." Try to do that today.

They say I don't deal with social problems. Who am I? Amy Vanderbilt?

All I know is that life is just a series of mixed-up, disconnected one-liners interrupted by birthdays.

For example. You're born. You're Jewish. But you're too young to understand. So they have the Bris. *Then* you understand.

At thirteen, while you're still too young to use your handkerchief, they tell you that you're a man and hold a Bar Mitzvah.

Even Bar Mitzvahs have changed. You used to have to have a boy. Now all you need is a caterer.

Your next important step, if you're Jewish, is to get married. Then you have kids and as soon as they find out they're Jewish, they become Quakers.

A Philadelphia rabbi told me that so many of his congregation had converted that most of his best Jews are Friends.

Mr. Reiter turns to me and says, as if he's expressing a great new thought, "Kids today."

"What'll you do if you find your kid?" I asked.

"Depends," he said. "First I'll see if I like what he's doing."

"Then what?"

"Well, if I like it, I'll wire his mother I won't be back."

Here I am, sitting on a thirty-million-dollar airplane, minding my own business, and I have to run into a switch on my own joke, "Take my wife . . . please!"

"Don't you drink?" he asked me.

"No. Why?"

"I thought maybe you'd order your two drinks and give them to me."

"Be my guest," I said.

"Thanks. Who *are* you?"

"Henny Youngman."

"Who's he?"

As he drank my two drinks and as I looked down on Des Moines, I continued to think about myself, to wonder how I got into the crazy life I lead in which everybody knows me but nobody knows who I am. Not even me.

So I decided to write this autobiography and find out.

Let this be a warning. Never ask a man why he writes his autobiography.

And never fly to Los Angeles.

*"Money isn't everything," Sinatra said to me.
"You're right," I told him, "but you can't be
rich without it."*

2

It Happened One Morning

IT was about a quarter of eleven on a nasty rainy New
York morning. I was walking through Times Square on the way to
see my agent. It was in the early forties.

There was a long line of young girls in short skirts, saddle shoes,
and bobby sox standing in front of the Paramount Theater waiting
for the doors to open. Why? Frank Sinatra, their "Frankie Boy,"
was making a personal appearance.

"Personal appearance." When talking pictures and radio nailed
the lid on vaudeville, people began to get hungry for the sight of real
flesh-and-blood human beings, even Sinatra, who didn't look as if
he had much of either flesh or blood. So the picture palaces began
booking film stars for what they called "personal appearances" to
distinguish them from impersonal appearances, which were called
"talkies."

I'd played on the same bill for a couple of weeks with Frank when
he was with Tommy Dorsey's band. We got to be friends because I
used to stick up for him in his fights with Tommy. So I figured I'd go

backstage and say hello and wish him luck, not that he needed any. At that point, if he had any more luck, it would have killed him.

When I walked into his dressing room, I was surprised to find him on the couch. I was surprised because he was *alone* on the couch. I said, "Hello. What's wrong?"

He didn't look up. He just moaned, "Henny, you gotta help me."

"Sure," I said. He was lying down. "I'll help you." And I lay down next to him.

"It's my choppers," he groaned. "I don't think the guy I just came from is really a dentist."

"What happened?"

"He drilled so deep I think he's a proctologist."

"You just had a doctor who was tying to make both ends meet."

"Very funny. But I can't go on till this pain wears off. Will you do the first show for me?"

"I'm no Bing Crosby."

"If you *were*, do you think I'd let you sub for me? Just go out there and tell a few jokes. The kids'll love you. What's one show to them? They all brought enough bubble gum to stay all day, anyway."

"Okay. But if one of those bobby-soxers pops her bubble on a punch line, I'm gonna climb right over Jesse Crawford and spank her."

Let me interrupt this yarn for a few words about Jesse Crawford. He and his wife, Mrs. Jesse Crawford, played duets on what the Paramount Theater called their million-dollar matched consoles. They figured if they were going to have a man and a woman working on one organ, they'd better get a couple that was married . . . to each other.

Now back to Frankie and his aching teeth.

The kids are all expecting him. His music is playing. And I walk on. For a second there was a stunned silence. Then the house began to buzz like a beehive. And *I* got stung!

I let them buzz till they were all buzzed out. Then I told them that Frankie was resting. I said he'd been having some dental work and the dentist had drilled a small hole in his tonsils.

The audience groaned. I didn't mind. I knew they'd groan at anything I said. So I told them, "If you're good kids and let Frank rest a little, while I play the violin, you can all stay for the second show." Then the manager groaned.

But they finally quieted down, and I went into my routine. When

I came to the part where I started to play the fiddle, there was a big yell and wild applause. It wasn't for my fiddle playing. Frank had walked on. The noise nearly blew me off the stage. He let them holler and scream, and when they finally quieted down, he said to me, "Play something on that. If it's anything you know, I'll recognize it and try to follow you."

I started to play "All or Nothing at All," and that did it.

During the bedlam that followed I just walked off and continued on my way to see my agent.

Frank told me, the next time I saw him, that when he came on for the second show, the kids all began hollering, "Where's Henny?" Instead of going to see my agent, *he* should had come to see me.

That was something like thirty years ago. I wonder if Frankie remembers? If he does, I hope I remembered it right.

*A writer mailed me a synopsis of a comedy
routine. I mailed him a synopsis of a check.*

3

A Short Life

I see most of the movies at previews in screening rooms.
It's great. When you come in, they hand you a piece of paper that
tells you what the movie is all about. While you're waiting for them
to run it, you read the paper. Then, as soon as the lights go out, you
can go to sleep.

I figure if this is a good idea for motion-picture companies, it's a
good idea for me. So this synopsis is for people (and movie producers) who haven't time to read this book.

It's a matter of record that I was born. It's all written down in a
book. But the book's in London. This is because I was born in the
London Jewish Hospital. The year was 1906.

Whenever I tell people I was born in London, they think I'm
kidding. They think it's a joke. Believe me, being born is no joke. I
wouldn't want to go through *that* again!

My mother wasn't too happy with the results either. She had a lot
of pain. I was glad I was able to be with her when she was suffering
so.

I suffered a little, too. We had a nearsighted doctor. When he
held me up and slapped me, he gave me a nosebleed.

In reply to drunks who holler at me in nightclubs, and Jersey drivers who yell when I make a U turn on the Long Island Expressway, my mother and father *were* married.

When I was about six months old, they brought me to America. The immigration laws weren't so tough then. Anyway, the United States is where I grew up. Some say it never could have happened in England. I would have made it just as big there. Why not? Larry Olivier did. Alec Guinness did. Ralph Richardson did. It might even have been easier in London. Think about it. Sir Henny.

One of the problems I had breaking into show business was that I wasn't brought up on the Lower East Side of Manhattan. I was brought up on the Lower East Side of Brooklyn. So it was years before I learned to speak English.

Schoolbooks say that Brooklynites speak English. It's not true. Have you ever listened to Buddy Hackett?

Naturally the first thing every kid in Brooklyn wants to do is to go to New York and learn the language. That's why they built the Brooklyn Bridge. And that's why I used it.

So now, if you want to know more about me, go ahead and read the book. If you don't, take it back. The guy in the bookstore will be glad to sell it to someone else. Or you can cut out the middleman and sell it yourself. You'll only have one small problem. To whom?

Of course, you could always spill a little tuna fish salad and coffee on one page and tell everyone it's a dirty book.

If you decide to read it, it must mean that you've enjoyed my life so far. That makes two of us.

I took Milton Berle and his mother to a farm where a friend of mine raises thoroughbred pigs. I was just casting Berles before swine.

4

Uncle Miltie

A fella brags to his wife that he's a self-made man. She says, "Why didn't you finish the job?"

It's an old joke. But it's true. Truth is what makes old jokes live. I've helped a little, too.

But that old joke says a truth you'd better keep in mind when you're writing about your life.

No man is self-made. Everybody needs help. No matter who you are, look back over your life. You'll remember someone who did or said something that marked a turning point in your career. Who'd have ever heard of Adam if it hadn't been for Eve?

My father wanted me to be a printer. I tried to be one in the worst way. You'll read about that. I even went to school to learn to be a printer. But all the time I really wanted to be in show business. Then I met Milton Berle. Even that didn't make me change my mind.

I guess Berle really helped me more than anybody else. Well, he didn't really help me. But he didn't hinder me . . . too much.

What he did for me was to give me encouragement. Whenever he was playing in New York, for instance, he'd encourage me to try to get a booking in Traverse City, Michigan. You know that must be true. How else would a guy from Bay Ridge, Brooklyn, ever hear of Traverse City?

But Berle has mellowed a lot since we first met. He says he still thinks I'll make it in show business. I hope he's right. To show he meant what he said, a few weeks ago he asked me to do a two-man show with him.

It's interesting how he had the show routined. When I finished a bit, I'd go off. So that while Berle was working, I was changing my clothes. Then, when I was working, Berle was changing his clothes . . . behind me.

The truth is, Berle's a great artist. Not only is he very funny, but he can also play serious dramatic roles. The trouble is, it's hard to tell which he's doing. I saw him in a Broadway show where he actually made men cry . . . the playwright, the producer, and the director. It was called *The Good-bye People*. He played the part of a seventy-year-old man. What a makeup job! You wouldn't believe they could make Berle look that young. At the end of the first act the play made its title come true, *Good-bye People*.

But let me tell you how Berle helped me. He's a real pioneer, you know. (He doesn't do bad with pie in the *face* either.) He was the biggest thing in television when there was no one else in it. People who can still remember when he was called Uncle Miltie now have families of their own—one for each divorce.

But he really was Mr. Big in TV and before that in vaudeville, even though he got a late start. A lot of comedians like Eddie Cantor and George Jessel and Georgie Price started in vaudeville as children in Gus Edwards' kid act. It was called "School Days." Milton didn't. He couldn't pass the entrance exam.

But I was saying how Milton always encouraged me. When he had his big TV show, he could have had me on it with him regularly if he wanted to. When I suggested this, he said, "I wouldn't do that to you, Henny. I want you always to be free to get your own show any time you can."

I just laughed. What was a TV show to me? I had my own radio show before Berle knew which end of the mike to giggle into.

Well, it wasn't exactly my *own* show. They called it the *Kate Smith Show*. That's because in those days she was bigger than me. She still is. Besides, it *was* her own show. But I used my own jokes. Of course, when Berle got his TV show, he also used my own jokes. I recently thought I'd get even with him. I stole one of his gags. It turned out to be mine.

Right here I must admit that Milton also had his own radio show at one time. What a cast! He was co-starred with that great, late British actor Charles Laughton. The music was by Bob Crosby and his Dixieland Bobcats. It worked out fine because Berle and Laughton fought like bobcats.

The final blowoff came when Berle told Laughton that he would not do the show on Yom Kippur. Laughton screamed at him, "I command you to be here, Mr. Christian." Naturally this got Berle's Irish up.

What a hothead! People say this was because he wasn't born until his mother came to the Berling point. People say that. I never would. Maybe because of his temper and the fact that he realized the danger of uncontrolled anger, he took a great interest in law and order.

He did a lot to help train policemen. When he was in New York, he'd go down to the Police Academy on East Twentieth Street regularly. That's where they train the young recruits in all sorts of crime prevention techniques, like how to fool muggers and mashers and prostitutes. Nobody was better at teaching the rookie cops how to dress and walk like girls.

In case you're a friend of Berle's and think he may be hurt by these insults, I just want you to know that they're not insults. They're true. Besides, insults are part of Berle's business. Berle has used insults so long in his routines as savers that he has fallen in love with them. He gets such laughs with the insults he uses to squelch hecklers that when an audience likes him and doesn't heckle him, he insults them anyway.

For years, to protect his act and be sure of always getting at least one laugh, he carried his mother around with him wherever he went. At nightclubs she always sat at ringside. In theaters she was always in the third row on the aisle . . . laughing and applauding. When it got so that she couldn't take it any longer, he got a new mother.

As I write this, with love, it seems only yesterday that I saw him. As a matter of fact, it was only yesterday. We were having lunch at the Friars' Club. "What are you going to say about me in your book?" he asked.

"Just what you'd say about me."

He said, "You wouldn't dare!"

I'll have more to say about Milton Berle and me and the *Kate Smith Show* and how I happened to get Abbott and Costello to take my job when I left it . . . when I can remember how it happened.

My mother-in-law went to get her face lifted. They couldn't do it. They had to lower her body.

5

In-Law and Order

ONE day I was at my desk sorting out some stuff for this book when my friend Joe Franklin called up to say he had two tickets for a fight at the Garden if I wanted to pick them up at his office. I don't care too much for fights. I like my kind of jokes better. But anything's better than working, even walking. So I pulled on my pants and started down Broadway to WOR.

Hum a few bars of "Intermezzo" to denote a lapse of time.

When I walked into Joe's office, he jumped up and greeted me in that wild way he has . . . sometimes I wonder if it's possible to be as glad to see anybody as he seems to be to see everybody. I imagine him waking up in the morning and jumping out of bed and saying to himself, "Wow! I'm alive!"

On second thought that's not bad, when you consider the alternative.

Joe and I talked for a little while about old times. As far as Joe is concerned, there are no *new* times. For him, if it's not nostalgia, it doesn't exist. As I'm about to walk out he says, "Oh, wait a minute, Henny. Here's something I've been meaning to mail to you. I pulled it off the UPI teletype in the newsroom the other day."

Here's the dispatch he handed me:

STUDIO CITY, CALIF. (UPI)—ROCK BAND LEADER KIM "PIED PIPER" RICHMOND DIDN'T COMPOSE THE MOVEMENT THAT ENDED HIS LATEST NUMBER, BUT IT LEFT HIM—AS AN OLDER GENERATION OF MUSICIANS MIGHT SAY—FRACTURED, MAN, FRACTURED.

RICHMOND, 24, MARRIED ONLY FOUR MONTHS, WROTE A SONG IN HONOR OF HIS MOTHER-IN-LAW AND PLANNED TO SERENADE HER WITH IT AS AN EARLY MOTHER'S DAY SURPRISE.

HE GATHERED HIS 10-MAN GROUP IN THE GARAGE OF HER HOME ON TUESDAY. WHEN HIS WIFE, BARBARA, SIGNALED HIM THAT HER MOTHER'S CAR WAS TURNING INTO THE DRIVEWAY, RICHMOND STRUCK UP THE BAND.

MRS. BATES DROVE INTO THE GARAGE AND WAS SO ASTONISHED AT FINDING IT FILLED WITH MUSICIANS IN FULL TOOT THAT SHE DROVE INTO RICHMOND AND BROKE HIS LEG, A SPOKESMAN FOR THE BAND LEADER REPORTED.

"HOW CAN I TOP THIS NEXT YEAR?" RICHMOND ASKED HIS WIFE, A DANCER WITH THE CAROL BURNETT SHOW.

MRS. BATES SAID SHE FELT BADLY THAT HER MOTHER'S DAY SURPRISE HAD ENDED AS IT DID.

"THIS IS AN AWFUL WAY TO START A RELATIONSHIP," SHE LAMENTED. "IT SOUNDS LIKE SOME HENNY YOUNGMAN MOTHER-IN-LAW JOKE."

Joe saved the item for me because he thought it was flattering. I guess it is. So what? I usually throw things like that away when people give them to me. But it would have been rude to throw it away right there in front of Joe, so I stuck it in my pocket.

When I found it again, I decided to include it in this book. I thought it might help me to make a point. *Then* I threw it away.

The point is, someone else probably would have pasted it in his scrapbook. But I can't understand why. Why should he want to put something about *me* in *his* book? I know I wouldn't paste an item about someone else in *my* book.

The main reason for this is I don't have a scrapbook. I don't believe in them. The only thing they prove is how old you're getting. I find *that* out every morning when I wake up.

The first thing I do is turn to the obituary page. If I don't find my name, I get up and dress for breakfast. The day I *do* find my name, I'll put on my tuxedo and lie down.

When a little girl says, "I'm a girl and you're a boy" and the boy says, "I'll go ask my mother," that's research. When he says, "Let's see," that's sex!

6

Research and Destroy

AS far as I'm concerned, a scrapbook is just a bunch of clippings that you look at later and wonder why you saved them. It's a book of scraps that shows you how many times you've been clipped.

When I was young, I subscribed to one of those services that send you clippings everytime your name appears somewhere . . . anywhere. They charge you by the hundred clippings. Get a mention in a syndicated column and you get a hundred identical clippings. Well, they're not exactly identical. They have this advantage. Read them and you'll find out how your name is misspelled in every large city. Then when you play that town you know whether they spell your name Henny, Henry, Heiny, Haney, or Hunny. One spot spelled it Honey. I canceled that date.

But getting back to scrapbooks, when you finally find what you're looking for, what you find is that it doesn't say what you thought it did. And if you ever really find exactly what you want, it's taken you so long to find it you've forgotten why you wanted it.

Why am I telling you all this? It's because I want to give a guy credit for an idea and I can't remember his name. How's that for human nature? I can remember the name of every son of a bitch who was lousy to me. Here's a guy who gave me a good idea, and I've forgotten his.

He was on a newspaper somewhere in the Middle West. That's all I remember. Sorry, pal. Let me hear from you, and if the book goes into a second printing, I'll put your name in. Or better still, I'll send you a ball-point pen, and you can put your name in it yourself. That way you'll get it spelled right.

By this time you've probably figured out that I couldn't find the clipping. I couldn't even find the scrapbook. It disappeared with all the others when we sold the house in Brooklyn. So here I am, trying to *write* the story of my life and I can't *find* the story of my life. But that's the story of my life.

And if you think I'm not going to tell you what this Midwest newspaper guy wrote, you're wrong. The interview said that the first thing you have to do when you leave Henny Youngman and walk out into the normal world is straighten your glasses. He said, "After talking to Henny for a little while, you get the feeling that everything is either upside-down, back-wards, or both."

But the big idea he gave me was when he wrote that I was "the kind of man whose life is measured by a thirteen-inch ruler." For a long time I thought he meant my feet were too big.

Then the whole thing was explained to me by my grandson, Larry Kelly, when he got Bar Mitzvahed. *Kelly* Bar Mitzvahed? And how about me having a grandson named Kelly?

Larry's father was Jack Kelly, one of the finest accompanists in show business. He used to play for Sammy Davis, Sinatra, Vic Damone, all the great ones. He was wonderful. And the most wonderful thing about Jack was not that his name was Kelly, but that it *wasn't*, and how he got it.

His name was Jacob Schneiderman. Of course, everybody but his parents called him Jack. But there was a Jewish cop in his neighborhood who liked him and called him by the Yiddish pet name, Jackele (pronounced Jack-ell-la). It means little Jack.

From Jackele to Jack Kelly was an easy jump. And from Jack Kelly and my daughter, Marilyn, I got my grandson, Larry. Larry doesn't play the piano. He just plays on my sympathy. It's good practice for him.

Larry's taking a lot of English courses at school and, in time, will learn to speak the language fluently. English! The language of the land where his grandfather was born.

What Larry said he thought the man meant is that I carry everything just a little further than most people do. "People are always trying to prove a point," Larry went on, "by coming up with some dumb statistic like, every four seconds a woman gives birth to a baby. You knock the whole thing down and make it look ridiculous by saying, 'Our job is to find that woman and stop her!' That's what makes you funny."

I asked, "My face isn't enough?"

"There you go. When you were on the radio with Kate Smith, people couldn't see your face and they laughed at your jokes."

"You weren't even born yet when I was on the radio. How do you know I made people laugh?"

"You told me."

"Better you should hear things like that from your grandfather than from the kids in the street," I told him.

"The jokes you did then must have been different from the one-liners you tell now."

"Don't be silly. They were the same jokes."

"But they were new then."

"No. They were old *then!*"

"Did you ever try telling new jokes?"

"There's no such thing. Jokes keep repeating themselves generation after generation."

"No kidding," he said, "isn't it lucky comedians can only repeat themselves for one generation?"

If I'd made a crack like that to my grandfather, I'd have got a crack right back . . . in the skull.

"Larry," I said, "in ancient Rome a senator came down the steps of the Forum and said to a slave, 'Call me a chariot.' 'Very well, sir,' said the slave, 'you're a chariot.' "

"Many years later Sherlock Holmes came out of Thirty Baker Street and said to an urchin, 'Boy, call me a four-wheeler.' 'Righto, guv'nor,' said the lad, 'you're a four-wheeler.' "

The other day I walked out of the Algonquin and said to the doorman, "Call me a taxi." He just looked at me and said, "I don't have time to stand here trading old jokes with you, Henny. Besides, it would be quicker and cheaper to walk."

Everybody at the Hotel Algonquin gets into the act. I guess it's been that way ever since the days of the famous Algonquin Round Table, where New York's literary wits used to sit around at lunch and cut up everybody, including each other.

When I asked Ben Bodne, who runs the Algonquin, if I could sit at that famous Round Table, he said he'd take care of me personally. Then he said something to the maître d', who led me to a table.

In a few minutes Bodne came over to ask if everything was all right. "Fine," I said. "But how come the Round Table is square?"

"I've heard your jokes," he said, "and decided to give you a table to match."

But I like Bodne. He has answers. When I complained about how high the prices were in his dining room, he walked me out to the sidewalk and explained, "See that Rolls-Royce? How do you expect me to operate that car on Automat prices?"

He was right. So I bought him a drink . . . of gasoline.

But as I was saying, almost all jokes come down through the years sometimes switched, sometimes unchanged.

Flip Wilson has a great story that I remember hearing on an old 78 record back in the days when "Cohen on the Telephone" was a hot recording. It's about a man who comes home from a trip and asks his gardener if anything happened while he was away.

The gardener tells him his dog died. The record used to be called "No News or What Killed the Dog." I'll just give it to you fast. The dog died from eating burned horsemeat. He got the burned horsemeat when the barn burned down. The barn caught fire when the sparks blew over from the house. The house burned down when the candles around the coffin set fire to the draperies. There were candles around the coffin because the man's mother-in-law died of a heart attack. The heart attack was caused because the man's wife ran away with the chauffeur.

Another version of the same story is about a guy who had a pet cat. He loved the cat, and the cat followed him around like a dog. One day the man had to make a business trip, and he left the cat with his brother. Every day he called his brother to find out how his cat was. The fourth day he called up, and the brother said, "The cat died."

The guy was terribly upset and scolded his brother for being so blunt. "You shouldn't have come right out, like that," he said. "You should have started by telling me that the cat got out on the roof, that he fell and broke his leg, or something, so that I could get used to it gradually." So the brother apologized and said he was sorry.

His brother said, "You're forgiven. Now tell me, how's Mother?"

His brother answered, "She was on the roof. . . ."

Another way to tell the same story deals with a bunch of guys who played poker together every night. One Friday night one of the players, Sam Jones, fell dead of a heart attack. The other players had to notify Mrs. Jones but they didn't know how to break the news to her.

Finally, one of them picked up the phone and dialed. When Mrs. Jones answered, the guy said, "Mrs. Jones, I just called to tell you that Sam lost eight hundred dollars playing poker."

Mrs. Jones screamed into the phone, "Eight hundred dollars? He should drop dead!"

"He did!" said the man, and hung up.

A different finish for the same story is: the man calls up and says, "Is this the widow Jones?"

She says, "I'm not a widow."

He says, "Wait till you see what the undertaker's bringing home to you."

Or you can make it a golf story about the foursome that played every Sunday.

One of the men comes home more tired than usual and all disheveled. His wife asks, "What happened to you? You look awful!"

He says, "You remember Sam Jones in our foursome? Well, he died on the eighth hole, and for the next ten holes it was hit the ball, drag Sam, hit the ball, drag Sam. . . ."

Give you another golf version. A man hits a terrific slice that goes off the fairway and through the windshield of a passing car killing the driver.

That evening he's telling his wife about it, and she asks, "What did you do?"

He says, "I broke eighty."

"Thanks for the lesson," Larry said, "but what good does it do me to have a grandfather who knows how to switch jokes? One kid in my class has a grandfather who's a writer. He gets A in English. Another kid's grandfather is a CPA. That one gets A in math—"

"Don't say another word," I interrupted. "There's another kid in the class whose grandfather's a furrier."

And together we said, "And he gets A in zoology."

But I didn't start out to explain what a good relationship I have with my grandson. It was about that thirteen-inch ruler. I liked the idea so much I had a lot of them made. They were made of heavy brass. They looked and felt pretty good. Everybody wondered why I was giving out rulers. They didn't notice they were thirteen inches long. So I took them back to the shop and had them engraved with the words, "Everyone can use an extra inch." Guys broke up when they read it.

I gave one to a pretty gal who was the receptionist in a television station. She looked at it, read it, and said, "You're so right! Thanks. It's just what I've been looking for to give to my boyfriend as a going-away present."

"Where's he going?" I asked.

"That'll be up to him. When he gets this ruler, he'll understand." She stopped for a minute to think; then she said, "You know it's a big disappointment to a girl to play hard-to-get for a long time and then find out that what she got wasn't worth fighting against."

Shows you how times have changed. When I was growing up, if a girl said that to a man who was practically a stranger, he wouldn't stay a stranger for long . . . if he really *was* practical.

But then when I was going to school, who could have guessed that a conversation between two pretty high school girls would sound like a reading from the walls of a BMT men's room?

They used to say that it was better for parents to be frank with their children than to let them learn the facts of life from the kids on the street. Nowadays parents can't wait for their kids to get home from school so the kids can tell *them* the facts of life that they learned in their sex education class.

Mothers and fathers who once thought that there was only one position, and that was in bed, are finding out a lot of things that can be done even on the buddy seat of a speeding Honda.

A guy once told me his parents were a couple of wondering Jews. I said, "Don't you mean wandering Jews?" He said, "No. They were always wondering why they got married."

7

Family Get-Together

THE reason everything was either given or thrown away when we sold the house in Brooklyn was that I didn't have the time or the patience to sort things out. The furniture and the pictures and things I knew were more important to my aunts than they were to me. So I let them take their choice. And I couldn't see the need of saving the scrapbooks.

It's not that I'm modest about the success I've had or ashamed of the failures. It's just that there's a tomorrow that you can do something about and it's more important than scrapbooks full of yesterdays. Besides your real life never gets into a scrapbook. It never tells what you did for your wife and kids. It just tells *how* you did in Cincinnati or Columbus.

Luckily my family, like every family, has a few pack rats. Those are people who, when they move, pack everything including the rats. And it is because of these types that I happen to have proof that my father was not an Englishman, but a Russian who emigrated to England. It wasn't that my father didn't like Russia. He must have because he stayed there a year longer than his father—my grandfather. The only reason he left was that he didn't see eye to eye with the Russians on how they ran their Army. He believed the Army should be recruited through typecasting, and he didn't think he was the type.

There were other little details, too. He didn't like the wardrobe. He didn't care for the working conditions. And, above all, he objected to the fact that they didn't keep a kosher kitchen. But it wasn't so much that he was an orthodox Jew; he was an orthodox coward.

So when it was almost time for him to take up arms to defend Mother Russia and Czar Alexander Alexandrovich, he told the czar what to do with the big mother and split for France. That was in the year 1893, or one year after my grandparents and my uncle left the Holy Russian Empire. This we know because my Aunt Sarah, one of the family's most successful savers of everything, saved my grandfather's "papers."

Actually it's not the original. It's a page from a supplement of the March 18, 1892 edition of the London *Jewish Chronicle*, which is a copy of a copy of the "passport," translated into English:

By Order of His Imperial Majesty Alexander Alexandrovich, Monarch of All the Russians. . . . The holder of this passport, burgher of Friedrichstadt, Government of Courland. . . . The Jew Lieb Yungman, married, cap and hat maker, is allowed to reside in the different cities and towns of the Russian Empire for his own purposes for two years from the undermentioned date, that is, until the 18th of January one thousand eight hundred and ninety-two. . . . At the expiration of which term he must return, in default of which he will be dealt with according to the law.

Given, according to the document entered in the book under Nov. 19 from the Friedrichstadt Department with seal attached, January 18, one thousand eight hundred and ninety.

Then there was a NOTE that says:

This passport is valid only in those governments where Jews are allowed to reside.

The document was signed by two men, R. Ulman and another whose signature has become illegible.

Under "Special Remarks" the paper says:

His wife, Hannah, 41 years, his son Yonkel, 17 years and his son Aaron, 14 years.

Yonkel was my father. There was another note saying that he had a passport dated 1891, which gave him a year longer to remain in Russia than his father and mother and brother, Aaron.

In case you'd like to know where Lieb Jungman and family lived during their two-year stay in St. Petersburg, in 1890, they lived on Stremj Street and in 1891 they lived on Nevsky.

And in case you're wondering, as I did, why my grandfather, a Russian, had a German name and was referred to on his passport as "burgher," in case you wonder why the Russian city he came from had a German name, it's because a lot of German knights went through that part of Russia early in the eighteenth century and liked the land, the water, or the women.

It must have been the women because in 1710 Princess Anne, who was the niece of Peter the Great and finally became Empress of Russia, married one of the krauts whose name was Duke Frederick William. For marrying the boss' niece he got a city named after him.

How's that for information you never expected (or wanted) to find in this book?

Now, as they say on TV, back to my father.

He knew what he wanted. He wanted out of Russia. And the one out he wanted after that was to get out of the hat and cap business. Shows you how smart he was, how visionary.

Way back in 1891 it was clear to him that by the 1970's the hat business would be lousy, that the only male members of the human race who would be wearing hats were the kids who carry the coffee from the deli to your secretary's desk. (Not a bad song title, "The Kids Who Carry Coffee from the Deli." In 1930 someone would have written it, and Al Jolson would have become a co-author.)

The one thing my old man had no way of guessing is that in 1972 a lot of women would be wearing the kind of stupid-looking caps he made for the St. Petersburg garbage collectors.

You can guess what else Pop wanted when I tell you he went to Paris. Actually, he wanted to find himself, and he figured Paris was a good place to look. He might even find something better. As the candy butchers in the old burlesque houses used to say, "Each and every box of these *dee*lishious choc-oh-lets has a little novelty in it . . . a clever little device that comes to you *digh*-rect from Paris, France . . . and I don't have to tell you men . . . you're all men of the world . . . I don't have to tell you men what goes on in Paris, France . . . now then . . . who'll buy the first box?"

Even though he made the words "Paris, France" sound like an obscene phone call, I never saw anyone buy a box of that candy, and to this day I have no idea how he made a living.

The first thing a young man looking for adventure is apt to do is get into show business. And that's what happened to Yonkel (who changed his name to Jacob) Jungman, who changed his name to Youngman. And from what you've just read, you're probably thinking that he became a butcher in a burlesque house. Wrong!

He hated everything about burlesque and everything about show biz in general except opera. This he loved. When he got engaged to my mother, he didn't give her a diamond. He gave her the Wagner Ring. But that was years later when he was spending all his spare cash on opera recordings. If he could hear the quality of the ones today, he'd flip.

So, to be near the music he loved, he got a job in the opera claque. The pay was about two francs a night. But it meant he got paid for attending performances he used to spend money to hear. Back in the thirties, when press agents hired teenyboppers to show up and scream and squeal and giggle wherever Frank Sinatra was appearing, everybody thought it was some fancy new kind of promotion. It was just an updated version of the opera claque that was formed in Paris early in the nineteenth century.

If you were a tenor opening in *Rigoletto* and you wanted to be sure you got a good hand on all your cadenzas, you went to the office of the claque and hired as many enthusiastic "fans" as you figured you needed . . . or could afford to pay. This made sure that you got just the right number of encores and curtain calls that you felt you deserved.

And although that was my father's specialty, the claque was not just for opera. You could hire claquers for any kind of situation you were up against, the way a movie director casts extras by calling Central Casting.

If you were the producer of a sad play or an actress with a heavy emotional scene, the claque would rent you a few *pleureurs*. Don't bother calling your nephew who's majoring in French at CCNY to ask him what that means. My grandson, Larry, looked it up. It means, literally, "rainers." *Pleureurs* were mostly women who sat in the audience, and when the right time came, they got out their handkerchiefs and sniffled and cried it up.

Girl reporters who were assigned to cover sad human interest stories for the newspapers used to be called sob sisters. But the *pleureurs* of the Paris claque were the original sob sisters. Some of them actually cried, they got so sad thinking about what a rotten way they had to earn a living.

You could also hire what the French called *chatouilleurs*. They were congenial types, and their job was to keep the audience in a good mood. They'd talk to their neighbors, make little jokes, and say good things that they said they'd heard about the play before the curtain went up and during intermission at the bar. Years later at the resorts in the Catskills they called men who did the same kind of work . . . but all day . . . "toomlers."

If you were a Parisian comedian, you could go to the local claque's rent-a-laff division and ensure your weak monologue with a few *rieurs*. They were laughers. Milton Berle always had one. He paid her regularly to laugh at his act. He called her Mother.

Naturally the members of the claque were strongly organized, and you can see how they could practically control the success or failure of any performance in Paris. People who can cheer can also boo! It was like a military operation when they went to work at a show. The whole thing was handled like an army in the field.

There was a *chef du claque*. He was the chief of claque, not the man who cooked for them. He was in charge of dispersing his people strategically around the audience. And he gave them the signals when to do their stuff. Most often the claque was made up mainly of *bisseurs*. That's what my father was. *Bisseurs* were people who applauded and hollered "*Bis! Bis! Bis!*" until the artist was "forced" to come out and do an encore.

He told us that one soprano was such slow pay they couldn't get the money out of her for weeks. So the *chef du claque* set it up with the membership to clap and holler louder and louder after every encore until she was forced to take so many encores she lost her voice.

It might have been Papa's involvement in that claque racket that caused him to leave Paris. Or maybe he got tired of having blistered hands from applauding.

Whatever it was, he took a boat across the Channel to England to join his parents, who were living in London's East End. Funny, isn't it, the way Jews always seem to live on the East Side . . . the Lower East Side of New York, the East End of London, and there are nothing but Jews in the eastern part of Tel Aviv.

*While in London, I went to Harrod's to buy a
dress for my wife. I couldn't remember her size,
but there was another customer there built just
like her. So I said, "Excuse me, sir, what size
are you?"*

8

London Broil

AS this is being written, I am in the middle of the Atlantic
Ocean aboard the *Queen Elizabeth II*.

It's Wednesday afternoon, and this is the first chance I've had
since coming aboard Monday morning to do a little work. I like to
get a certain amount done each day. If I don't, I have to take a day
off and catch up. This puts me two days behind on everything else I
have to do.

That's the trouble with taking a vacation, and I wish this trip was
a vacation. It's a job. Playing a voyage on the *QE II* is just like
playing the Mountains, but with sea breezes. I'm supposed to do
four regular shows a day, two in first class and two in second class.
But all the time I'm working, I'm worrying. What if I do a first-class
show in second class and a second-class show in first class? Next
time I take one of these jobs it'll be on a one-class ship.

In between doing the regular shows, I'm supposed to mingle with
the passengers and entertain them. Again it's like the Mountains,

only the food isn't kosher. Another trouble about entertaining the passengers is when I watch how they act, I don't know who's entertaining whom.

In the first place, nobody seems satisfied with the cabin he has. Late every night I see them going from one to the other in pajamas and bathrobes. First I thought maybe the plumbing didn't work. Then I remembered a story Ed Gardner used to tell on himself. Ed was the Brooklyn piano salesman who became famous on the radio as Archie, the manager, of Duffy's Tavern.

Ed said that one night halfway between New York and Cherbourg, his wife stepped out of their cabin just in time to catch him coming out of a wealthy widow's stateroom right across from theirs.

"I was backing out very quietly, and when I turned around, there she was," Ed used to say. "Well, she had me. There was nothing to do but tell the truth. So I confessed, I said, 'All right. Now you know my secret. I'm an international jewel thief.' "

There's another problem to being a comedian on a boat. The passengers follow you around the deck and pester you for autographs the minute you tell them who you are. If you don't get a chance to talk to them, you have yourself paged. I haven't had a minute to myself.

I'm on deck every chance I get checking the lifeboats, measuring off which one is closest to my room, and trying on life jackets. The way people stand and watch me doing this and laugh only goes to prove that once you get the reputation for being funny, people will laugh even when you're doing something that's really serious.

For years, when I was a young man just starting out in show business, I wouldn't go to England. I was afraid I'd get seasick. Of course when transatlantic flight came along, it gave me a way to avoid seasickness. Now I get airsick. But I've gotten used to both. Actually I travel so much that sort of thing doesn't bother me. I have a pill for seasickness, a pill to get over the pill, a pill to put me to sleep, and a pill to wake me up. I even have a pill to tell me when to take each pill. If I took all the pills I have, I'd be sick.

Thinking about it, I guess I now prefer traveling to Europe by boat. You don't have to sit strapped in a narrow seat and keep your eyes fastened on the wings for signs of metal fatigue. On a boat, you sit strapped in a deck chair, wearing a Mae West and sitting on a big, round white thing that says on it HMS QUEEN ELIZABETH II. They had smaller, more comfortable ones in the hospital where I had my last operation.

But just being aboard the *QE II* is great. Anyone who spent the first six months of his life—for me the formative years—in London gets a wonderful sense of homecoming when he steps aboard a British ship and hears people speaking English he can't understand. Really, though, the crew's Cockney chatter is music to my ears. And if you've ever heard me play the fiddle, you know how I understand music.

The anticipation of arriving at Southampton and taking the boat train to London and the thought of the hospitality of the Dorchester Hotel is blunted, however, by the fact that I'm only going to Cherbourg. From there I take a plane to Le Bourget, a Paris taxi to Orly, and a jet for JFK in New York. This is because I have to be back in New York City Sunday morning to start work on a TV pilot.

It's an Americanized version of P. G. Wodehouse's *Jeeves* stories. I play the part of Theeves, the Brooklyn valet to the playboy son of a Chicago gangster. The casting is a natural. Everybody has always said that I'm the Jewish Arthur Treacher.

The story is about how the kid's mobster father hires me because he wants his son to have a typical Brooklyn gentleman's gentleman to take off the smooth edges the boy picked up at Princeton. I'm supposed to keep him on the crooked road. He has a tendency to go straight. He wants to be a used-car salesman.

Sorry, I have to stop writing now. But you can go right on reading. It's getting a little too rough. I can't keep my hand steady. Or my stomach. I'll try to stand up, and if I don't fall down, I'll go to my cabin and lie down. This makes me the first man ever to get seasick writing his autobiography . . . with the possible exception of Captain Bligh.

Later.

I'm happy to tell you that I wasn't forced to stop writing just because the normal motion of the ship made me feel a little sick. What happened was, it suddenly became spring aboard the *QE II*, and everybody turned green. We ran into such a terrible storm in the North Atlantic that it slowed us up for two days. We were forced to skip the stop at Cherbourg and go directly to Southampton. The passengers will be flown from there back to Paris. Not me. I may take the boat train to London and lie down for a little while if I can find a hotel that isn't rocking too badly.

It was really very bad. Captain Hehir didn't leave the bridge for four days. I told him he should force himself. He said he was proud of the way his ship "held the sea." The ship's doctor said he should have seen the way the passengers held their heads.

The captain said it was the worst weather he'd ever experienced.
He said, "Looking around the liner from the bridge, there was
nothing to be seen, at times, but spume and spray." He was right.
Even when you opened your eyes.

But you learn something even under the worst conditions. Until
this trip, I thought spume was an Italian fruit they used to make
spumoni.

Of course I did a little hero stuff. There were a lot of scared
people aboard. I went from cabin to cabin telling them not to be
afraid, that everything was all right. Then I'd faint, and they'd be so
busy trying to do something for me they'd forget about themselves.

During the worst of the storm Sadie said, "You're always getting
a laugh with that line, 'Take my wife, please.' Try it now. If
anybody's going to take me, this is the time. Take me anywhere as
long as it's off this ship."

But the Cunard Line was great about everything. The last night on
board all the ladies got bouquets and champagne. All the men got
their bar bills.

Among the passengers who didn't seem to suffer at all from
topsy-turvy tummy were Natalie Wood and Robert Wagner. They
were once married but had been divorced for several years. The
storm threw them together again.

When we arrived in Southampton, they announced that the trip
had been so rough they figured if they could live through such an
experience, they could live through anything. So they decided to get
married again.

The delay caused by the storm meant that I couldn't get back to
New York in time to start shooting the *Theeves* pilot as planned. But
that didn't bother me too much. I figured they could put it off for a
few days. They decided to put it off forever.

I got a wireless telling me the project had been abandoned. If
there had been no storm, that message would have been enough to
make me sick. The reason the deal was off was that P. G.
Wodehouse got wind of it.

I was glad for a little unexpected time in London. I like it there.
And they like me. I had a chance to see Sir Alec Guinness, Sir Ralph
Richardson, and Sir Laurence Olivier, but I didn't take it. Every
time I phoned one of them his line was busy. I asked the London
operator what they could be talking about for so long. She said,
"The Lord knows." I finally got through in the usual way. I prayed.

Every important show business personality in London seems to
eventually get a title if he just sticks it out long enough. It's a nice

idea. When you start out in the business, you're dazed. Why shouldn't you end up knighted?

If the queen should ever decide to confer knighthood on me, she'd have to say, *"Mah neesh-ta-no ha-lei-loh ha-seh mee-kol ha-lay-los?"* which means, Why is this night different from all other nights? It could happen.

They even confer titles on agents. Years ago I used to do business in London with a man named Lew Grade. Now he's a big-time producer and he's Sir Lewis Grade. But I talked to some people there who said he hadn't changed a bit. It reminded me of the days when he was my London agent and I wasn't working. My friends kept asking me why. I told them I was suffering from a Lew Grade infection.

But I've always done well at the London Palladium. I've played there once or twice a year for the past ten years or more. I get big laughs. It isn't that they understand the jokes. They just think I sound funny when I talk. But it took me a long time to get up courage to go to England the first time.

I was booked to play the Palladium seven or eight times, and every time I canceled. I was afraid of being seasick. Now that I know what it's like, I'm not afraid anymore. I don't like it, but I'm not afraid of it.

When they threatened to sue me if I canceled again, I had a choice of an ocean trip or jail. I figured jail would make me sick, too. And it's much better, if you have to be sick, to get that good healthy sea air. So I sailed.

Was I surprised! I felt fine all the way over. But the last day on the return trip, just before we got to New York, I was having tea on deck and the deck steward showed up looking like the Jolly Green Giant. That did it. I flipped. And I don't mean my lid.

During my first run at the Palladium, a reporter named Geoffrey something called me late one night and said, "I say, Henny old boy, I do believe I know the very place where you were born." He could have shown me anywhere, and I wouldn't have known the difference. But I made a date for the next morning. He took me to see the Cressy Houses in Whitechapel, which was a ghetto area when I was born there. Since then the neighborhood has run down.

I was interested to see that the same thing happening at the time (it's since happened) to the Jewish section of the Lower East Side of New York, where men like George Burns and Irving Berlin came from, was also happening in Whitechapel. The Jews were being displaced by Indians, Pakistanis, and Jamaicans, and stores that used to have a Star of David on the window were selling curry and spices.

But there were still some old-timers around the Cressy Houses. It's hard to move old people out of a place that they've lived all their lives. I talked to an old lady named McCarthy. She talked Yiddish with a brogue. She said she remembered my family. She said that my father had a big collection of opera recordings and that she helped my mother diaper me when I was a baby. I couldn't help saying that she'd never recognize the old place.

She told me about a time she and my mother took me to Hyde Park to play. They got to yakking while I was crawling around in the grass and I crawled right out onto the roadway. There were still a lot of horses in those days. People who have since told me what they thought I was full of would have been right if they'd seen me then.

Do you think Berle could have stolen that joke about the mother who told her kid to go out and play in traffic from *my* mother?

He might have. She was a funny lady. She had a terrific sense of humor and knew how to use it. The first time I came home with money I made as a comedian she said, "How? You're not funny."

She didn't want those few dollars to go to my head. And they didn't. They went right to Poppa's pocket.

Momma's favorite story came, she insisted, from a time when she was on jury duty.

An old Jew was on the witness stand. The bailiff placed his right hand on the Bible and swore him in with the usual "Do you swear to tell the truth, the whole truth, and nothing but the truth, so help you God?"

The old man said, "Would I lie to you?"

The prosecuting attorney began his questioning with: "How old are you?"

"*Kayn aynhoreh* seventy-three," he answered.

"If it please the court," objected the prosecutor, "the witness is adding words to his testimony."

"Ask the question again," said the judge.

The prosecutor did and again the old man answered, "*Kayn aynhoreh* seventy-three."

The magistrate said, "Will the defense counsel please instruct his client to answer the question without adding extra words."

The defense attorney said, "If it please the court, I think I can ask the question so as to get the proper answer."

"Please do," said the judge.

The defense attorney said, "*Kayn aynhoreh*, how old are you?"

The man answered, "Seventy-three."

For the information of the few Gentiles and those not in show business who may read this book, the words *kayn aynhoreh*, sometimes spelled *kine-ahora*, mean roughly "thank God." Literally it used to mean "I cast no evil eye." How do I know it? Being Jewish isn't enough? No. It wasn't. I had to look it up.

I was telling Momma about our trip to Israel. We left early in the morning on an El Al plane. As we started to ascend, the handsomely dressed gentleman who was sitting next to me began winding *tefillin* on his wrists. He saw me watching him. I smiled. He smiled and said, "Would you like me to do the same for you," indicating the phylacteries. I don't exactly look Arabian. I said, "I'd be proud if you did."

"The pride and pleasure will be mine, sir," he said in the most beautiful English I'd heard since the last time I'd seen Larry Olivier.

When I told that to Momma, she said, "Why not? Do you think all Jews talk like you?"

Then I told her how impressive it was on the way home to see ten devout Jews holding a minyan in the cabin of the plane. "Think of it," I said, "thirty-five thousand feet in the sky over the Atlantic Ocean they're praying to God."

Momma said, "That high over the ocean, I'd pray, too. If they'd been much higher, it would have just been a local phone call."

Again for any WASP's who may be present, "tefillin" (also called phylacteries) are leather straps with a small box that contains certain scriptures attached to them. They are worn for morning prayer by all orthodox males past Bar Mitzvah age.

When she was living with all the other old people down in Miami Beach, she wrote me, "Where can I get in touch with Myron Cohen? I want to sell him this joke. A new couple moved into our building last week. He's sixty-seven. She's sixty-three. We're getting a much younger crowd this year."

Another time she wrote to ask for Jackie Gleason's phone number to tell him about the old couple that lived in the next apartment. Momma said, "The way they love each other after all the years they've been together! It's beautiful. Just think! Fifty-five years married. Every night when they go to sleep he holds her hand. But he's aging fast. He's eighty-one. Last night he didn't hold her hand. He just said, 'Not tonight, dear. I'm too tired.' It's sad." Momma never sent *me* any gags.

She died in Miami in 1965. She had so many friends we had to hold two funerals, one down there and one in New York. She might have said, such a sendoff was worth living for.

She would certainly have been proud of the following notice she got in the house organ of the Chase Bank. She dealt with their North Beach Office.

> The following poem was written by Mrs. Olga Youngman, mother of famed comedian, Henny Youngman.
>
> Mrs. Youngman was a customer of our office before her death last year at age 88. More than that she was a lovely little friend to your NBO Reporter.
>
> Her visits to our office were always those to which we looked forward. A second son, Mr. Lester Youngman, has given us permission to put this poem in the Chase Chatter.

I believe everyone is talented in their own way
It takes lots of talent living day by day
It takes talent to know how to get along
It takes talent to admit when you have been wrong
It takes talent to be alone and to enjoy a book
It takes talent to cook the things your family likes you to cook
It takes talent to be a good parent to your child
It takes talent to be patient and not to go wild
It takes talent to understand the moods of others
It takes talent to get along with your sisters and brothers
It takes talent to select the right clothes to wear
It takes an abundance of talent to know how to share
It takes talent in knowing how to take care of your health
It takes talent in knowing how to enjoy your wealth
It takes talent in developing a sense of good taste
It takes talent in knowing time is not meant to waste
It takes talent in seeking, the right mate to find
It takes talent in appreciation of peace of mind
It takes talent in knowing how to employ leisure time
It takes talent to be frugal with a dollar or dime
It takes talent to accept yourself as just you
It takes talent to understand real friends are few
It takes talent not to nourish any part of the past
It takes talent to make a healthy life really last
It takes talent to see the humor of each day
It takes talent to accept what does not go your way
It takes talent not to live on the avenue of hate
It takes talent and tolerance to understand your mate
Every person is talented in their own way

By virtue of healthy living day by day
Even though you do not have to be an artist of great fame
The real talent of being a good you, is just the same

Not long after I tied up traffic around Marble Arch, Mrs.
McCarthy told me, Jacob and Olga Youngman packed up their
meager belongings and headed for America. I don't remember the
sea voyage at all. Possibly the subconscious memory of it was what
made me keep postponing the boat ride back to England to play the
Palladium.

I have no idea why my father decided to leave London. Maybe
the cap and hat business got so bad he was afraid that instead of
selling hats, he'd be passing one.

There's no more way to tell the real reason for his coming back to
America than there's any way of knowing why he left Paris for
London. Or why he left London for his first trip to America. He just
had itching feet and couldn't do anything about it because Dr.
Scholl was still in medical school.

But if Poppa's feet hadn't itched so much or if he could have
found foot powder, he might never have gone to New York in the
first place. And I might not have inherited that same inner need to
keep moving which I suppose a psychologist would tell me I
sublime by hopping around the country doing shows the way I do.

On Poppa's first trip to Manhattan, he naturally headed right for
the Jewish section on the Lower East Side and wound up in the
area's most famous spot for newly arrived immigrants, the Mills
Hotel. The rate was 25 cents a night and worth every penny of it.
The Mills Hotels were the idea of a rich California philanthropist
named Darius Ogden Mills, so that a poor man could find a decent
place to stay. Lucky he wasn't a *poor* California philanthropist. He
might have had to charge more for the rooms.

Mills should see what happened to his idea. The one on Bleecker
Street, next to Art D'Lugoff's Village Gate, in Greenwich Village,
is now a welfare hotel, a nest of bums and addicts.

But there was no disgrace connected with it when Poppa stayed
there. He soon got a job at his trade, making caps and hats. He also
made a few friends. One of them was an immigrant girl, one of a
family of two brothers and six sisters, that had just arrived from
Riga, Russia. Poppa didn't pay much attention to the two brothers.
Philip turned out to be a doctor. The other became a very successful
businessman. Poppa liked the six girls, Helen, Fanny, Marie, Rose,
Gusta, and last, but not least, Olga. At least Poppa didn't think she

was least. He figured "last the best of all the game"—remember that? "First the worst, second the same, last the best of all the game." Kids used to say that when they lost. But Pop didn't lose. He liked Olga so well and she liked him back so hard that she became my Momma. They were married in 1904 and went to London on their honeymoon. Nowhere does it say where Poppa got the money for all the traveling he did. There was no "fly now—pay later." American Express was just a baggage service.

He might have borrowed it from Aunt Marie, Momma's sister, who married a rich businessman named Morris Kaplan, who was the one who brought all the other sisters to America. Aunt Marie really ran the family . . . with Uncle Morris' money.

Maybe Poppa and Momma just lived very frugally, saved, and did what they wanted to do. It must have taken them a year and a half to save up enough loot to get back to New York because that's how long they stayed in London, where I was born. Some honeymoon!

When my father met my mother, Marie had just brought her and her sisters to New York. They hadn't had much time to learn English. So it was tough on her when Poppa took her to London where the words she was learning in Brooklyn didn't sound quite right. Of course they lived in Whitechapel, an area where anyone could get along on Yiddish. It's a universal language. No matter where in the world you go, if you know Yiddish, you can find someone to talk to. Spreading the language might have been why the Wandering Jew was made to wander so much.

I can remember back in New York when I was little, my mother was still learning English. There was a dressmaker named Mrs. Kramer because that was her name before she married an Italian dude. He seemed to have no means of support except the money his wife earned making dresses. He used to strut around the neighborhood all dolled up in a pinstripe suit and a wing collar, looking like a cross between a floorwalker and a Packard salesman. Maybe he had a night job as a spaghetti cook in some beanery. Sometimes on Sundays he'd invite us all over to their flat for a spaghetti dinner.

My mother and Mrs. Kramer had a nice arrangement. Momma who spoke four European languages—French, German, Russian, and Yiddish—taught Mrs. Kramer to speak French and Mrs. Kramer tried to teach Momma to speak English. Most of the time they just talked to each other in Yiddish.

We lived in Brooklyn because that's where Aunt Marie and Uncle Morris lived. Uncle Morris was doing all right. And when Aunt Marie married him, she didn't do badly either. Naturally my mother and Marie were very close. But not as close as Uncle Morris.

At that time Brooklyn was called "the bedroom of Manhattan." People used to say they built the subway under the East River so those who lived in Brooklyn could sneak home without being seen. But it had a lot of beautiful neighborhoods with large homes set in lots of land. To a kid from the slums of London it was like a new world. I used to just walk around looking at the big houses and the wide green lawns. And I hated the whole scene. Because I didn't live there.

We lived at 223 Fifty-first Street in a cold-water flat, and I used to wander over to the fancy neighborhoods because it was easier for me to hate them if I was looking at them. Our flat was on the top floor of a tenement we happened to live in because Uncle Morris and Aunt Marie owned it. He owned a couple of crummy buildings where poor people like us had to live. And besides the real estate, he owned a couple of liquor stores on Third Avenue in Brooklyn. Later, when I was about twelve years old and Prohibition was in effect (but ineffectual), I think Uncle Morris did a little bootlegging on the side.

Whenever we went to their house, Aunt Marie would offer Poppa a glass of slivovitz. "Don't worry," she'd say. "Would I offer if it wasn't good? This you can trust. Morris made it himself. I saw with my own eyes. Just this morning."

Naturally, when we came from London to Brooklyn, which for us was like jumping from the frying pan onto the fire escape, Uncle Morris wanted to do something special for his wife's sister's husband. He was very sentimental, especially when it came to money. So when he had an empty apartment in one of the tenements he owned, he let us have it. He gave it to us at a price he wouldn't give it to anyone else. He didn't raise the rent. It was tough. Because my father couldn't raise the rent either.

Uncle Morris tried to instill his philosophy about money in my father. Uncle Morris felt having it was better than not having it. That far Poppa could follow him. But when it came to the part about how getting it was better than anything, he lost Poppa. Poppa thought opera was better than anything.

But I shouldn't knock Uncle Morris. If you really needed anything, you could count on him. He'd give you the shirt off his back . . . at a good price. And if you couldn't pay, he'd trust you for the interest for a little while. Every comedian has a routine about some guy who's "so stingy that. . . ." That guy was Uncle Morris.

"He's so cheap that when he goes out to eat, the restaurant changes hands three times before he pays the check."

". . . he files his nails before he goes to a bar so he won't be able to pick up the check."

". . . he sends his mother a Mother's Day wire . . . collect."

". . . when he takes his girl to a motel, they go Dutch."

I was playing violin in an orchestra. I hit a clinker. A guy in the balcony hollered, "Kill the son of a bitch on the fiddle!" The leader hollered back, "Who called the violinist a son of a bitch?" The guy in the balcony came back with: "Who called that son of a bitch a violinist?"

9

Violin Obligato

WE only lived for a few years at No. 223 on Fifty-first Street. We felt we had to move into a better neighborhood. So we moved to No. 281 on Fifty-first Street.

You know how they say, "In New York you move around the corner and you're in a different world"? We didn't quite make it around the corner. But the move brought us closer to the wealthy Shore Road section and the other expensive home areas of Brooklyn where I used to wander around hating the people who lived there.

At the rate we were moving—about a block every three years—it would have taken us half a century to move into one of those big Shore Road homes.

Now I'll tell you the real reason we moved. Someone offered Uncle Morris a better price for our top-floor flat at 223. Why I'll never know. Maybe they kept pigeons. And that's another thing I'll never know. Why do slum kids keep pigeons? Could it be revenge? Better than keeping a dog? Dogs just dirty the sidewalk. With pigeons you have an air force that can bomb civilians.

What's more, dogs cost too much to feed. With pigeons you can always get someone to give you a handful of corn. Then you take it home and pop it. If things get really tough, a squab can be sold as a delicacy.

The interesting thing about our new flat was that you could step out of a bedroom window and be on the roof of the tailor shop next door. In summer I used to go out there to practice on my violin. It was a present from my Aunt Marie. Every time the tailor pressed a pair of pants a puff of steam would come sneezing out of a little pipe near where I was playing. That's how I happened to become a hot fiddle player.

Of course, having that roof right next to our window made the place easy to rob. But we didn't worry. Everybody knew we didn't have anything worth stealing. And Poppa was glad for the roof. He was the one who had the idea I should practice out there. He got the idea one evening when my scratching interfered with the sounds of his opera recordings, which he listened to night after night.

Come to think of it, I might have been the original "Fiddler on the Roof."

I think the people in the neighborhood really loved to hear me play. I know in the winter when it was too cold to go out on the roof and I had to play indoors, the neighborhood kids used to throw stones through the window just so they could hear me better.

My father had great plans for my future. I was to become so good on the violin that I'd play in the orchestra at the Metropolitan Opera. But after listening to me practice for a while, he revised his plans a little. He was willing to settle for the Metropolitan Life. But just to be on the safe side, he said, it would be a good idea, when I got out of grammar school if I learned a trade. That's the way fathers are. I'm taking an hour violin lesson at a dollar a week, and he's already thrown me out of the pit at the Met.

I remember a series of violin teachers who are to blame for the way I play today. They say I'm to blame for their hearing problems. The first man who was supposed to make me into a concert violinist was a dapper little dandy named Anthony Di Trinis. People who remember the band singers around the time of Russ Columbo, when Bing Crosby was just getting started, will remember the name Tony Trini. He was my violin teacher's kid. You note he didn't try to teach *his* kid the violin.

Signor Di Trinis used to show up to give me lessons all dolled up in striped pants and a Prince Albert coat. Real swell. He'd take his fiddle and bow and stand opposite me with my fiddle and bow, and he'd say, "Do this." Then he'd demonstrate what he wanted done, and I'd try to do it. Then he'd hit my knuckles with his bow. He nearly crippled me.

I tried to distract him from trying to give me a lesson by talking to him. I'd say anything that came into my head. He was the first one to say that I ought to give up the fiddle and become a comedian. But he only told that to me, not to my father. Di Trinis wasn't about to lose that buck a week just because he thought that what I said was even funnier than my fiddling.

Finally he got a charley horse in his bow arm, or something, and gave up on me and my father got me another teacher, Mr. Conrad. As far as I know, "Mister" was his first name. I never heard him called anything else but Mr. Conrad. He was a much better teacher than Di Trinis, I thought, because he gave my knuckles a chance to heal. He quit coming to Brooklyn to give me lessons after the time he showed up with one of the pockets completely cut out of his pants. Someone had done it in the subway during the rush hour, and Mr. Conrad didn't even notice it was gone. It just happened to be the pocket he carried all his money in. Shows that being robbed on the subway is no great big modern improvement. They were doing it way back when I was a kid.

My mother had to give Mr. Conrad a nickel to get back home. A nickel. That's all it cost then to ride on the subway. That's all it cost then for a loaf of bread. Sometimes in those days, I'd find a copy of the New York *Times* lying on the street and I'd take it to the nearest subway entrance and sell it for a penny. That was a pretty good price to get for a secondhand newspaper because that's all it cost when it was brand-new.

After Mr. Conrad had the pocket cut out of his pants, he dropped me as a pupil. He wouldn't travel on the subway anymore. A lousy excuse.

The next teacher I had made me come to see him. He had a back room in a boardinghouse about a mile or so from where we lived. I think he was Hungarian because there was always a little goulash on his vest. I don't remember his name anymore, and if I did, I probably wouldn't be able to spell it.

One of the kids who also "took" from this guy told me that he got his room and board for nothing in exchange for playing every Sunday night in the front parlor for the other guests, who, from what I could see on my weekly visit, were mostly old ladies. Maybe they were young ladies when they moved in.

Just listening to my teacher play "When a Gypsy Makes His Violin Cry" could have aged them.

When I figure out how much money Poppa spent on my career as a violinist, I feel sorry. Imagine! A dollar a week for about forty weeks for about five years. (It took Poppa that long to give in that Stradivarius didn't have me in mind when he was making his violins.)

Poppa could have used that two hundred dollars, too. He should have tried to get the dough back from Aunt Marie. It was all her fault for giving me the instrument in the first place. And look what Poppa got for it. A comedian. Maybe if I'd spent all that time and money learning to tell jokes, I'd be playing in the Philharmonic today.

It wasn't safe then (and I guess it still isn't) for a kid to walk through the section of Brooklyn where I lived carrying a violin case. That's why there were so many violins for sale in the pawnshops in the neighborhood. It was nice that the fiddles never left the neighborhood. All you had to do was find out where yours was hocked and buy it back.

Of course, when Prohibition came in, things got better. If you were a big kid like me and you carried a violin case, you got a lot of respect. All you had to do was hold it as if you were aiming at somebody.

The first thing that kids who grow up in run-down areas of any city have to learn is that they have two alternatives. They can stand and fight, or they can learn how to run very fast. Running is safer! I found that out the hard way.

One day a tough Irish kid stopped me on my way to my violin lesson and said if I didn't give him my fiddle, he'd punch me in the nose. I knew if I came home without the fiddle, my father would punch me in the nose. And I knew how hard he punched. So, as the kid grabbed for the violin case, I took a wild swing at him and landed a lucky punch on the kid's jaw, and he went down and out, spitting two teeth.

News of events like that travel fast in communities where there's a lot of ethnic antagonism. That means that the Poles fight with the Germans and the Irish fight with the Italians and everyone fights with the Jews. (We were one of two Jewish families on our block.) So knowing how to fight makes it easier to grow up enough to move away.

Pretty soon all the big kids started coming around, telling me they were going to make a prizefighter out of me. I began to see myself as another King Levinsky. (When another King Levinsky came along, his name was Max Baer.) I dreamed of dancing around the ring in

Madison Square Garden with my hands clasped over my head acknowledging the cheers of the crowd. Then I had my first fight. When I woke up, my seconds were working over me. I had earned the title of One Punch Henny. One punch, and I was out. Out of the fight racket.

I gave up the idea of being a fighter and learned how to run. I got to be so fast that I eventually made the track team at Manual Training High School in Brooklyn. The girls' track team. Too bad the kids who were chasing me when I was in training didn't chase me farther. If they'd kept after me until we came to the river, I might have made the swimming team, too.

The first school I went to was P.S. 2 on Forty-sixth Street in Brooklyn. I don't remember too much about it because of a game I used to play with some of the other pupils. It was called hooky. This brought me in contact with the principal a lot. He was a man with one arm named Memmot. No. I don't know the name of the other arm. But I do know this: If he'd had two arms and handled me the way he did, I might not have survived.

I really only remember one of the teachers in P.S. 2. His name was Julius Laderberg, and I don't remember him because of anything he contributed to my education. It's because he later went into business with a cousin of mine named Herman Davis. They bought a resort hotel in the Catskills. It was on a pond called Swan Lake, so the genius schoolteacher and my genius cousin, after weeks of thinking, came up with this catchy and creative name for their new hotel . . . Swan Lake Inn. This was particularly bright because the nearest resort was called Swan Lake Manor. You'll come to more about this place later.

The Swanee Syncopators, under the direction of Henny Youngman, eventually wound up playing at the inn. The fact that we worked cheap and the joint was owned by my cousin had nothing to do with it. The manor, next door, also had a fiddler. His name was Pinky Pearlman né Jacob Pincus Perelmuth. While the leader of the Swanee Syncopators was busy becoming the King of the One-Liners, Pinky Pearlman laid down his fiddle and became a concert and opera star named Jan Peerce. And just to make the whole thing come out right, while I was busy being a running gag on a TV show called *Laugh-In* ("Oh, *that* Henny Youngman?"), Jan Peerce was singing Tevye in *Fiddler on the Roof*.

Too bad we never got together to do a double. He could sing while I told jokes, and I could fiddle while he sang. That way there'd always be something funny to laugh at.

I have no idea how I ever got out of P.S. 2. What with playing

hooky and taking violin lessons and going to Hebrew school to get
ready for my Bar Mitzvah, my spare time was all used up. I had no
time for homework. Maybe the school just got tired of seeing me
around (or looking for me when I wasn't around) and decided to
pass me on to another school.

But about my Bar Mitzvah. They weren't such big things as they
are today. It used to be that all you needed was a rabbi, a minyan,
and a boy thirteen years old. The rabbi said a few Hebrew words the
boy didn't understand. Then the boy pronounced a few Hebrew
words in such a way that the rabbi didn't understand. Everyone had
a little drink of Manischewitz or schnapps and maybe a piece of
herring, and that's all there was to it.

Today it's different. First you have to have the affair on a day the
rabbi isn't playing golf.

The competition between Jewish families to put on the most
elegant Bar Mitzvah for their son the doctor has reached idiotic
proportions. I say "Their son the doctor" because if you show me a
Jewish mother who doesn't want her boy to be a doctor, I'll show
you the mother of a lawyer.

There's a story—it probably isn't true, but I'll tell it to you
anyway—about a wealthy man on Long Island who wanted to do
something really different for his boy when the kid became thirteen.
After a year of thinking and planning, they finally invited two
hundred and eighty-three of their intimate friends to the boy's Bar
Mitzvah, which was to be held on safari in Africa.

The invitation included first-class air travel, accommodations on
top of an elephant, and rooms in some jungle hotel run by a
syndicate of Hollywood actors. Very classy. Very pem-pem.
Nothing was omitted from the plans. Every guest got a supply of
Dramamine for air and elephant travel, a snakebite kit, an assortment of antihistamine pills to handle any allergies, and every girl
got a whistle in case she ran into Tarzan.

Everything was going fine. The safari was moving slowly
through the jungle. Manischewitz was flowing like wine. Everything was going great. From the lead elephant the father of the boy
was playing "Sonny Boy" on a portable Japanese hi-fi record
player. And from the children's elephants, way in the back, came
sounds of Eddie Fisher singing "Oh, My Papa." It was beautiful.

Then, all of a sudden, the safari stopped. At first nobody noticed
because a safari moves very slowly. But then someone realized that
he'd been reading the same Burma Shave sign for three hours. They
still have Burma Shave signs on the jungle trails. They're out to get
the bushman business.

After about six hours of no moving, the mother of the Bar Mitzvah boy said to the father, "Well, if you're not going to do something about this delay, I am. I told you not to take the bid from the cheapest caterer." Then she called a Great White Hunter, supplied by Hertz-Rent-a-Hunter and asked him to find out what was holding up the safari.

In less than an hour, the bearer the hunter had sent ahead to determine the delay came back with the news. They had to wait because there was another Bar Mitzvah ahead of them.

Who said I only know one-liners?

There's another Bar Mitzvah story about the elaborate buffets that are a feature of so many of them.

Two ladies were admiring a life-size statue of the Bar Mitzvah boy done in ice.

"It's beautiful," said one.

"A perfect likeness," said the other. "Who did it? Epstein?"

"Don't be silly. Epstein works only in chopped liver."

The night my grandson, Larry, celebrated his Bar Mitzvah at the Hotel Regency on Park Avenue in New York, we had a six-piece band, a twelve-course dinner, and a guest list that looked like an ad for the coming attractions at the Sands Hotel in Las Vegas.

Earl Wilson covered it. Stiller and Meara were there. I think the William Morris office booked it. They tried to charge me my salary, less 10 percent commission for them, because I was there.

It used to be okay to give a Bar Mitzvah boy a fountain pen. Now he doesn't have to accept anything less than a block of stock in the Schaeffer Pen Company.

I know all about Bar Mitzvahs. That's how I really made a living in show business for a while . . . playing at them. People would want to get Milton Berle to entertain. He thought he was too big a man—he was a lot older—so he'd send me. It was great. If I was good, I'd take all the credit. If I was bad they blamed Berle.

My education didn't really begin until I entered Manual Training High School and then Brooklyn Vocational Trade School. At both those excellent institutions of intermediate education I majored in vaudeville.

"The trouble with going to school is it breaks up the whole day."

10

School of Hard Knucks

I found Manual Training High much easier than P.S. 2 . . . to get out of. And it looked to me as if they planned it that way.

Right in front of the building they had this great big door with the one word "Entrance" carved above it in stone. But when you got inside, everywhere you looked there were doors with red signs over them that said "Exit." So I did.

I must say the school had a fine reputation. Friends of the family were always asking me where I went to school as if they didn't believe I could get into one. When I told them, they'd shake their heads in surprise and say, "You go to Manual Training? Fine school." Then they'd shake their heads some more. Everyone had something good to say about that school except the kids who went there.

There were a lot of *them*. When my class from P.S. 2 got inducted, it brought the number of inmates at Manual Training up to 2,000. Of that number, 1,999 were working to get a diploma and go to college. The other one was working to get out of the building and go to the early show at the Orpheum on Flatbush Avenue.

51

There were only two things I didn't like about all vaudeville theaters. They had a woman sitting behind a window who sold you a ticket and a man standing in front of the door who wouldn't let you in without it. I'd have seen a lot more vaudeville if it hadn't been for them. I figured those tickets were a big waste. If they'd eliminated the woman who sold them and the man who took them and the cost of printing them, they'd have saved enough money to create scholarships to let students like me in free. I mean students of vaudeville.

I only got a quarter a day allowance. That was supposed to pay for my lunch. So I had to moonlight to get enough dough to support my vaudeville addiction. One way I found for picking up a lot of change was to become a telephone inspector. It's an easy job. You do it on your own time, and you're practically your own boss.

What you do is you go around to all the pay telephones and inspect the return coin slot for money. For every nickel you find, you get to keep five cents. I still make a couple of bucks a week at it in my spare time. Experienced inspectors know that if there are no coins in the return slot, you have to give the phone a good hit.

In the old days there were very few phone booths on street corners. They were in drugstores mostly. One druggist saw me coming in and going from booth to booth every day and caught on to what I was doing. He grabbed me and told me if I didn't give him half of what I found, he'd call the cops and report me to the telephone company. He scared me so I spent my half for aspirin. But at a different drugstore.

The kids today have a much better system. They pull out the whole phone, drop it in a shopping bag, and take it home and crack it open. The only danger in doing it that way is that your old man will come home from the welfare office, catch you, and demand his cut.

I know about all this because I go back to the old neighborhood once in a while. Some men climb mountains. Some men explore the jungles of the upper Amazon. I go back to my old neighborhood.

It's not easy to get to by cab. If you can get one to stop for you, when you tell him you want to go to Brooklyn, he tells you he'll take you to the Bronx because that's where he lives.

Then there are the student drivers. They don't ask you, "Where in Brooklyn?" They ask, "Where *is* Brooklyn?"

I don't mind kids wearing long hair. But the other day the cab I was in almost hit a bus because the driver was driving with only one hand, while he adjusted the bobby pins that held on his yarmulke.

The guy who finally stopped for me was one of those old-time cabdrivers who know more about running things than the President, the mayor, and my wife.

When I told him I wanted to go to Brooklyn, he said, "Hey! Henny! Want to hear something funny?"

"I'll tell you something funny," I said, "it's the dough it's going to cost me to get to Fifty-first Street in Brooklyn. I may have to mortgage my home. I can remember when you could get from Times Square to Flatbush for a couple of dollars. Now it's cheaper to buy the cab."

He said, "Yeah. I remember those days. You used to crab about the two dollars, so tell me something funny."

"What's funny is that suckers like me pay to ride in filthy cabs like this. There's a puddle of dirty water and a beer can on the floor. The upholstery's ripped, and a spring is sticking me in the ass."

"It ain't my cab," he said. "Want to hear a one-liner?"

"I've heard one."

"Get this," he said. "It's one of those 'bad news-good news' jokes."

They were very popular at the time. "Can I stop you?" I asked.

"You already stopped me when you got in the cab."

Anybody who attempts to have a sensible conversation with one of those characters should have his head examined. I may have some cards printed that say, "I'm deaf and dumb. Please take me to ————" Then when I get into a cab I won't have to listen to the gab that comes from the front seat.

I thought those bulletproof glass partitions that they now have between the driver and the fare would help. But it doesn't. The driver just talks louder. And when you want to tell him where to go, he can't hear you.

They put those safety glass partitions in because so many drivers were being hit on the head by people in the back seat. The police thought robbery was the motive. Not true. The mugger just wanted a little quiet.

"You ready for this?" the driver asked. Then he blew his horn so he couldn't hear my answer.

"Listen. First the bad news. The Japs have landed on the moon. Now the good news. *All* of them!"

It's a good joke. I ought to know. I made it up. I've used it in clubs. Taxi driver jokes aren't generally that good.

"Did you hear," he asked, "about the Poles' march on Washington to protest against all the Polish jokes?"

"Yes," I said, "they got lost in downtown Seattle."

He said, "Somebody told you."

I said, "Right! It was the same guy who told me about the Polish couple that had a big family fight. It lasted all night. Finally, exhausted, the wife went to the bedroom. In a minute her husband followed her with a gun in his hand.

"She paid no attention to him. He put the gun to his head. She started to laugh. He said, "Don't laugh. You're next!""

That shut the driver up for a while. He had to think about it. But as we rode through the familiar parts of Brooklyn, *I* got to thinking about when all dumb jokes were about Brooklyn people and wondering why the Polish became the target in 1972. Actually, most of the so-called Polish jokes were "Italian" jokes in 1969.

Every minority group has had its turn. Years ago in London the dumb jokes were called Irish bulls. That one about the guy threatening to shoot himself before he shoots her is just a switch on a famous London *Punch* cartoon. It showed an Irish laborer hanging from a fourth-floor windowsill on the handle of a pickax. Hanging from the first man's feet is another man. The first man says, "Let go of my feet, or I'll hit you over the head with this pick." Think about it.

The driver finally figured out the shooting joke and asked, "Did you hear about the Pole who got thirty-two holes in his face from trying to learn to eat with a fork?"

Before I could answer, the cab stopped. "Here we are," he said. "Don't forget that Jap joke. It's a killer."

I paid him and gave him a twenty-five-dollar tip. It sounds like a lot, but it's only 15 percent of the meter on a ride to Brooklyn.

Of course, I couldn't use those jokes on the air. That's one of the problems with all the gags taxi drivers tell you. They have the kind that Archie Bunker would think were too bigoted. Actually you have to go along with the idea that the Japanese are our friends. And nowadays on TV, we're not even allowed to offend our enemies.

The censors . . . excuse me, there are no censors. The man from the program acceptance department explained to me exactly what was wrong with that joke about the Japanese. If we offend them, they'll stop sending us electronic equipment and we'll have to rely on the stuff we make here. The networks would then break down, and we'd all be out of work.

When I got out of the cab in Brooklyn, I started to walk around the old neighborhood, trying to remember old landmarks and how they looked years before. As I was walking along, I saw a cop stop a kid who was carrying a telephone in a shopping bag. The kids explained that his old lady was sick and he'd gone to the telephone company to get a phone so that his mother could call the doctor in case of an emergency. I thought it was wonderful and showed how wrong people are, saying that kids today have no regard for their parents. Here was a boy staying out of school and doing the best he knew how to make things easier for his mother.

When I was in high school, radio was just beginning to come on. It hadn't hit real big yet. A few kids fooled around with a cigar box and a galena crystal and made their own sets. They didn't get much, mostly static that sounded like a cat howling which we could hear by just opening a window. Some of the wise guys with their little homemade radios used to compete with each other on getting "distance." That meant you could get KDKA in Pittsburgh and hear "Dardanella" through a lot of static or get WEAF in New York and hear "Dardanella" through just a little static. Some stations were so bad even their static had static. Kids like me who had no idea how radio worked thought kids who said maybe they'd be able to send pictures, too, someday were crazy.

I remember there was a kid on the block named Solly Dineen. He was also in one of the classes I didn't go to. Sometimes we'd sit in the park together. The park was Ebbet's Field. He'd tell me that someday they'd have it so you could not only hear the ball games on radio but be able to see them right in your own home. Know what Solly's doing today? He's driving a truck for a Brooklyn bakery. The dumb kid had no vision. He never even thought of commercials.

But seriously, folks, as Berle so often says, I still have no idea why it is that when a little red light goes on in a box in Radio City, New York, people can see you bomb in Mason City, Iowa. They've got television now so that you can even see a guy drive a crazy-looking automobile all over the moon. There's only one thing they haven't figured out yet: how to keep people from switching off.

To give you an idea of how mystified I am by TV, I still don't know how the telephone works. I know if you don't pay the bill it *doesn't* work. People say I have telephoneitis. If I have, it's due to my early association with the company. I love to pick up a phone in New York and dial someone in Hollywood and wait to see what I get. I once got a casting director at Columbia Pictures, and he turned me down for a job I didn't know he had. Over the phone he knew I wasn't the type.

Another time I got a pregnant woman in Bergen, New Jersey, who was trying to dial her doctor but couldn't get a dial tone. I asked her for her doctor's number, dialed it, got him, told him the problem, and he told me to start boiling water.

But, as I started to say, when I was a boy, if a kid wanted some entertainment, he had to do more than just switch on a radio or TV set. He had to get out of the house and look for something to do. Some guys did this by getting together in groups and standing on corners whistling at girls. I was told that was the way you got to learn about women. My problem was that first I had to learn to whistle.

When a pretty girl came along, the inside of my mouth would get so dry cactus would grow between my teeth and make my gums sore. And I knew no girl would want to have anything to do with a guy who had sore gums.

Some kids liked to go to the movies. That was no problem for me. My rich Uncle Morris owned a movie theater. Often film distributors would save money by booking the same film in two theaters that weren't too far apart and make both theaters use one print. In a case like that I'd bicycle the print from one house to the other, rotating them all day. When Uncle Morris' house was playing the third and fourth reels of *Orphans of the Storm*, I'd be carrying the first and second reels on my bike to the other theater that was playing the last two reels. One rainy day I almost got hit by a Brooklyn *Eagle* truck. I turned quickly to get out of the way, the back wheels of my bike caught in the trolley tracks, and the two reels of the Hoot Gibson picture I was carrying unreeled all over Prospect Avenue. By the time I picked it up off the wet street and wound it back on its reels, got it in the cans and to the theater, the people had been sitting for fifteen minutes looking at a sign that said, "One Moment Please While We Change Reels." When I showed up, I thought the manager would kill me. And that was before he ran the film. It had got so wet that *West of the Peco Mesa* looked like *20,000 Leagues Under the Sea*.

Another way I made money at my Uncle Morris' theater was to sell half-price tickets to my friends. It was a great racket. Uncle Morris would let me in free as part of my pay for the bicycle work. Then I'd open a side exit and slip in my paying customers. Uncle Morris finally caught me and put me out of business. He damn near put me in the hospital.

All this hustling was just for one thing: to get money to go to vaudeville shows. There were a lot of vaude houses around Brooklyn in those days. There were a lot of them everywhere in those days. It was the common man's entertainment, and a lot of it was very common. The commonest they called burlesque.

There were basically two kinds of vaudeville houses, big time and small time. Frequently they played the same jokes. The acts graduated from the small time to the big time. The jokes never graduated. In the big time they could be heard only twice a day instead of three, four, five, or even six times a day. Generally speaking, a lot of it wasn't as bad as the rest of it, and the worst of it seemed better to me than anything that was going on at Manual Training High School.

I even learned to read and spell hard words while watching comedians. Words like "pharmacy" and "delicatessen." Most of the smaller theaters had one curtain they let the audience see at least once every show. Generally it was used as the backdrop for some monologist working in one. It was full of ads for neighborhood stores. "After the show go to Solly's Delicatessen—the biggest sandwiches in town." Or maybe "After the show go to the Nellis Drugstore—sodas, sundaes and aspirin." The sign served two purposes: It was advertising for the neighborhood businesses, and it gave the people who didn't like the jokes something to read so they wouldn't go to sleep and snore.

They had a system at Manual Training. If a kid did something a teacher didn't approve of, he was sent to a room they called Detention. It's different today. Now if a teacher says something the kid doesn't like, the teacher goes. I remember once in an ancient history class the teacher asked why Hannibal crossed the Alps with two hundred elephants. A kid said, "To sell them to an Italian circus?" He was sent to Detention. If a kid said that in school today, he'd be sent to the High School for the Performing Arts and become a talk show host.

I was sent to Detention so often a kid who took woodwork made a sign and hung it over the door. It said: "Henny Youngman Slept Here." It wasn't true. I never slept in Detention. I used my time to better advantage. I never went near the Detention Room. Nobody ever checked up on you. They had the honor system. So I took advantage of the many exits and went to see a show.

Nobody had the idea, yet, of selling all kinds of goodies in the theater lobby. The popcorn machine probably hadn't even been invented. So if a guy expected to spend the whole day seeing a show over and over again (how else can you learn the jokes?), he'd get in early before the prices went up and bring his lunch. I'd buy a corned beef sandwich at Solly's Delicatessen. With the sandwich, just like today, you got garlic pickles free. This was great. The corned beef was nourishment and the pickles guaranteed privacy.

There were enough vaudeville theaters around school so that I could go to a different one every day. The Orpheum was the big-time house that changed its bill only once a week. Then there was the Fox, the Flatbush, the Prospect, and a lot of other houses that changed their bill twice, sometimes three times, a week. I saw all the great acts of the day like Frank Tinney, Pat Rooney, Ted Healy, Lew Hearn, Joe Laurie, Jr., Bert and Betty Wheeler, Williams and Wolfus, Harry Watson, Eddie Cantor, Willie and Eugene Howard, Joe Howard, Al Jolson, Finks Mules, and I figured I really belonged in show business when I caught a bill that opened with an act called the Youngman Family. No relation. Can you picture any of my family walking thirty feet above the floor on a tight wire? But those other Youngmans were wonderful. I guess great talent goes with the name. They did somersaults on the tight wire. That's no trick now, but it was great then. It was doubly great to a kid who couldn't walk a crack on the sidewalk without falling.

Years later, I remember talking to Joe Laurie, Jr., who wrote a book about vaudeville. He called it *Vaudeville* so everyone would know right away what it was about. This was just before he died. And speaking about how vaudeville had declined, Joe said, "The only thing that's improved is the acrobats. Today they start with tricks they used for their big finish." That made me notice. And it's true. Of course when the Ed Sullivan Show folded on TV, there was no place left but the circus and carnivals for acrobats to do their stuff.

Acrobatics wasn't the kind of work I really wanted to do, anyway. If they were good, they got gasps. I wanted to get laughs. The first audience I appeared before must have thought I was a member of the Youngman Family. I got gasps.

I used to try out the jokes I'd heard on some of the bigger guys who hung around a candy store. They called themselves the Rowing Club because they had a rowboat that they kept at one of the piers along the East River. It was a big rowboat that looked something like a lifeboat. On the bow it said SS *Mary Lou*, New Orleans. Every day or so they'd take it for a practice row in the river, and sometimes they'd take me along. I enjoyed it. Sometimes I'd go down to the dock looking for a ride, and they wouldn't be there or they wouldn't take me with them. I'd stand and watch while they rowed out to one of the big freighters anchored in the harbor and come back with one or two big heavy bags that they'd carry to a truck.

One day I went looking for a ride, and I saw them coming in. A police boat was coming toward them, so they threw two big bags overboard. That didn't bother me much. I figured it must be booze. We had Prohibition then, and everybody was a bootlegger. A few weeks later I saw pictures of some of the members of the Rowing

Club on the front page of the Brooklyn *Eagle*. The "stuff" they were bringing in in those big canvas bags was Chinamen. Then I thought about seeing them dumping the bags overboard, and I got sick.

The one thing good about vaudeville as a career was that you didn't have to worry about the cops unless you were doing your act in one of those theaters where the girls took their clothes off as they danced. It was considered very daring then, but what the strippers in those days stripped down to, after the sports in the audience had clapped their hands full of calluses, was more than the average girl today wears to the office. I don't know any way to describe it except that it was a long suit of heavy cotton underwear (like what they call a body stocking today) with a round neck and short sleeves. The legs came all the way down to the ankles. And around their stomachs they wore a kind of big fluffy pink bow made out of stuff that was called tulle and was pronounced tool. Very daring. You could see more exciting things in the Sears, Roebuck catalogue.

While I was doing all this running around to variety shows, I kept my position as the best fiddle player in the family. This made my father angry because when he heard how I played, he was sorry there was *any* fiddle player in the family. He'd cut off my lessons, but it was too late. I'd found out the same thing about the violin that Jascha Heifetz found out. You can make money with one.

Before unionism really took hold, when you began working at something, before you could get a job that paid any money, you had to get some experience. So the only way you could get experience was at a job that didn't pay. For instance, if you wanted to play in a band, you had to find some band that would let you play with them so you could learn what it was like playing with a band. You see, it's one thing to play lousy violin all by yourself, but if you're going to play in a group, you have to learn how to make your lousy violin fit in with their lousy playing so that the whole thing will sound good.

I got my first "band" practice playing for nothing at Uncle Morris' movie theater. I was allowed to sit in with the three-piece orchestra he had in the pit. It supplied the mood music for the pictures.

The pictures Uncle Morris booked generally stank, so the mood music was perfect. It did, too. The three-piece combo consisted of a piano, a stool and an old lady who had arthritis so bad her fingers looked as if they belonged to a veteran knuckleball pitcher.

The pit, of course, was below where the stage would be. But there was only a little narrow piece of stage and then the screen. You had to look straight up to see the picture. It made Fatty Arbuckle look like Slim Summerville. The old lady tried to fit what tunes she knew to what seemed to her was happening on the screen. From her angle it was sometimes hard to tell. If she saw something that looked like a baby, she'd play Brahms' Lullaby. If there was no baby, she played something else, if she could think of it. Her only other rule was: If there seemed to be excitement, play loud. If there was a love scene, play soft. It never occurred to her to play good. My talent and hers blended perfectly.

As a rule, I could generally follow whatever she did, and we got no complaints from the audience because they were generally more interested in each other than in the film or the music. So we worked it out. She played in the only key she knew, and I played in the only key I knew. Anyone who said it didn't sound bad was either stone deaf or a liar.

I might have still been playing there, which would make the old lady about a hundred and eighty-two, if my uncle hadn't come into the theater one day and heard us. He generally didn't show up at the theater, and when he did, he rarely came into the house to look at the picture. All he looked at was the books.

He spent most of his time managing his real estate holdings and investing all the money anyone in the family would give him in Florida swamp. I think one of my uncle's alligators modeled for the picture of the little alligator you see on all those tennis shirts. The beast made so much money he's now selling tennis shirts with little men on them to alligators.

The day Uncle Morris dropped in and heard us we were playing some big romantic drama. I've forgotten the name of the picture, but Percy Marmont was making passionate love to somebody whose name I've forgotten. The old lady at the piano was softly playing her own arrangement of something Chopin would have wished he hadn't written if he'd heard what she did to it. On the violin, with my glasses all steamed up by what I was watching, stretched out on the screen above me, I was scratching out "There'll Be a Hot Time in the Old Town Tonight."

Uncle Morris fired me on the spot, saying, "And don't ask for a week's salary either." When I told him I didn't get any salary, that I was just doing it for practice, he offered to hire me back at half the price, provided I did the practicing at home.

I don't want you to get the idea that Uncle Morris was crazy. He just was so full of schemes that half the time he didn't hear what people were saying. He was rich when Aunt Marie married him, and he did a lot for the family, when he wasn't taking a lot away

from them. He was one of the first people to see what a great future
there was in Florida—about twenty years too soon. He got everybody in the family to chip in with him and invest. Only my father
held out. The trouble was, what Poppa held out was too little to
matter. Pop thought it was better to have a small house in Brooklyn
than a lot in Florida. So he bought a small house. Guess who sold it
to him.

It was on Fifty-first Street in Brooklyn. For about the first
seventeen years of my life I thought it was illegal for a Jew named
Youngman to live on any street but Fifty-first.

While everyone was mind-spending the money he was going to
make on Morris' Florida deals, Poppa used to tell them the story
about the man who bought a thousand dollars' worth of stock in a
gold mine. It was all the money he had. And he told everyone that
when they started to take the gold out, he'd have a beautiful buggy
with a patent leather body and red wheels. His little boy interrupted.
"Daddy, can I ride in the front seat?"

"Quiet," the man would say to the child. "As we ride up Fifth
Avenue on a Sunday, everybody will stare at us and say, 'Who's
that in that beautiful buggy and matched pair?'"

"Daddy, can I ride in the front seat?"

"Quiet! Then, after a few months everybody will know who it is
who drives up Fifth Avenue on a Sunday in such a handsome buggy
with a spirited matched pair of horses."

"Daddy, can I ride in the front seat?"

"Don't bother Daddy. We'll ride out into the country or we'll
take the ferry to New Jersey—"

"Daddy, can I ride in the front seat?"

"Abie, get out of the buggy!"

"You see," Poppa would say, "it's better we have our own roof
over our heads." But there were times in the summer that it rained
so hard he wasn't too sure we had one.

After my experience as a pit musician I branched out into playing
every Thursday night with a small combo at the weekly socials in
the high school. The combo was whoever showed up with an
instrument. One night we had two drummers, a trumpet player, and
me on the violin.

They had these socials so the teachers and the parents and the
pupils would get to know each other better. The trouble was that as
soon as they did, they hated each other.

They had games like bingo in some of the rooms and lectures in
some of the rooms. Most of the rooms were dark. Those were where
the boys and girls were taking night courses in sex education.

In the gym we played for what passed for dancing. It was all right because we played what passed for music.

There was also some old folk dancing. The young folks were down in those dark rooms. I got three dollars a night. That financed a lot of my theater going.

Uncle Morris' son, Jim, was in vaudeville—sort of. That is, he *wanted* to be on the vaudeville stage, and occasionally he made it. He got himself an act by "borrowing" material from a popular small-time vaudeville monologist who billed himself as D.D.H.? He went so big in the spots he played that today he'd be called DDT because he killed the people. Everybody thought he was out of this world . . . and with the material he used and Jim stole, before long he was.

His name was David D. Hall, but he was never billed any way but by his initials and a question mark. His delivery was sensational, and Jim copied it: every gesture, every inflection. He had a little book that he carried in his back pocket. He wore a black robe, like a judge, and a flat hat with a tassel on one side, like a professor. To show you how times have changed, even an amateur like me got laughs with his jokes.

I asked my cousin Jim, who was in the circulation department of the New York *Post* before he retired and moved to Miami Beach, to send me as much of the routine as he remembered. It may explain why he went into the newspaper business. Here it is:

LADIES AND GENTLEMEN, standing here, as I do, before you without even the protection of a net, I can see by the expression on the backs of your necks that you're sorry your seats are fastened to the floor.

HOWEVER, it will do you no good to try to get your money back, for when I get on this platform, the cashier, accompanied by his bodyguard, leaves by the back door.

FOLKS, I've been known to talk for hours without saying a word. I have been promised life insurance and life imprisonment. Of course, I could tell you more about myself, but there may be police in the house.

NOW, no doubt you have all heard of the *Encyclopaedia Britannica*. But today we have what is known as the hip pocket edition of the *Encyclopaedia Brizannica*. The best part of this holdup which I hold up is that we do not ask you to pay one cent. We would not accept it. It's not enough. Now, after five years, you find you've been stuck, send the book back prepaid, and we'll send you in return a nutcracker, beautifully engraved. Use it on yourself.

Now, if you should buy this book—you shouldn't, but if you should—and you pay ten dollars down and ten dollars for life, and at the end of seven years you should die—what the hell do we care?

To GIVE YOU AN IDEA what we have in this wonderful book, on page one we have the names of a few jewelry stores that were robbed this week. On page twelve we give you the names of *people* who have been robbed this week. And on page seventy-two, we tell you that twelve Mexican bandits attacked ten American women below the Rio Grande.

Now, should you want to know anything about etiquette . . . for example . . . should you ask . . . is it proper for a woman to go to a card party in a low-cut gown. Our book says no! At a card party it is only necessary to show one's hand. And, if you are walking in the street and see people riding in automobiles and you are tired, you are absolutely within your rights to go home.

So YOU SEE, FOLKS, let's start with our friend Al, Al Phabetical, and pull a wheeze on asthma. Asthma is a disease that makes it difficult for the patient to breathe with ease. But by following our advice, the patient passes away and leaves the asthma behind him. *A* also stands for ammonia. Ammonia, one whiff. Pneumonia, one stiff. *B* stands for bum, booze, and bootlegger. When a bum buys bum booze from a bum booze bootlegger, he becomes a bum booze bootlegger himself. *C* stands for courtship, courthouse, and cemetery. What is courtship? Courtship is the beginning of a young boob's life when he takes his salary, buys two tickets to a show, a dinner, and a taxi, so he can take his future legal ball and chain and legal watchman home. Courthouse is where the same young boob comes, in a lacerated condition, and tells the judge he can't live with her. Cemetery is the place that people are dying to get into. *H* stands for hash, husbands, and hospitals. What is hash? Hash is something that a ouija board can't tell us. Husbands, otherwise known as poor fish and sometimes used as blotters for baby's mashed potatoes, are the people who eat the hash. Hospitals are where they go. Now let us all go to *L* together. *L* stands for love, liver, lawyer. If I were to ask any of you folks the meaning of love, not one of you could tell me. There is only one woman who knows and that woman, God bless them, are our mothers. The beginning of love is like having one's rib tickled. The end is like having one's adenoids taken out. Liver is something the butcher used to give us for the cat. Nowadays the only thing he gives is his gall. When I speak of lawyers, I must be brief. *M* stands for money and marriage. What is money? Money is the thing you want most and throw away as soon as you get it. Marriage is like the red light on the back of an automobile. It's a warning to people not to follow you. Statistics show us that for every seven marriages there's one divorce. So you see, men, the odds are seven to one against you. *P* stands for polygamy, profanity, and prohibition. I do not believe in polygamy. I believe that one wife is punishment enough for any man. Neither do I believe in profanity in front of a woman. If you're married, hell, that's different. Prohibition. Years ago if a man walked down the street drunk, people would follow him booing and jeering. Today he has crowds following him to see where he gets it.

DEAR FOLLOWERS! And what does a man usually follow? A woman. WO Man. Again were I to ask you where woman comes from, the chances are you'd tell me she comes from the rib of a man. But our book says no. Our book says that woman comes from a mulberry tree and let me prove it. Doesn't a mulberry tree have worms . . . doesn't a worm come from a caterpillar and doesn't a caterpillar become a silk caterpillar . . . and doesn't a silk caterpillar become silk and doesn't silk become a dress and doesn't a silk dress become a woman and doesn't a woman become a mother and doesn't a mother become a mother-in-law and doesn't a mother-in-law become the damndest nuisance around the house!

NOW, where does man come from? Our little book tells us that man comes from everything that creeps and crawls around the ground. And let me prove that to you. We all know he has the brain of a fish, is as dumb as an oyster, as meek as a lamb, parrotlike in his ideas, yet on the other hand, he may have the courage of a lion, the heart of a tiger, be as wise as an owl, yet when he meets a pretty woman, he makes a jackass of himself.

SO YOU SEE, FOLKS, our little book gives it to us in a dirty four-letter word, and that word is "bunk" . . . B-U-N-K. When you come into this world and the doctor says, "It's the handsomest kid I've ever seen," that's BUNK! When you're three years old and they tell you to eat spinach, it puts hair on your chest, that's BUNK! When you're sixteen and you know it all, you're full of BUNK. And when you get married and she tells you all the rich guys she might have had . . . that's applesauce! And when you're seventy-five and you say you feel like a kid again, that's palsy. Bottled in bond on a bottle today, that's bunk! Homemade pies, that's bunk! Walk up one flight and save ten dollars, that's bunk. And sawing a woman in half—that's clever.

SO, FOLKS, YOU SEE, you start your life in a bunk and you'll die in a bunk. In 1776 it was Bunker Hill, in 1927 it's still bunk, so take our encyclopedias and Bunk diddle dee yonk . . . Bunk Bunk!

Maybe Jim has a bad memory. Or maybe D.D.H.? had something you had to see to appreciate. Or maybe audiences in those days were easier to please. Anyway, armed with "surefire" stuff like that, I used to face full-grown men and women at neighborhood parties, block dances, and political clubs. I'd work anywhere they'd let me. And with that routine I'm surprised I worked anywhere. Sometimes they let me pass the hat. Once I didn't even get the hat back.

I just gave you that routine so you'd know what the word "corny" really means. And when you put the words to that routine together with D.D.H.?'s gestures and delivery, you have more than corn. You have succotash.

Nevertheless, on the strength of that stuff, I did get an offer to appear as a contestant in an amateur night at the Sixteenth Street Theater in Brooklyn. I got the job through a guy who did nothing but book contestants for amateur nights. He had a regular stable of professional amateurs who played a regular circuit. But he always had to be on the lookout for new faces. Occasionally one of his troupe would get killed by an angry mob. Anyway, I was a new face. To look at it today, it's hard to believe.

He told me he'd give me three dollars, I'd already established that as my salary while playing with the combo at school, so I took it. How much he got out of it never entered my head until years later when it was foolish to ask. His name was Jack Linder, and he later managed Mae West, which was nice work in those days. I hear it's still not bad.

When I finally began to get into the Broadway scene, I met a lot of agents who hung around what was then called Columbia Beach because it was on the corner of Forty-seventh Street and Broadway, where the Columbia burlesque house was. All the actors who were "on the beach"—out of work—would get together there and tell each other how lousy their agents were. Naturally there were a lot of agents hanging around to pick up some new business from an actor who had just fired his best friend. One of these was a guy named Solly Shore who booked amateur shows as Linder did, but on a bigger scale.

Solly used to book whole units of amateurs who would play the houses on the Columbia wheel and in any other places that could be reached by subway or ferry. In those days a ferryboat was the only thing that would take you to New Jersey. They were just building the first tunnel under the river, and there was no George Washington Bridge.

Sometimes on Sunday afternoon, I'd take my fiddle, and for a nickel I'd get on a ferryboat and play. The people would give me money. As long as I split with the captain, I could ride back and forth. I never made very much, but it was a nice way to stay out in the open and have a boat ride. The only difference between playing on the ferryboats and the jobs I do crossing the ocean or on cruise ships, like the *QE II*, is the money, the food, and the accommodations.

Although I never worked any of the burlesque theaters that Solly Shore booked his amateurs into, I saw some of the shows. The "amateurs" would take turns at being lousy. Then they'd get the hook, and that was the big laugh of the show. Solly told me if I came with the show, I wouldn't have to *try* to be lousy.

To determine who would be the winner on each show, they'd pick out one act and bill it as being from the area in which the theater was located. Like they'd introduce, "Ladies and gentleman, young Danny Driscoll, a musician who really uses his head. Young Danny will play Beethoven's Fifth Symphony using nothing but two spoons and his skull. Incidentally Danny's a Washington Heights boy, so let's give him a great big Washington Heights hand." That would do it for Danny. I must say I never heard Beethoven played better with two spoons.

Of course if the theater was in Brooklyn the "Flatbush Avenue boy" or the "Bay Bridge boy" would win the big prize, which was generally about ten dollars. Naturally the contestants didn't get to keep the dough. All they got was the three dollars.

When I found out the pay was three bucks, I was very proud. I'd started out in the amateur show field at the top salary. But I never played any burlesque houses except occasionally on Sunday, when they had what they called concerts, which were really nothing but vaudeville shows. It was while working one of these dates that I met a comic named Buddy Walker. He came on carrying a cat, and he'd say to the audience, "I stole this cat from a guy who runs a poker game in the President Hotel. I heard someone say there was fifty dollars in the kitty." Years later, he was still doing that same tired joke, and he asked me for some material. He told me to meet him in front of the Lobster, a restaurant on West Forty-fifth Street, and he'd give me fifty dollars for whatever I had.

He showed up driving a great big fancy Stutz Bearcat, which in those days was like driving a Jaguar—very sporty. He got out, and passed right by me. Gave me a brush bigger than anything the Fuller brush man ever saw. So I got mad. I had to do something to this son of a bitch.

There I was with exactly fifty cents in my pocket, waiting for a man who promised me fifty dollars and he wouldn't speak to me. I started looking around for a stone or something to throw through his windshield. The first thing I spotted was a sign painter's truck parked in front of a tailor shop. Two painters were painting a sign that said "Pants Pressed While U Wait—35¢." It was a theatrical neighborhood, and an actor might get a call for a job and need his only pair of pants creased.

I walked over to the painters and told them I was broke and wanted to sell my car, that I'd give them fifty cents if they'd paint "For Sale—$25" on the side of it. We made a deal, and I had them paint the sign on the side of Buddy Walker's Stutz. He never spoke to me again. That's the thanks you get for helping a man to sell his car.

But to get back to my first appearance as a paid amateur. It was not an unqualified success.

My father was not what you'd call a highly religious man. Like most of the immigrant Jews who came to this country from Eastern Europe, he was inclined to be a Socialist. This meant that he wanted all people who needed something to get it by some arrangement that gave equal opportunity to all for equal work. Not a bad idea. First you've got to find equal. Then you've got to find work.

Poppa read and argued the teaching of Robert Ingersoll. For years I thought he was in the watch business. Then I found out he was an agnostic. Someday I'll find out what an agnostic is.

But Poppa kept a Jewish home. I guess Momma made him do it. He sent me to Hebrew school, and when I was thirteen, I had my Bar Mitzvah just like every other little Jewish boy. I'm writing this book with the last of the fountain pens I got as Bar Mitzvah presents. I outgrew the blue serge suit two years ago.

We all went to B'nai Israel Synagogue on Twenty-fourth Street and Fourth Avenue in Brooklyn on the High Holy Days. Beyond that the religion Poppa taught was be good to your parents, read books, and listen to opera. I think I did all right with the first one, but the second two kind of threw me.

To make a living, Poppa was a show card painter. He gave up making caps and hats when the factory he was working for put him to work making sweatbands and made him supply his own sweat. I don't know. I guess he got bored with caps and hats.

So he learned show card writing where so many of the newly arrived in this country went to enlarge themselves, at Cooper Union in what is now called the East Village in Manhattan.

As far as I know, he must have been a good show card painter because he seemed to make enough money to take care of us. I think the reason he did well was because he could misspell as well as any show card writer in the business. In fact, he was so good that kids just learning would come to him for wrong spellings.

We had our own house, Poppa saw to that—instead of a piece of swamp in Florida—and he probably ran our whole family just on the money he saved by giving me such a small allowance. He figured if he gave me too much money, I'd become a bum. I fooled him. I became a bum anyway. At least that's what he thought. And when I got married, my father-in-law agreed with him.

There's only one reason for going into all this. The job I got at the Sixteenth Street Theater happened to be a matinee. It was Saturday. Not only Sabbath but Yom Kippur. If there are any people in the world who still don't know that Yom Kippur is the holiest day in the whole Jewish calendar, let them know it now. It's the day you fast to atone for your sins, one of which is usually not fasting last Yom Kippur. So that's the day I picked to do an amateur show in a cheap vaudeville theater.

Anyway, I went on, and things were going great. The gags I'd picked up from Lou Holtz, Richie Craig, Jr. (I had some trouble with him later on in my career), Jackie Osterman, and some of the other headliners I'd caught, plus D.D.H.?'s material that I got through my cousin Jim, were clicking fine. I was beginning to feel the sweet flush of success when a policeman appeared on the stage followed by my father, and I began to feel the hot flush of embarassment.

What happened was, I'd been standing out in front of the synagogue before going off to make my three-dollar debut and I had to tell somebody about the great event. So I bragged about my job to another kid, who was also standing in front of the temple trying to get a little fresh air.

There seems to be some old Hebraic law that says it must be

unbearably hot on Yom Kippur. And even if the little *shul* we went to could have afforded air conditioning, there wasn't any made for it. All the air-conditioning people knew how to do was chill big places like the Paramount Theater and the Roxy and places like that. If B'nai Israel could have afforded one of the available cooling systems, they'd have had to rent another building to put it in, and if they'd turned it on, it would have immediately turned a lot of religious Jews ice blue.

Poppa had come out looking for me and to get some air, and when he asked if anybody'd seen me, this kid I'd been bragging to told him where I was. Some years later that kid turned out to be the announcer on the *Kate Smith Show*, André Baruch, when I was one of its stars.

To this day I really don't know whether it was because I was working on a Holy Day or because my father thought that any kind of show business that wasn't opera was unholy that made him have me hauled off the stage by the scruff of my neck. I was the first amateur ever to play that house that was given the hook by the fuzz. It was shameful. It was embarrassing. And worst of all, it cost me the three bucks. It was my first contact with the standard show biz arrangement, no play—no pay.

I tried to be a printer but I wasn't the type.

11

Balance of Trade

DURING my second year at Manual Training, the news that my scholastic career had only one way to go—down—began to reach my father. Evidence was presented by various teachers. They told wild stories of how my classroom deportment upset their routine, made the other pupils laugh, and in every possible way destroyed discipline. In those days schools had it.

Poppa talked the situation over with Momma, and she said he should talk to me. He said *she* should talk to me. They finally compromised. *He* talked to me. Both of them were convinced that the Lord had punished them by giving them a first son who was some kind of nut. They didn't know what would become of me, but they thought I might wind up in a Hershey bar.

So one day Poppa called me into their bedroom, which was his private office when he was home. Actually Poppa had two private offices at home. The other was where he locked himself in to do all his studying. Sometimes he studied so long, I couldn't wait and would have to run down the street to the Shell station. Sometimes I didn't run fast enough.

Poppa sat me on the bed, stood over me, and said, "Henny, you act like a nut. You talk like a nut. You even play the violin like a nut. What am I going to do with you?"

"I don't know, Poppa. Maybe you should try to find a place for me with the Cushman Bakeries. They might be able to work me into a fruit cake."

"See what I mean. Nothing's serious to you. All you want to do is laugh. Here you're getting to be a man, and what kind of man are you getting to be? Tell me, who ever heard of a nut becoming a doctor?"

"I did. There's a headliner in vaudeville, named Doc Rockwell."

"Vaudeville! Show business! That's all you think about."

"It's a good way to make a living, if you're good."

"In the kind of life you have to lead, by the time you're good, you're bad. Traveling all the time. Staying in cheap hotels. Eating cheap food. You call that living? And if times should get bad, God forbid, who will go to see a show with nothing in it but to laugh at? Because in times like that, what's to laugh at?"

"In bad times, that's when people need something to laugh at."

"Henny, when times are bad and people have to be careful what they do with their money, a man doesn't spend a dollar to get a laugh. If he wants to laugh, he gives himself a little tickle and spends the dollar to put some food in his family's mouth. Sooooo . . . as long as you're not going to college to become a doctor or something smart that your family can be proud of, the next best thing for you to do is to learn something useful with your hands. When you know how to do that, you can thumb your nose at the world."

"I learned how to thumb my nose when I was in third grade, and when I did it, you slapped my face."

"That wasn't thumbing your nose at the world. That was thumbing your nose at me. At the world it's different."

"But I can do something with my hands. I can make music with a violin."

"Don't ever tell that to anybody. He may ask you to prove it. Then what will you do? I'm talking about a person who can really do—make—something with his hands, something that people need. If he can do that, he'll never starve."

"I haven't made any plans for starving, Poppa."

"Well, if you're going to try to make a living with that violin, you'd better start making some plans along that line. When I left Russia, I knew I could get along anywhere that people wore hats and caps because I knew how to make them."

"Hats and caps? In Paris you made your living as an opera claque."

"That wasn't my living. That was for fun and to see the opera for nothing. I made my living making hats. And when I wanted to, I wasn't afraid to leave Paris and go to London because I knew that there they also wore hats and caps. Sometimes very funny ones. And if you think I was brave to come to America, I wasn't. Because I had a trade. And I made enough out of it to bring the rest of my family to America. That's what a trade can mean to a man."

"Poppa, I'm not going into the men's millinery business."

"I would never let you. It's no good."

"That's because in the hat and cap business it isn't the man, it's the product that has to get a head."

"You should have told me that before I was married. By the time I found out you couldn't make much money in the hat business I was already comfortable."

"Comfortable" was a word Poppa used for "doing well." He wasn't the only one. There's a joke about the old man who was hit by a taxi. He's lying on the street. People have called an ambulance. From somewhere people have brought a pillow and a blanket. An old lady leans over him and asks, "Are you comfortable?"

"I make a living."

"What was I going to do," Poppa rambled on, "by the time I found out I didn't like making hats, what was I going to do, give it up and do something I didn't know how to do?"

"That's what you did. You learned something else. You went into the show card business."

"That was later, and don't contradict your father."

"Okay. But I want to go into show business because I think I'm learning something about it."

"Just from going to shows?"

"How else can you learn?"

"Can a man learn to be a dentist just by watching someone grind teeth? No. For you, Henny, I want something more in the intellectual field."

"When I was a little boy and tried to read books in bed at night, you wouldn't let me. You said I'd hurt my eyes. You made me turn off the light." (The light I was talking about was a gas light with one of those Welsbach mantles that made them shine brighter.)

"It wasn't that you were reading. It was *what* you were reading. *The Rover Boys in Honduras*! Who cares what three fellas with a crazy name like that did down in a country where they don't know how to do anything but grow bananas. For you I want a career that's more intellectual, that has to do with journalism or books maybe."

"I could never learn to write." (When I said that, I never thought I'd be trying to prove it.)

"Who's talking about writing? I want you to be a printer. No matter where he goes, a man who knows how to set type will always be able to get a job. People will always have to read."

Poppa had no way of foreseeing television.

"So you'll go to the trade school and learn to be a typesetter. Someday, then, I can pick up a newspaper or a book and be proud to say, 'My son set that.' "

"Anything I ever set in type is sure to get a laugh."

"They have proofreaders to fix that. Someday, maybe, you could even have your own printing plant and print great magazines like *The Literary Digest* and *St. Nicholas*."

"Poppa, now *you're* talking like a nut."

"So get me into Cushman's Bakeries and they'll put me in a fruit cake. Tomorrow we go to the trade school and get you started on a career as a printer."

And that's how it happened that for a time I combined the thrill of trying to get into show business with the problems of learning how to set type. As a matter of fact, I can still set type and to prove it . . . fum thez poyt don, thus tipe wuz said buy me.

I kid a lot about my printing career now, but if it hadn't been for printing I might never have met my wife, and I probably never would have gotten on in show business. Without the woman I've lived with for forty-four years (at this writing) I might never have thought of the joke, "take my wife, please!"

The Brooklyn Vocational Trade School was really two schools. In the morning you were in one building where you learned your trade. Then you had lunch. After lunch you went to another school a few blocks away for more academic studies . . . like gym.

I started taking my lunch to school, and sometimes, on my way from one building to another, I'd stop in to see my father, who was working as a show card writer for a McCrory store that happened to be right on my way between the two schools. The Brooklyn Vocational Trade School was an entirely new kind of school experience for me, and I think it did me a lot of good.

One of the first things I learned was how to get along with people I thought weren't meant to get along together. We'd always lived in a mixed neighborhood, and I got the idea, at an early age, that the Irish, the Poles, the Italians, the Chinese, and the Jews—to name just a few—were put on earth to fight with each other. But I had all this thinking changed for me in trade school because there happened to be a lot of orphans in my group.

I discovered this—you can't tell just by looking at a kid that he's an orphan—when I noticed that at lunchtime some of the boys didn't have anything to eat, and I felt sorry for them. But there were so many of them it gave me a problem. I couldn't give part of my lunch to one of them without giving some to all of them. And if I gave to all of them, I wouldn't have anything to eat, and they'd think I was an orphan, and it would get confusing.

I finally worked it out. Instead of bringing my lunch to school after that, I made arrangements for all of us to eat lunch together. This is how I did it. I knew how Poppa felt about helping those who needed help, so I got all these Irish, Polish, Italian, Chinese, and black orphans together, and we all went to Poppa's office. He'd send one of us out for a couple of cans of sardines, and we'd all have lunch and talk. Long before there was a United Nations Building on First Avenue in New York, Poppa had meetings going in his little office in Brooklyn.

Listening to what those orphan kids had to say taught me the truth of an old saying my mother used to tell me so often: "If you think you have trouble, stop complaining for a minute and listen to the other man's."

By listening, I found out that when winter comes, an Italian without an overcoat gets just as cold as a Jew without one. And a Pole with holes in his shoes comes home with just as wet feet as a black man with worn-out shoes. One of the little Chinese kids pointed out—he must have been one of Confucius' great-great-great-great grandkids—that there wasn't a whole lot of difference between ravioli, kreplach, and wonton, and they were all equally desirable if you were hungry.

There's no question that we all got something out of those United Nations-type sardine lunches in Poppa's office. And if I had to put what it was in just one word, I'd have to say it was indigestion.

One of the things I learned in this world while I was still young is that you can learn something from everybody, if you just pay attention. Of course, I couldn't learn how to pay attention. But I tried.

I even learned something from the knob-knuckled piano player I fiddled with—make that played with—make that played the violin with—in the movie theater. She told me how I could get free music. She'd send me to New York, to Broadway, where all the music publishers had their offices. There were a lot of them in those days and they had pretty crummy offices. Now if you go to see a music publisher, he's a vice-president of one of the big conglomerates like Gulf and Western. And he has a beautiful office. The trouble is, he doesn't know a damn thing about the music business.

Publishers' offices all used to have rehearsal rooms open to anyone who wanted to learn one of their songs or could write a song that might be worth taking a chance on publishing. All I had to do was tell someone at one of these places that I had an orchestra in a Brooklyn movie theater and they'd give me free professional copies of their Number One Plug and all the standards in their catalogue. Their Number One Plug was what they called the song the house was working on to try to make it a hit. And there was a lot more to it in those days than just knowing a few disc jockeys and getting them to play it for you. Sheet music was still the big selling item for publishers, and the way they got plugs was to work on the vaudeville stars and near stars to sing or play the tune.

They used to spend thousands of dollars entertaining the big bandleaders. I couldn't get them to pay my subway fare back to Brooklyn. And then it was only a nickel.

One of the best ways to get a song plugged was to put one of the top stars on the cover of the sheet music and give him writing credit and a piece of the royalty on the song. In that way you got him to sing it better and more often because the more popular he made the tune, the more the tune made money for him. That's why when you see an old piece of sheet music you'll see Al Jolson's or Eddie Cantor's or some other big star's name and picture on the cover.

Of course, all the fancy illustrations on the covers of songs were an additional gimmick to get people who probably couldn't play or even read music to buy a copy of a song and put it on the piano at home. In those days pianos were a status symbol the way having a loudspeaker on your radio (instead of listening with earphones) used to be. Then, of course, television became a status symbol. Some people in Brooklyn near where we lived couldn't afford TV, but they spent two dollars to buy something that looked like a TV antenna to put on the top of their house or stick out of the window of their flat so people would think they had a TV set.

But to get back to pianos, families spent a whole lifetime paying off on an upright piano that no one in the family could play unless it had a pianola attachment. It was boom time for piano teachers. They got fifty cents to a dollar an hour and were worth every cent of it. A real smart kid could get his parents to lay out four or five dollars for piano lessons and learn enough to play better than the teacher.

Going to Broadway to get music was what really started me learning things about show business. One thing I found out about was something called agents and how, if you had one, he could get you jobs that paid more than three dollars a night, which was my top take up to then.

From the agents I found out that if I could get my own band together instead of playing in someone else's band, I could get as much as five dollars a night. Of course the agent got 10 percent. But four dollars and fifty cents was still better than three dollars. Shortly after that my Swanee Syncopators came into existence. I picked the name "Swanee Syncopators" for a couple of reasons. In those days some of the biggest songs were called "coon" songs, and they were all about a river called the Swanee. Another reason was that we could always get a date to play at my cousin's resort Swan Lake Inn in the Borscht Belt.

But my group wasn't called the Swanee Syncopators all the time. We changed our name to fit in with the surroundings. If we played at the Bay Ridge Social Club dance, we were the Bay Ridge Society Orchestra. When we worked at the Flatbush Athletic Club, we became the Flatbush Five, which was a clever name for a band that only had four men in it. By giving ourselves a name that sounded as if we were from the neighborhood, we got a more friendly reception than outsiders would get. And, also, after the gig was over, we were safer going home with our money.

Not only did we change names, but we changed leaders. We took turns. If you got the date, it was your turn to lead. But I was always more impressive when I was leading because I had a violin and a bow to use as a baton the way big bandleaders like Paul Whiteman, Guy Lombardo, and Ben Bernie did. But those three great bandleaders were smarter than I was. They never tried to play their fiddles.

One of the stars of the Swanee Syncopators was a crazy kid who played an awful lot of trombone. His name was Mike Riley, and the first time I heard him he was marching in some saint's day parade with the band of the St. Michael's Catholic Church, which was on Fifty-ninth Street and Fifth Avenue in Brooklyn.

I must have been a pretty good judge of talent. About ten years or so later, Mike was one of the big attractions at the Onyx Club on "The Street." That's what everybody called the block on West Fifty-second Street in New York between Fifth Avenue and Sixth Avenue. That was before Sixth Avenue became the Avenue of the Americas. It still had an elevated railroad running along it.

The Street was a row of nightclubs, one right next to the other where you could hear all kinds of entertainment: the greatest jazz in the world, some of the funniest comics, and everything else from female impersonators to exotic dancers, one of which had a snake for a partner—a real snake! But mainly the Street was where you went to hear the greats of the pop music field do their stuff. There were always two kind of musicians on the street: the ones who were working and the ones who were hanging around looking for work. You'd never know when someone would get sauced up and there'd be an empty chair on the bandstand in some spot. There was always someone somewhere on the Street to fill the vacancy. Out-of-work cats hung around spots just waiting for a chance to sit in for a couple of sets with the hot combos. It was in this scene in 1934 or maybe '35 that Mike Riley became a very big figure. And it was while playing at the Onyx Club that he wrote the tune that every band in the country played over and over again on New Year's Eve, "The Music Goes 'Round and 'Round (Oh-oh-oh-oh-oh-oh and it comes out here)." I played the Street too—but not as a musician. But I'll come to that.

Looking back on my life, as I am, I don't know where I got the time to do all the things I know I did. And I know I really did do all of them because I can't remember half of them. Of these things I'm sure. I went to school. I learned how to be a printer. I had my band that played for evening parties and on weekends. And on weekdays and Saturdays after school I held a job in a printing booth in some of the five-and-ten-cent stores. It was a little sort of a box with a printing press, a chair, and a telephone, and we turned out business cards and letterheads while you waited for businesses that were just getting started and would probably be finished before very long.

I even had my own little business. When nothing was going on, I'd print up batches of cards in sets of ten with jokes on them, one joke to a card. Then I'd peddle them around the store for ten cents a set. They were great jokes like: "If you want to know how to make a pair of pants last, make the coat and vest first." There were other biggies like that. They weren't the best jokes in the world, but anyone dumb enough to buy them would be dumb enough to like them and tell them. I got most of them out of *Variety*.

In the "Vaudeville" section of that show business paper, they used to run a column called "Released Jokes." I thought this meant that whatever act was using them didn't want them anymore and was willing to have anyone take them. This was better than stealing jokes. It was sort of being given them.

It wasn't until years later that I found out that "Released Jokes" were jokes that the editors of *Variety* decided had been used enough, were old enough, and tired enough to be retired. But what I didn't know at the time didn't hurt me. And it didn't hurt business any either. I'd walk around whatever store I was working in, hollering, "Get Your Fun Cards! Ten Big Laughs for only ten little pennies! Be the life of the party for ten cents." Sometimes I'd sell as many as forty sets on a busy day. Deducting what it cost me for the cards and to print them, it meant that I made a net profit of three dollars and ninety cents.

The man I worked for, who owned the printing concessions, was a gentleman named Atkinson who claimed he invented the press we used. It was just a regular job press, but smaller than most, and he called it "automatic." If I turned the handle, it was automatic. That meant that it automatically fed the paper through the press so that the operator didn't have to stop after each impression and put another sheet on the platen.

Atkinson had five or six of these presses operating in variety stores around Brooklyn, and he must have done very well. When one of his regular operators in any location was sick or had a day off, I'd fill in for him. This was good for my funny card business because I kept getting into new territories that had yet to be flooded with my gags. Another advantage of the job was that I could use Atkinson's telephone to book band dates. Atkinson never objected. Probably because he never heard about it.

One day I got a call from a man in Coney Island who told me an agent had told him that I had a great band and he wanted to hire it for a Saturday night dance he was running if we were free. I told him we weren't free, that it would cost him five dollars a man. He said that would be all right as long as we didn't have more than six men. But before he hired us, he wanted to hear how the band sounded.

"What do you mean, 'hear it'?" I asked, not knowing what to do. "We don't audition for dates."

"It's not that," the guy explained. "I was told that this number I called was the place where you were rehearsing."

Go explain to someone not in show business that agents lie. Or that bands don't just sit around rehearsing all day hoping someone will call up and book them. Another thing I wasn't crazy about explaining was that I didn't really have a band in the first place. What I did, when I got a call like this, was to book the date and then hire whoever I could get to fill it with me. But when you're hungry and ambitious, even an evening in Coney Island looks big, so you think of something.

"Hold the wire," I said, "While I get the phone closer to where the band is and I'll let you hear how they sound."

Across the aisle from my printing booth in the Kresge store where all this action was taking place was a booth where they sold sheet music and phonograph records. It was run by an Irish girl that I had a silent crush on, the kind only growing boys understand. I used to steal looks at her, and every time I tried to get up courage to speak my tongue stuck to the roof of my mouth. But necessity makes heroes of us all. So I asked her, just as if I'd been talking to her all day, if she'd put a dance record on the phonograph she had there for demonstrating records. She did, and I told my man to listen. He liked the sound and closed the deal. He never knew that he hired Rudy Vallee and his Connecticut Yankees. What he got was the Coney Island Ramblers.

There was one thing we had to be careful about. All scratch, or pickup, bands like mine did. Sometimes we'd meet for the first time in a week or so. Sometimes some of the guys would be total strangers to the rest of them. So I'd warn everybody who was coming to play a date like the one I just described, not to shake hands when we got together. It always had to look as if we were together all the time.

Don't think that "my boys" didn't rehearse. In those days every bandleader referred to the musicians in his company as "my boys." Why? Like in Westerns, the sheriff always forms a posse by telling someone to "get the boys." Even in World War I, which I was lucky enough to be too young for, they talked about "our boys in France."

But me and my boys were really boys, and we did rehearse. The problem was finding a place. As I've said, we used to rehearse sometimes on the roof over the tailor shop that was next to our apartment. But people higher up sometimes threw things out the window that weren't nice to get down the bell of a trombone. So we were always looking for free rehearsal space. I hired a drummer for one date, a kid who called himself Riffs Parker. He said we could practice in his parlor.

We'd never practiced in a parlor before, but we were willing. It turned out that his parlor wasn't far from the Prospect Theater in Brooklyn on Ninth Street and Fifth Avenue, and it was some parlor to practice dance music in. It was a funeral parlor that his father owned. Nobody minded that we played there between jobs, except us. We didn't rehearse very well. I guess we were scared that it might be sacrilegious to play our kind of music where they kept the dead. Anyway, the riffs and the stiffs didn't work out.

Another place we used to get a lot of rehearsing done was in subway trains on the way home from a gig late at night. We'd play for the conductor. Whenever a guy would come to his station, the rest of the guys wouldn't let him get off. We used to ride around for hours playing and keeping each other from getting off. Sometimes there'd be a passenger or two that would applaud, and occasionally a drunk, feeling no pain, would peel off a dollar bill and hand it to us. It wasn't much, but it covered the carfare.

The wonderful thing about the Coney Island Ramblers date was that it broke the ice for me with that Irish girl who ran the record booth. The next time I showed up for work I brought her a box of candy. Not the kind of cheap candy you could buy in our five-and-ten-cent store. It was high class Loft's candy at seventy-nine cents a pound. I got her a half a pound. And ate most of it. She really had me hooked. It was the first present I ever bought for anyone, even myself.

When I wasn't at the store, I used to dream about taking her out to fancy places like Reisenweber's or Shanley's that I couldn't get into even if I could afford them. I guess I figured if I had a pretty girl like that with me, I could crash anywhere. But one thing I thought about most was what my mother would say if I told her I was dating an Irish girl. Dating? I hadn't taken her out. But just knowing I was *thinking* of it would have made Momma unhappy.

There's a story about two Jewish mothers. One asks the other, "What would you do if your son brought home a shiksa and told you he was going to marry her?"

"What could I do? If that's what's going to make him happy, who am I to stop him? I'd fix him a nice dinner with chicken soup and matzoh balls, wish him *mazel tov* and go in the other room and cut my throat."

I once saved a girl from being attacked. I controlled myself.

12

Dates with Sadie

I was excited. I was young. I was in love. I was out of work. I was nuts!

That's what being in love means. Being nuts.

The fact that the girl was Irish, I knew, was going to be a problem. But I had to live with it. So I let it move in with all the other problems that were living with me. Among those the most important was money.

You can't come on strong with a girl when you're working night and day and weekends. I was doing this to make enough money to take the girl out. If I stopped doing it to take her out, I'd be broke. If I were broke, I couldn't take her out.

What was I doing night and day? I was either hustling printing orders, printing printing orders, hanging around with musicians to get a job with someone's band, selling business cards to someone who had a band, or looking for bookings for my own band. A man tries everything when he's in love and needs money. To me, love was feeling about a girl the way Milton Berle feels about Milton Berle. Beautiful.

But there was one bright side to the situation: When I got brave enough to ask my little Irish rose what her name was, it turned out to be Sadie Cohen. Of course, George M. Cohan, with an *a*, was Irish. But Sadie Cohen, with an *e*, that's Jewish all over the world.

I was a lot happier. Not that I have anything against the Irish girls. But it meant my mother wouldn't have to cut her throat. When she found out about us, she wanted to cut Sadie's.

Nothing unusual. She was my mother. They're all the same. They all want their sons to get married, if only there was a girl good enough. Girls' mothers are the same. But there isn't a man worthy of their daughter. They're all saving their daughters for the second coming. "Don't marry the first man who asks you. Wait for the second!"

So what's happening? Girls are going with girls and boys with boys. It's getting worse and worse. It could be the solution to the population explosion. It could also be the end of the world.

When I told my parents that Sadie and I hit it off, they told me to knock it off. They asked me where I met her and I sang, "I found a million-dollar Sadie in a five-and-ten cent store."

What I saw in her puzzled my parents. What she saw in me puzzled *hers*. And in all the years of our marriage they never solved the puzzle. We had trouble no matter whose parents we lived with.

There was only one thing her parents and my parents agreed on: that we should live with the other's parents. This puzzled us.

At this writing we've been married forty-four years. Where did I go wrong?

Not long ago I was reminded of the sort of dates Sadie and I had. I couldn't take her to dinner, theater, and then dancing for two reasons: two dollars, that was what it cost in those days to take a girl to dinner, theater, and dancing. Chinese dinner, seventy-five cents (with tip), theater fifty cents, dancing (seven dances at ten cents a dance) seventy cents, carfare home, five cents. That covered me. She paid her own two dollars.

There was another reason why Sadie and I didn't do all these things that are called courtship. We knew that they led to marriage, which leads to the divorce court. The other thing that kept us from the conventional dating game was that I was usually playing my violin where people went to dinner, theater, and dancing.

How was I reminded of all this? Some joker at the Friars' Club walked past my table, dropped a clipping in front of me, and disappeared so fast I thought he was the waiter serving me a quick lunch. So I put ketchup on it. When I saw it was a clipping, I knew it was left by one of my friends. They're always clipping me. But I was glad to see it was just a clipping. The guy got in and out so fast I was afraid it was a subpoena.

Later that afternoon while taking a *shvitz* (that's the same thing they call a steam bath at the New York Athletic Club), a guy next to me with a towel over the old neighborhood said, "How'd you like that thing I left on your table?"

"Great," I said. "Thanks. I'll use it in my book."

"Some bookmark! What book are you reading?"

"Reading!? I mean the book I'm writing."

"You're kidding. Only college boys know how to write. It's part of their survival training. They have to know how to write home for bail money."

(That's the trouble with talking to people at the Friars. You're always tangling with some joker who thinks he's funnier than you are. I don't mind his thinking it, but I get damned mad when he's right!)

"Haven't you heard?" I asked, for vanity makes straight men of us all. "I'm writing my autobiography. My life."

"I didn't know you had one," he said, finding an opening. "I didn't even know you knew how to write."

This was an out-and-out lie. He'd seen me sign his lunch check just the day before. "Do me a favor," he said, "if you use the item I left on your table, don't mention my name."

"Why not?"

"I'll sue you for defamation of character."

"Is that possible?"

"To sue for defamation of character?"

"No. To defame yours."

"Too bad the *Ed Sullivan Show* has folded," he said. "I think we just wrote an act. He'd book us for next Sunday."

"And the show would close next Monday."

I hope that explains why I'm not mentioning the man's name. But I'll give you a hint. Two of his initials are in the alphabet.

A few years ago, to celebrate its fifty-sixth anniversary, *Billboard* got out a special edition, one of those things that's full of nostalgia to remind you of how lousy the "good old days" really were. What this character had dropped in front of me was a Xerox copy of one of the pages from that special issue. Right in the center of the page there's a three-inch story with the headline HEN YOUNGMAN AND SYNCOPATORS OPEN CONEY ISLAND BOARDWALK. It reads as if we were the carpenters who built it. The date line was July, 1924.

The reason Al . . . well, that's one of the names he used. For a while he had a pen name—No. 42-391-220. The reason he gave me the clipping was that he knew, when he saw "Hen Youngman" that it marked a turning point in my career. (A career is anybody's life, if he makes money.)

That "Hen Youngman" headline caused me to change my name, for the first time. I almost changed it a second time, but that was later, so hang on. All my life the guys used to call me Hen, short for Henry. It wasn't until I saw it in print like that I realized it was a bad name for anyone in show business. A hen can lay an egg.

So I changed it to Henny. With a name like that you could only lay a little egg. That's why they made me a Friar.

I think you ought to read the rest of the item. It says, "Hen Youngman and his Original Swanee Syncopators have been engaged for the Boardwalk Hotel in Coney Island." How do you like that "original Swanee Syncopators"? When you hired Youngman, you got the genuine article. That line also cleared it up that we were not playing *on* the boardwalk. We'd played on sidewalks. We'd even played on subway trains. We'd played in school playgrounds. But this was in a hotel. It meant we were moving up in class. We were going to play inside a building where people paid to hear us. But I still don't think it was fair for *Billboard* to warn people who were planning to weekend at the Boardwalk that we were going to be there. With a band like mine, it was best to surprise them. It was a very surprising group.

I'm surprised the hotel didn't complain. But judging by the money they paid us, they couldn't have expected us to play very good. Nevertheless, you notice, they tried to come on swell by putting in that word "original" in front of Swanee Syncopators. They didn't want their classy clientele to think they'd have to accept any Brand-X Syncopators.

The item goes on to say, "The seven piece combination"—how did *Billboard* know we could only play seven pieces?—"is making a specialty of novelty stuff, including eccentric clowning, singing and dancing. Hen Youngman, violinist and leader, is also doing comedy songs." I got to be the leader because I had a bow to wave in front of the band. Then I'd turn and wave it in front of the people to ward off attack.

As for the comedy songs, I did romantic hits like Billy Rose's first smash hit, "Barney Google with the Goo-Goo-Googley Eyes," and "Yes, We Have No Bananas" and parodies of comedy songs like "Dear Old Pal" ("Dear Old Gal"), which fortunately I've forgotten.

For one show I did both parts of the big hit, "Oh, Mr. Gallagher! Oh, Mr. Shean!" Then I got a call from Gallagher and Shean's lawyers, and I decided to cut the song from my program. Gallagher and Shean were one of the top acts in big-time vaudeville. Al Shean was the Marx Brothers' uncle. I had to have an uncle who was in real estate.

It was while playing the Boardwalk date that I got a nice offer to do a single. But I didn't take it. You know how those things are in the movies. I wouldn't take it because I was loyal to "the act."

One of the officials of the Old Fall River Line heard me and wanted to hire me to sing on one of his boats. The line ran night boats to Boston, that were as famous, for the same thing, as the Night Boat to Albany. The boats didn't really go to Boston. They went to Providence. You took the train to Boston . . . if you wanted to go to Boston. Not many of the line's passengers did. You see, a cabin on the Old Fall River boats was as cheap as a hotel room—motels hadn't been invented yet—and you didn't have to register. Besides, you got the added pleasure of a little sea air. Most of the guys who took the trip hoped that would be the only heir they got out of it.

The only reason I know so much about this is because when I was a kid there was a hit song called "On the Old Fall River Line." It spelled out the whole operation in such a nice way that I didn't understand it until I was twenty-five.

The official of the line told me they didn't usually book singers. He said most of those who took the ride brought along their own entertainment. But he said I was different, that he felt a real need for a voice like mine on one of their boats. The foghorn was broken.

What the man who wrote the *Billboard* story didn't know was that what they called "eccentric clowning and dancing" was just the way I normally moved when I was leading a band.

The *Billboard* story even listed the sidemen I had with me on that date. They were Jack Meyer, drummer; Frank Carroll, piano; Jack Henderson, sax and clarinet; Mike Riley, trombone and sax; and Frank McGlynn, cornet. What memories. I met them all again later when we were all working on the Street.

More than forty years have passed since those days. You'd think seven men, no matter how close they'd been in their youth, would sort of drift apart over the years. You're right. We did.

The one person who was on the date that I still see all the time is Sadie. I think maybe she's the original groupie.

Groupies are girls who are turned on by musicians and bandleaders. You notice I make a distinction. Bandleaders don't have to be musicians. They just have to be handsome, suave, and debonaire. That's how I got to be a leader.

These groupies follow their favorite group wherever it plays. That's how I dated Sadie. When I had a date, she came along. My date was her date. Like when we played a spot like the Boardwalk Hotel, she and the girlfriends of the other members of the band would sit around the table reserved for us to use between sets. The girls would drink ginger ale. None of the musicians liked ginger ale, so they used to put something in it to kill the taste. I never touched the stuff. I had trouble enough when I was sober.

When we were playing, the girls clapped like crazy. When I got up to sing, they clapped louder and didn't stop till I sat down.

For jobs that weren't close to home, like a five-cent subway ride, I had to figure out some way to get Sadie there, too. I couldn't afford the train fare. I couldn't even afford the subway fare, so what I did was figure out ways she could come along as part of my organization and do some work.

Like when we played Swan Lake Inn in the Catskills, which could be anywhere from several weeks to a whole season, I'd talk the management into giving her a job taking care of the guests' children so their parents could get the rest they paid for. I figured it would be on-the-job training for when we could afford to get married and have kids of our own.

Oh, yes, we had 'em. Marilyn and Gary.

You go to the country for a change and rest. The bellboys get the change, and the hotel gets the rest.

13

Borscht Belt Follies

FROM the very beginning the Mountains was the birthplace of talent. You may have heard the show business expression "it's amateur night in Dixie." Well, the Mountains was Dixie North. But it was a great training ground. I couldn't begin to name all the great young writers, actors, singers and musicians who worked in the Borscht Belt learning the best ways to present what they had and letting the audiences tell them what it was they lacked. There was Danny Kaye, Beatrice Kaye (no relation), Buddy Hackett, Red Buttons, Don Tannen, Jerry Lewis, Eddie Fisher—you pick a name. Almost anyone you can mention in the "variety" field is someone the Mountains gave to the theater, the films, radio, and then television.

Of course, they didn't all work in the same place. The Mountains was an area in the Catskills of maybe fifty square miles. And, luckily for the entertainers, it was where a lot of squares came to have fun. We gave it to them. *Boy*, did we give it to them!

The region was dotted with large ponds, called lakes. And the shores of these lakes were dotted with boardinghouses, called hotels. Some of these resorts were small, some large, some good, some not so good. But talent was everywhere. The littlest dump could have the hottest entertainment. Everybody got a chance to work because so much of it was needed and the pay was so little that only newcomers had to accept it.

It used to be that when an actor established a salary, he couldn't take less or it would hurt his prestige. I hate guys who make a living telling Joe Frisco stories. But this one explains what I mean. Frisco had been a great star in vaudeville. But he had a bad habit. He bet on slow horses. While he was using his heavy money to do this, he also got older and vaudeville died, and he finally found himself holed up in the Hollywood-Plaza Hotel, across from the Brown Derby on Vine Street.

His agent called him from the Derby to say that he had a job for him, but it only paid about one-third of a thousand dollars, his old salary. Frisco turned it down. The agent pleaded with him, saying, "Just come across the street. I'm eating with the guy now. Just talk it over with him. Come on over and see him."

Frisco's answer was: "And get locked out of my room!"

Just to make the point about new talent, there was a young Puerto Rican busboy at one hotel. There weren't so many Puerto Ricans in New York in those days, so he was a kind of novelty. The hotel was not far from the Swan Lake Inn where I was. He couldn't speak English very well, but after dinner, when he'd cleaned up the dining room, he'd play the piano in the parlor. Lots of times the waiters, bellboys, and busboys were also the entertainers.

This character played so well that he attracted guests from all the hotels in the area. As an encore he did an imitation of the famous symphony orchestra conductor Walter "Papa" Damrosch. It was very funny. Damrosch at that time was very popular for his Saturday afternoon children's concerts at Carnegie Hall, where adults could go to get the music explained to them. This young man would talk and swing his arms, pretending to conduct the orchestra and make noises like the orchestra, all in a Spanish dialect. It went over very big. Today that young man is the composer of *West Side Story*, about Puerto Rican street gangs in New York, and one of the world's most famous orchestra conductors, Leonard Bernstein. Would I lie to you?

The truth is he wasn't really Spanish. He only pretended to be so the guests wouldn't try to make friends with him, as they tried to do with most performers. Half the job at any hotel in the Mountains was "mingling." I did a lot of it.

There was another hotel that had a great big tall, frecklefaced, pug-nosed bellboy. He also entertained. He had bright red hair, big blue eyes, did an Irish jig, and when he closed singing "Danny Boy," every Galitzianer in the hotel felt as if he were an Irishman. Everyone who caught this tad's act knew he'd make it big someday. And he did. First he became a Jew. Then he changed his name from Dinty Doyle to Sammy Davis, Jr. You must have heard of him.

And there was a little fat black man who told Jewish dialect stories. He worked at a place about a mile and a half from where I was, and I'd try to sneak away to catch his act. His timing of a joke was perfect. Some Hollywood talent scout caught him one Saturday evening, and the next thing I heard he was in pictures. They changed his name to John Wayne.

Those are just three of the "names" that broke in in the Mountains. I could describe a lot more, but you'd just think I was making it up.

The American language is funny. When a Westerner speaks of the Mountains, he means the High Sierras or the Rockies. When a New Yorker speaks of the Mountains, he means the Concord, Browns, Grossinger's, or some other place like that. And if you think Grossinger's isn't bigger than the Rockies, did Pikes Peak ever serve fifteen hundred kosher meals three times a day?

When I go up to the area now, I can't believe my eyes. Every resort now has half a dozen professional tennis courts, a couple of eighteen-hole golf courses, a skating rink, a ski slope, and an all-weather indoor swimming pool.

There was a time when the Mountains didn't even have all-weather indoor toilets. The most expensive rooms were the ones that were the shortest walk to the grape-covered path that led to the outdoor pavilion. But anyone could spend a couple of weeks at any of the spots in the Mountains for a few bucks.

Today those same people can fly to Israel for what a weekend in the Mountains could cost them, and meet the same people.

A lot of my Gentile friends have been amused by the fact that so many Jewish immigrants wound up in the Catskills and, of all places, Sullivan County. That's just a crazy accident. General John Sullivan once owned all the land in the county. He got it because he was one of General Washington's executive officers. George Washington, you may remember, was the Father of His Country. The way the girls act, today, when they get into the Mountains, anybody could be the father of his country. But it wasn't the Irish name that attracted them.

Those who came were frugal people, peasants, who couldn't stand the cramped, noisy canyons of New York's Lower East Side.

They tried to find jobs and become city people, but they really couldn't adjust. All they knew or liked was farming. So they sent scouts out into the country around New York City to find a place that was more congenial. Before long the word came back that the southern hills of the Catskills had the same kind of climate as Galicia, a province that was then in Austria. That's where many of them came from. So those who could scratch enough money together bought farms in Sullivan County. They would have bought farms there if it had been called Egypt County. It was the land and fresh air they wanted. As it turned out, the land wasn't very good, so they put on airs. And those who couldn't afford to buy land made like swells and came up to board with the farmers.

As you may have guessed, buying worn-out land in Sullivan County wasn't too tough, or these people never could have made it. It was like the actor who was buying a showplace in the hills of Bel Air. He found just the place he wanted. "It has five master bedrooms," he said, "each with his-and-her bathrooms and dressing rooms. There are two children's rooms, each with its own bath, a kitchenette for preparing their meals, and a playroom. Also upstairs there's a drawing room and an office for me. Then there's a large living room—all rooms have practical fireplaces, of course—a music room, a playroom with wet bar and regulation snooker and ping-pong tables, a library, a dining room that will seat twenty-six, a kitchen and butler's pantry large enough for three butlers, three servants' rooms, a heated pool and pool house with a two-room guest suite complete with small kitchen, two dressing rooms in case anyone's fussy about sex, a tennis court, a badminton court, a croquet court, a five-car garage with chauffeur's quarters, and a stable for two horses with rooms for their grooms. I was just about to buy it. The price was right. A hundred and fifty thousand dollars. But the owner wanted two thousand dollars down, in *cash*."

And that's how Grossinger's was born. They wanted to get out into the country so bad they put all their savings to make a down payment on a rocky piece of farmland, where they hoped to raise chickens. They started with two chickens, but one of them got sick, so they had to kill the other to make chicken soup for it.

Then they tried raising vegetables, but they couldn't live on those, because the other chicken scratched up most of the seeds, so they had to eat it.

Little by little it became clear that if they were going to keep the land, what they had to figure out was how to raise the mortgage. By accident it turned out that Jennie Grossinger had a genius for running a resort hotel. She knew what the people wanted. Good food.

A lot of hotels in the Mountains were started by people who thought it was an easy way to get rich quick. Most of them lost their shirts, their sheets, their pillowcases, their tablecloths, and their land. There were a lot of fires.

I've already mentioned a teacher of mine named Julius Laderberg who owned the Swan Lake Inn with a cousin of mine named Herman Davis and a man named Joe Schroff. To show how much they knew about running a hotel, they figured to get free vegetables, milk, and eggs by taking a farmer in as a partner. At the end of the season, his payoff was to be a share of the profits, which they planned to have eaten up by the salaries they paid themselves for running the place.

To show you how much the farmer knew about the hotel business, when he found out that my band and I got twenty dollars a week plus room and board he almost popped his rutabagas. Whenever he saw us, he'd holler, "Bums! I get up early in the morning and work all day. You bums just sit around and play. I wouldn't ask my pigs to dance to your music." As I said, he didn't know much about the hotel business, but he obviously had a keen ear for music. He obviously didn't know much about Jewish people either, or he wouldn't have been hollering around the Swan Lake Inn about how well he took care of his pigs.

When I first worked at Swan Lake Inn, it was just as leader of the Swanee Syncopators. But then my comic cousin, Jim Kaplan, came up there as a comedian and turned me off the idea of just playing the fiddle. I'd tried telling jokes and wanted to try it some more. So pretty soon we were working as a team of "toomlers." In the Mountains that means a social director. I think it's a Yiddish word. I know it's a Borscht Belt word. It means someone who makes a tumult, creates confusion and excitement. We did!

We told jokes to the guests, and we instinctively followed a show business motto that Walter Winchell used to quote: "People don't get bored if you change the subject often enough." I'd go along the long porch where they'd all be sitting, rocking, and having their afternoon glass of tea and tell them about the new guests we were expecting that evening. I'd tell them that, "One of them's a big iron-and-steel man from Pittsburgh." Then as the ladies with marriageable daughters smiled smugly to themselves, I'd add, "His wife irons, and he steals."

It was an old joke then. But it worked because no joke is an old joke to people who haven't heard it. And most people who have heard jokes don't take the trouble to remember them. Thank God!

I guess it was working in the Mountains that taught me the value of one-liners. Up there, when you're toomling, you have to have something funny to say to everyone when you meet them. This meant you tried to have some kind of gag about almost anything they might talk to you about. A man at the bar might talk about what kind of whiskey he likes. You'd have ready for him, "Yes, whiskey improves with age. I know, because the older I get, the more I like it." Coming from a kid like me made it even funnier.

You ask a kid where he goes to school. His mother thinks you're nice because you take an interest in the kid and gives you a tip. The kid tells what school he goes to. You tell him, "I went to that same school. I was teacher's pet. She couldn't afford a dog." The kid looks at you blankly, but his mother enjoys it. She says to her husband when he comes up for the weekend, "This is a nice place. They take an interest in the children. They tell them jokes." He says, "Tell them to teach them to swim."

Somtimes the husbands who came up to join their wives over the weekend found out things they didn't want to know. The deer in the woods around the place weren't the only ones with horns. Everybody who worked in the hotel was young. And part of their job was keeping the lonesome wives happy during the week.

The waiters, busboys, bellboys, and musicians would dance with them, have a drink with them, or do anything they wanted. A lot of them wanted something their husbands were too busy, too disinterested, too tired, or too old to give them. So working in the Mountains had certain fringe benefits for a young man.

But getting back to one-liners, you had to have one on the tip of your tongue. There was no time for long buildups. Just say the joke and get away. Someone was always asking, especially on wet days, what the mean rainfall was. Your answer was always: "Whenever there's rainfall, the guests get mean."

A guest would complain to you about his room being too small. He was afraid to complain to the management for fear they'd rent it to someone else. They always complained because the rooms *were* too small. You'd say, "You should see my room, sir. I put the key in the door, and it breaks the window. When I complained, they changed my room to one without a window."

Sometimes the guests made up the one-liners for you. A woman complained to me about the food. She said, "Young man, I want to tell you that whoever runs this hotel should be informed that the food isn't fit to eat . . . and such small portions."

City people, in the country for the first time, were always pointing and asking, "What kind of flower is that?"

Our stock answer was, "How should I know? Am I a milliner?"

When someone said something you couldn't think of a joke for, you changed the subject. When you couldn't think of a subject to change to, you'd wave to some unidentified person in the distance and say, "Excuse me, please," and beat it.

For some reason almost everyone who came to the Mountains at that time expected to have little tricks played on them. Sometimes they brought their own "little tricks." Sometimes our tricks weren't so little and got us in big trouble.

When we played the wrong kind of trick, we got into fights with the guests. When we got into fights with the guests, they generally led to fights with the management. Frequently, after a big fight with the management, we went out and looked for a job. I'm surprised we ever got jobs anywhere. I'm surprised we didn't get jail sentences.

To give you an idea what we did, when newlyweds checked in, we'd sneak into their room while they were at dinner and find the groom's contraceptives. Then we'd fill them with water and hang them all over the room. If we couldn't find any, we'd supply some of our own. Nobody ever complained. They were too embarrassed. Thinking about outrageous things like that, I can't believe we did them. But it could have been worse. They didn't have the Pill then. If they had, we might have switched the pills for aspirin tablets.

Sometimes guests would be out swimming or fishing or something, and we'd switch all their clothes around from room to room. A man would walk into his room and find it full of lingerie hanging from the fixtures. A woman might find a jockstrap on a doorknob and all her dresses missing. But trying to find the people who had their clothing got the guests acquainted with each other, and pretty soon boys had met girls, the ice was broken, and anger had turned to friendship . . . sometimes love. That's what the whole Mountains scene was all about. And still is.

When there was an overflow on weekends, the management would pitch tents on the ground for the extra guests to sleep in. One night we thought it would be a lot of laughs to hitch one end of a rope to one of these tents and the other to our old Dodge and pull the tent down around the sleepers. Someone in pajamas, sneaking back to his own tent early that morning, hollered at us so loud we had to stop or he'd have awakened the whole neighborhood.

Lucky he stopped us. He saw that by pulling down the tent, we'd also pull down some of the electric wires, and the people would have been badly shocked or burned.

Another thing Jim and I used to do to keep the guests happy was to run raffles. Sometimes a local auto dealer would park one of his best cars in front of the hotel, lock it, and go away, just leaving his business card in one window. We'd tell the guests that this dealer had donated the car for us to raffle off at fifty cents a chance. The next day the car would be gone, and the winning number would turn out to be held by someone who had checked out without leaving an address.

We got the idea from the story about the man who sold chances on a dead horse. He sold hundreds of tickets at a dollar each. When his wife asked him what he planned to do when the winner found out that the horse was dead, he said, "Give him his money back."

Jim and I tried to sell punchboards to the other hotels in the neighborhood to make a little extra money. We saw the punchcards advertised in *Billboard* and sent away for them. One day a guy stopped us on the road. He had a face like an old catcher's mitt and asked us in the politest way, "What the goddamn hell do you punks think you're doing trying to place your punchboards in my territory?"

We told him we were just trying to make some extra money. He told us to take our punchboards and make our extra dough somewhere else, or he'd have us punched till we were stiff as a board. When we got back to the hotel, we described the guy to some of the locals who worked there during the day. They told us he was one of the paid killers for a big New York mob and that he controlled everything in the neighborhood that wasn't legal. We didn't even know punchboards were illegal. We just knew they were crooked.

Later the FBI did some digging around up there and found some bodies of certain Brooklyn and New York hoods who had been taken to the Mountains for a terminal vacation. I'd give you the guy's right name, but I'm not sure whether or not he's still alive and I am and want to stay that way.

Maybe the most idiotic thing I ever did as a toomler was at a spot called Cohen's Hillside Inn, near Liberty, New York. When you got off the train, the good hotels were all to the right. Cohen's was to the left. It was one of those "nature" spots where they had campfire sings every night with people sitting around a campfire, roasting marshmallows (and their faces) and singing those dull folk songs that say the same thing over and over again, to the same tune. One weekend it rained so hard the guests had nothing to do. Instead of sitting around a campfire, they were sitting around the lobby. So I built a fire in the lobby.

I planned to just make a little blaze, for a laugh, and then stamp it out. It got a big laugh, but it got to be such a big blaze that the Liberty volunteer fire department almost couldn't handle it. I met the owners again a couple of years later. The hotel had just gone broke. They said, "Where were you when we needed you?"

Of course, I worked other places besides the Swan Lake Inn.

One of them was Livingston Manor at White Roe Lake. This was where Danny Kaye got his start. Not far away at Kiamesha Lake, the guests were treated to plays and comedy skits by the hotel's social director, Moss Hart.

I was playing at Livingston Manor when an agent by the name of Paul Small came to see me and the next thing I knew he'd booked me into the Yacht Club, one of the best spots on West Fifty-second Street in New York.

That was the whole bit. That was the payoff if you were a young hopeful trying to break in. You had only two places to work. One was the Mountains; the other wasn't. I tried both. The Mountains worked for me.

But winters are cold, and you have to work all year 'round or you get very hungry by Memorial Day. You could get so hungry they might be holding the memorial for you.

*A comedian told a gag that bombed. To save it,
he said, "That was one of my mother's jokes."
A voice from the balcony hollered, "What are
you, one of your father's?"*

14

Small or Nothing at All

AS it got closer and closer to the end of the season up in
the Mountains, customers used to ask me, "What do you do in the
winter?" I said, "I wear an overcoat." Of course, those who were
going to school had no problem. That's why I wasn't going to
school. When I *went*, I had a problem.

Today I don't suppose anybody working in the Mountains has
anything to worry about when summer ends. The resorts now stay
open all year 'round. When I worked there and Labor Day came, the
places closed up, the jobs shut down, and you were left out with a lot
of empty time to spend figuring ways to fill your empty pockets.

Today the Mountains has become a place for all seasons. A golfer
can go up there in the summer and break eighty. A skier can go there
in the winter and break a leg. A guy who met a girl there in the spring
can go back in the fall to plan the divorce. In short, anybody can
now go to the Mountains any time of year and find just what he or
she is looking for . . . a congenial companion of the opposite sex.
Or the same sex if that's your idea of congeniality.

In some ways I was luckier than most. If I couldn't get a job fiddling and telling jokes, I could get a job printing. That also made it possible for me to be out of two jobs. Which meant I was also twice as broke. I didn't know what to tell people I did for a living because I never knew which job I was out of. Besides, who could call what I was doing living? Sometimes it would get so oppressive that I'd wake up in the middle of the night gasping for breath, almost choked by the fear of what my future might be.

I don't recommend poverty to anyone. Not that we were so poor. It was just that Poppa wasn't going to help me get into a business he didn't approve of. So I had only myself to blame. I had to make all my own decisions. And I knew anyone who had me making decisions for him had a right to be frightened.

My father was so anxious to have me settle down to some kind of work he understood and thought was sensible that he went into hock to buy me one of those Atkinson-type presses I knew how to operate. It wasn't very big, and we installed it in the basement of our house. I wanted to put a sign in the window: ''Homemade Printing Fresh Every Hour.''

Suddenly, I was in business for myself. But I didn't like it. I didn't want to be my own boss. I didn't have any confidence in a business that was run by a guy like me. So I led a very strange life.

We lived a long way from the show business section of Brooklyn, which was where my heart was. But Sadie's folks, the Cohens, had an apartment that was only a few blocks from where all the theaters and restaurants were. Here, of course, was where all the musicians and comics worked or, in their spare time, ate. The comics were playing dates in the local theaters, and the musicians played either in the pit of a vaudeville house or in a little combo in some Chinese restaurant. These spots would be open until two every morning. I'd go from one to the other trying to sell business cards to somebody so that when they were getting thrown out of a booking office, they could throw back a handful of cards in case someone changed his mind.

I charged a dollar for two hundred cards that gave a man's name, address, telephone number, and instrument. All spelling guaranteed correct. If any mistakes were found, I promised to do the job over for half price. I think the automobile manufacturers modeled their warranties after mine. Every once in a while I'd persuade some flute player to put his credits on the other side of the card and charge him an extra buck for the extra run. I also had an offer that I'd print his cards for half price if he'd put on the reverse side ''Henny Youngman—Funny Violinist'' and my phone number.

I got one answer to that. A man called up and said, "What do you do? Stand on your head while playing the violin?"

I said, "No."

He said, "Well, that's as funny as you can play it." And he hung up.

I've mentioned going to Broadway to pick up music for the lady who played the piano in my Uncle Morris' movie house. The place I went to was the Putnam Building. It was about six stories high and ran from Forty-third to Forty-fourth Street on Seventh Avenue right there on Times Square. They finally tore it down to put up the Paramount Building, which was still there when I passed it yesterday.

They're putting up new buildings so fast now that you go out for a paper and when you come back, the tenement full of poor people on the corner has become a high-rise luxury apartment full of rich people. What became of the poor people? I'll tell you. That luxury building full of rich people, after they've paid the rent, the cost of an interior decorator, and the grocery bills, becomes a luxury building full of poor people. It is then ready to be torn down and replaced by a larger building.

The Putnam Building was a real show biz bazaar like the Brill Building today. Even the smells inside were a little alike: stale jokes, agents' cigar smoke, and all the crap that out-of-work people hand each other. It was full of agents, song publishers, joke writers, songwriters, jewelry salesmen, necktie salesmen, and men carrying bass fiddle cases that were really full of gin at a dollar a bottle, which they peddled from office to office.

It was a New York landmark for other reasons. At night every tourist in town took a look at it. On the roof there was a block-long electric sign, at that time the biggest spectacular ever built. Today a spectacular means a special show on TV. Then it meant an animated electric advertising sign. In show business whatever's new gets called a spectacular. I just read that Jessel's given in and gotten himself a gray toupee. So, as of the moment, that's a spectacular. It was when those big signs began to light up Broadway that it got the name "The Great White Way." Maybe if I say that the sign on the top of the Putnam Building was for Wrigley's Gum, I'll get a lifetime supply of Spearmint. That's enough to cover the underside of every theater seat in the world. As I remember the sign, it featured more peacocks than NBC has all week.

There was also a very famous restaurant on the Forty-third Street side of the Putnam Building, Shanley's. It was where the show biz biggies went to dine and dance. I used to dream of the day I'd walk in there with Sadie and be given a big greeting by the headwaiter and be led to the best table in the room. The other stars would nod hello to me as the tourists (way in the back near the kitchen or the men's room) would stand on their chairs to get a good look at us. Dreaming that was better than gasping for breath. But when I was awake, I didn't have enough money to walk past the place.

Sometimes my dreams were a little more conservative. I'd see myself in white tie and tails, leading the orchestra, too proud to play for any but very special customers, who'd dance by and slip me a fiver to play their girlfriend's favorite number. It wasn't until more than twenty years later that I wore my first tail suit and played before a full-dress audience. It was in the Persian Room at the Hotel Plaza on Fifth Avenue and Central Park South, in New York. But you'll have to wait to get to that story.

There was another way, besides patrolling the Putnam Building, that musicians could get jobs. *Billboard* ran ads that read: "SMALL BAND WANTED—For flash act with 20 weeks." I saw one of these and called everyone who'd ever worked with me. The ones who weren't busy joined me, and we applied for the job and got it. This fact alone should have told me there was something screwy about the ad. We couldn't believe our luck. We didn't know what we did right.

The job was playing in an act starring Cunningham and Clemens, a dance team. A flash act meant that they carried their own scenery, props, band, and a line of girls. Very flashy! I don't remember anymore what this one looked like, but I'll bet it was either a cabaret set or a garden. I do remember that we opened at the Capitol Theater in Trenton. There were five acts and the new Al Jolson picture, *The Jazz Singer*. That was the picture that put Jolson back in business as a superstar after he'd been in a bad slump. Because it was the first talkie, it did capacity business.

The fact that Sophie Tucker was the headliner on the bill didn't hurt either. She took the Trenton booking because she was trying to break in her son as a dancer. I don't know whether he was too light or she was too heavy, but she went back to doing a single.

I tried to get the team we played for to let me introduce them with a few jokes. They told me what I could do with my jokes. So I just stood there in front of five men and waved my bow while they did all the work. It was beautiful but dull. I told myself jokes to keep awake.

One strange thing happened on that date. *The Jazz Singer* was the picture in which Al Jolson introduced "Sonny Boy." Well, there was a tenor on the bill whose wife had just given birth to their first baby, a boy. The song got to him so hard that he borrowed money from everybody on the bill to take the train back to New York from Trenton, to see his wife and kid. It was only the second day of the job, and none of us had much cash, but we chipped in. When the guy came back, he did a surprising thing. He paid us all back.

There was only one trouble with that twenty-week job with Cunningham and Clemens. It wasn't for twenty weeks. It turned out to be only for one week. Nobody told me it was just a tryout in Trenton. The bookers came there, and if they booked the act, *then* it was twenty weeks. This taught me what flash act really meant, an act that could close in a flash.

So it was back to hanging around the Putnam Building during the day and hustling printing at night. The way I'd do it was to drop into a spot, get an order or two, rush home, print the cards, and rush back to deliver them the same night, so I'd have some walking around money for the next day. By the time I'd done all this it was so late I'd go to Sadie's folks' apartment to spend the rest of the night on the couch they had in the living room. It wasn't too comfortable, but it was better than going all the way back home again.

They didn't like the idea that I used their apartment for a flophouse. It wasn't that they weren't hospitable. It was that they didn't like *me*. How could you like a guy who was running around all night till three or four in the morning and then woke you up to ask if he could spend the night?

This routine had been going on about as long as anyone could stand it when I ran into a man named Al Davis, an agent, who said he could get me a week in Montreal as a single doing my monologue. "My" monologue! Part of it belonged to every comic in the business.

Naturally I okayed the job. Sadie didn't want me to go because she knew I didn't feel well. Her parents urged me to take the job for the same reason. I'd been having dizzy spells and attacks of nausea. But eighty dollars was about seventy-nine more than I had in my pocket, so I headed for Canada. I was worried, though. I wasn't sure they understood English up there. I was half right.

By the time I went on to do my first show I felt so awful that I did a show to match, a real theater emptier. The boss called me in to see him. "I just caught your act," he said. "I'm going to pay you off and cancel you." Then he told me the week before there was an act named Archie Robbins who had done my whole routine. The guy did a very classy act, working in white tie and tails. And he got twice the money they were paying me for doing my monologue. It wasn't unusual for the joke writers who hung around the Putnam Building to sell the same act to more than one person. It was a chance you had to take.

I felt terrible. If you stole somebody's act, you got in trouble. If you bought an act, somebody else either bought it or stole it, and you were still in trouble. Not only did I feel terrible about *that*, I also felt terrible.

It wasn't till a long time later that I found out the truth. Sadie had called up the manager to tell him to keep an eye on me because I wasn't feeling well. He was glad to oblige. No manager likes to have an act that might die on his stage.

When I got home, I went to see my uncle Dr. Phil Chetkin, my mother's brother. He was a pretty fair medico. Phil and my father used to argue about socialism, and Poppa would tell Phil to practice what he preached saying, "You're a good GP. You do a good job in the neighborhood taking care of people, but you charge too damn much. You've got to remember GP doesn't stand for Greedy Physician." Poppa finally made him cut his fee in half, saying, "Do you need two dollars an office visit? That's a lot of money for such poor people to pay." When Poppa finally won, he and Momma and the whole family went around the neighborhood dropping gossip about the miracle cures Dr. Chetkin had made. But then, as now, his fee was more than some of his patients could afford. When you think about it—and if you've paid any doctor bills lately—there's only one thing a doctor can ever really cure . . . affluence.

But it was Uncle Phil who diagnosed what was wrong with me. It was a couple of infected teeth. So I did what every young Jewish fella does who has infected teeth, I went to my brother's wife's brother, Dr. Max Kohn, the dentist. He pulled the teeth, and I felt fine. I hope you noticed how we kept our sickness in the family.

Whenever I could get Frank Carroll to play a date with my band, we did a specialty together, two-part harmony. His harmony was in two parts, and so was mine. Together we sounded like a barbershop quartet that had been shaved too close. We sang songs like "That Old Gang of Mine" and "Show Me the Way to Go Home." One night they did.

But whatever it was we had, a bandleader named Chuck Holtzworth saw it. He caught us doing a club date and liked us well enough to book us with his band. He said he was getting solid twenty-week booking and offered us forty dollars a week each. I figured that eight hundred dollars playing violin and singing was better than an occasional five or ten as a comic or the leader of a scratch band (so called because that's what I did on the fiddle). So I took the job.

Except for the Mountains, it was the first steady work I'd ever had. It made me feel as if I were really in show business for good. My father thought it was for evil. There were some audiences that agreed with him.

But out of the forty bucks I got every week from Holtzworth I was able to pay my agent, send some money home, and still have a little walking-around money. Of course, I couldn't walk around very far. But I wouldn't have had *any* money if I'd been a cardplayer.

Chuck used to like to fraternize with his help by getting them into a little friendly poker game between shows. The way this worked out was that at the end of every week everyone was broke but Chuck. I didn't play. I didn't know how. But I hung around to watch.

One day a magician on the bill was standing next to me kibitzing the game. He nudged me to follow him, and we walked out into the alley by the stage door. "Does he always wear that ring or only when he plays poker?" he asked.

I didn't know what he meant, so he explained something about there being a mirror in the ring that made it possible for him to see the cards as he dealt them. I still don't know exactly how it worked, but it sure worked great for Chuck.

The magician must have told some of the other men in the band about the ring because one morning our leader showed up with two black eyes and that was the end of the poker games. Sore losers.

On one of the bills we were on there was a blind comedian named Ben Welch. He was so great I'd stand in the wings and try to learn his timing. He had one gag that always broke me up. He'd say, "I'm supposed to meet my girl here at half past six. It's now only five o'clock. I think while I'm waiting for her, I'll go home."

Everybody seems to have a certain joke he's a sucker for. A lot of people tell me their favorite is mine about the lady who runs out with her garbage pail and hollers after the truck, "Am I too late for the garbage?" The men holler back, "No, madame. Jump in."

Jimmy Durante once had a joke in a radio script that he tried to do for three weeks in a row, and every time he came to it he broke up so he couldn't finish it. It was about a window washer who stepped back to admire his work.

Ben Welch had, for me, one of the funniest Jewish deliveries I'd ever heard and I'd heard them all from Benny Rubin to Lou Holtz. But Welch couldn't do his act if he were around today. They'd say he was anti-Semitic. How could he be? He was Jewish. But in those days nobody thought it was wrong. You could do Italian, German, Swedish dialect, just so it sounded funny.

George Jessel once told me about a small-time comic from Brooklyn with a very Jewish name like Abie Ginsberg—something like that. This guy couldn't get himself arrested with the "Hebe" act, as they called what he did at that time. Blackface comedy, stemming from the old minstrel shows, was popular. So this guy caught Eddie Cantor, Frank Tinney, Eddie Leonard, Lew Hearn, Bert Williams (who really *was* black), and others and put himself together a blackface act.

His agent got him a split week at the Audubon in Washington Heights but told him to get himself a new name; that it was ridiculous for a man named Ginsberg to do a colored act. Abie said he would and went right out to telephone his mother that he had work. He invited her to come see him the next day when he opened but explained that he wouldn't be using his own name. He hadn't made up the new name yet, but she should just come to the stage door and ask for him and he'd have a pass for her.

When she showed up, the doorman asked her who she wanted to see.

"Who should a mother come halfway around the world from Brooklyn to Washington Heights to see? My son, of course."

"What's your son's name?" asked the doorman.

"I don't know," she said, "but he's a nigger."

A couple of guys in the Holtzworth band were even newer in show business than I was and even fussier about where they slept, so we three got together, and instead of each of us getting a cheap room in some crummy fleabag, we pooled our cash and got a suite in a better hotel for the same money. It meant clean towels and clean beds.

One night in Bethlehem, Pennsylvania, we're all packed up and heading for the hotel with our instruments under our arms when a nice-looking lady stops us at the stage door and says, "Hello, boys. How'd you like a nice home-cooked Jewish meal?"

We told her that sounded great after the stuff we'd been eating in Bethlehem hasheries. So she said, "Fine, come on to my house. I'd like to have you meet my girls."

We caught on right away. Another anxious mother trying to marry off her daughters. But for a good meal, it couldn't hurt to look. So we went. (It never occurred to us that no mother would ever try to marry her daughters to musicians.)

She took us to a big old house in a nice part of town. The place was decorated very ornately with a big parlor and a back parlor with a piano in it. She said, "Make yourselves at home. Play something if you like. I'll tell the cook you're here and go upstairs and tell the girls.''

So we started to jam a little, and pretty soon our hostess came down with her girls. It was the first time I'd ever seen a girl wearing nothing but a red corset and a pair of black silk stockings. My hand shook so with excitement that while I was trying to play "That Old Gang of Mine," it came out sounding like "The Flight of the Bumblebee."

One of the guys went over and whispered something to our hostess, and she said to us all, "Don't worry, boys. There'll be some more guests here tonight. Just keep playing. You'll get your supper free, and then the fun is on the house."

Frank Carroll leaned over and whispered to me, "You'd better take your fiddle upstairs with you. You could learn some new movements on the G string."

And that's what happened to some straight boys in the band from Brooklyn in "the little town of Bethlehem," Pennsylvania. The outfit was weak for a week.

As I write it down, I'm reminded of a story I heard in Hollywood. A star asked a friend of his, just in from the East, if he'd like to go to a house, meet a few girls, and have a good time. So, to cut it down to two reels, the guy showed up. He was plied with champagne, given a selection of girls, had a most luxurious time, and when it came time to leave and he asked for his check, he was told there was no charge. He was impressed with this free entertainment. So a few weeks later he went back there, went through the same routine, and was handed a check for more than three hundred dollars.

"I was here two weeks ago," he said, "and everything was free. How come it's now three hundred dollars?"

"Last time" he was told, "Porno Productions was shooting a picture."

It was a joke a few years ago. Today, with the kinds of films they're making, it could really happen.

But musicians didn't have to go to "houses" to get girls. Girls always hang around bands. And there were always enough to go around wherever the Holtzworth organization entertained.

One night, before we left town, a member of our group took a girl home and, when he left her, took with him the entire contents of her bag. She checked with the house manager on where our next date was, and the next day she showed up looking for her compact, her lipstick, and her money. For a whole week we had to protect our friend. Without him the arrangements were no good. We sneaked him in and out of the back door. The girl had flashed a knife and made it perfectly clear that if our colleague thought it was okay for him to take a cut of her cash, she thought she was entitled to take a cut of his throat.

Up to now it's sounded like a long road tour. That all happened before we finished our second week. I figured if that was a sample of the life, it was going to be some forty weeks. I shouldn't have worried. It was only some of the forty weeks.

After eight weeks the job folded, and Henny was back in the printing business.

A man asked, "Are you the leader of this band?" I said, "Yes." He said, "Well, lead them out of here."

15

Mob Control

I knew it was silly to hustle printing orders in downtown Brooklyn or Manhattan, rush way out to Bay Ridge, where my press was, to fill them and then back to deliver them the same day. So, once again I turned to the ads in *Billboard*. I found one that read: SPACE IN PENNY ARCADE FOR SHARE OF PROFIT. It gave a phone number.

I figured sharing the kind of profit I made was a lot cheaper than paying rent, so I called the number. A woman who talked like Jack Pearl doing Baron Munchausen answered the phone, and I made a date to meet her and look at what she had.

This turned out to be space in a penny arcade on East Fourteenth Street around Third Avenue, near the Academy Theater, in Manhattan. I knew that where there was a theater, there was bound to be actors and musicians. So I made a deal. She took 40 percent of the gross. The rest was mine. Then I moved my press from a cellar in Bay Ridge to a penny arcade on Fourteenth Street.

First thing I did was put up my sign: "Henny Youngman—Prince of Printers." Then I put my card and samples on the call boards of

the theaters in the neighborhhod. When the printing business finally
died, its prince ascended the throne and became king of the one-
liners.

There were three or four theaters within five or six blocks along
Fourteenth Street at that time. And I printed handbills free in
exchange for passes to see the shows.

That ended when I got the idea of printing my own passes. They
were easy to copy. And everything would have been great if I hadn't
printed some of the passes for the Academy Theater with the name
spelled "Academey." It made the manager suspicious.

Naturally I still had my line of "Fun Cards" to sell. My quota
was still to sell fifty sets a day. At ten cents each it was five dollars
clear profit which I never cleared. But I always sold *some*. Who
wouldn't buy ten cards to get ten jokes like these:

(1) His acting career was interrupted by illness . . . people
    got sick of him.
(2) Do you mind if I smoke? I don't care if you burn.
(3) Didn't I see your picture on an iodine bottle?
(4) I had a date with a Siamese twin, but she couldn't get
    away.
(5) He killed his wife with a bow and arrow so as not to wake
    up the children.
(6) My wife said it wasn't a fit night out for man or beast, so
    we both stayed home.
(7) Mother goes to the fortune-teller to get her palm read, and
    Father goes to the saloon to get his nose red.
(8) A gambler made a pair of dice out of Ivory Soap and
    cleaned up.
(9) "Waiter. This steak is tough." "Eat it! You need the
    exercise."
(10) Love story. He falls. She falls. Niagara Falls.

A couple of men named Schalk and Schaeffer ran a penny arcade
in the Times Square area on Sixth Avenue between Forty-fifth and
Forty-sixth streets. It came to me one day that if I could make
money with my spot down on Fourteenth Street, I could do better
uptown, where the main action was. So I talked to these guys. I
offered them the same 40/60 percent deal I had with the lady down
on Fourteenth Street. When they checked with her and found out
that I grossed about one hundred to one hundred and fifty a week, I
got the deal. It turned out to be more than they could figure to take in
on any of their penny peep-show machines.

You put a penny in the slot and turned a crank to see shows like "What the Bellboy Saw" or "When Girls Get Together." These shows ran about a minute and were considered very hot stuff. They weren't even movies. They were a series of still pictures. When you turned the crank, it flipped them very fast and made them look like movies. A smart kid could stop cranking at what he thought would be a real hot spot in the series and get an eyeful. The trouble was there wasn't anything to see.

The action would be a bellboy coming down a hotel hall. He'd stop, look around, and then peek through the keyhole. A woman would be undressing. She'd take off her hat, gloves, and dress, then her petticoat. Then she'd put one foot up on a chair to unlace her shoe, exposing about three inches of stocking and a complete bloomer leg. The bellboy would then jump up and down and go crazy with excitement, and that was the end of the show.

Sometimes a smart kid would put another penny in to see what happened from then on. Of course, he saw the same thing over again. At least that's what everyone told me.

Funny thing about my joke cards. Some of the guys who were always hanging around the Putnam Building to sell jokes to comics would sometimes buy printing from me, letterheads and envelopes. Mostly the jokes these guys sold they'd swiped from working acts. And they'd sell them over and over again to different people.

Once while I was cruising the arcade selling my "Fun Cards" for ten cents, I sold a set to the guy who'd sold me the jokes. How was that for business? I sold him ten of his own jokes for a dime. I'd paid a dollar apiece for them. I wouldn't have been able to lose that much on one deal if I didn't have such a big turnover.

Not only did I do pretty well with my printing business, but because they put me right in the middle of the arcade, I also got to talk to a lot of people. I'd throw jokes at the passing customers. That way I first got to meet Milton Berle. He liked one of the jokes. He claimed it was his.

He was, of course, just a kid like me, except that I was still in the printing business and he was working as the comic in a flash act with a team of dancers and a line of tired chorus girls. It wasn't that dancing made them tired. Berle made them tired. But after dancing six shows a day and running around between shows trying to avoid Berle, by the last show they had a right to be tired. They danced with all the zip and precision of a squad of trainees on their first day of basic.

Milton used to come in and hang around, and we'd exchange jokes. After that I used to go and see him wherever the act was playing. Sometimes he'd have to advance me the money to buy the ticket. But he was always willing to make the investment to be sure there was someone in the audience who was on his side. Occasionally someone would offer him a date to play a Bar Mitzvah. He felt he was too big already for that kind of work and he'd recommend me. He'd say, "This boy's experienced. He just went through his."

I'd say, "You talk to this man as if he were a Gentile."

"So what?" Milton would say, winking at the man. "It makes him feel good."

Of course, every day, shortly after noon, when the agents began to show up in their offices, I'd put a sign up on my printing booth that said: "Be back in 5 minutes." Then I had a box with a sign over it, "Leave Orders Here! All jobs finished by 6 P.M." Often when I came back I had a couple of orders. Today if I did that, when I came back my printing press would be gone.

Once I found a note in the box that said, "You should stay on the job. We needed you to print our first edition. You weren't here. 6 o'clock is too late. Too bad." It was signed "The New York *Tribune*." There *was* one then. I suspected Berle. There still is one.

On one of those afternoon trips to the Putnam Building I connected with a band job at a joint in Pinedale, New Jersey, called the Nut Club. The name appealed to me. The other act to be playing the date with me was a dance team called the Hartmans. They were pretty good. One night, however, they failed to show up, and Ed Ball, the manager, was tearing his hair trying to find a replacement. So I found him a replacement for the hair.

I said every prayer I could remember that he wouldn't find anybody and I'd have to go on in the star spot. I must have got through to God because Ball finally came to me and said, "Henny, you've got to help me out. Instead of the Hartmans, you go on and tell some of those jokes you've been throwing away around here during rehearsal. You've gotta save my life."

"If I go on and tell those jokes," I asked, "who's going to save mine?" What I should have said was, "Sure. But do I get the Hartmans' salary?"

I didn't ask. I was too anxious to get out there on the floor. And did I get the Hartmans' salary? This is an autobiography, not a fairy tale.

That night a large party came into the club, and I got lucky. They loved me. When the show was over, Ball came over to me, threw his arms around me, and I thought I was going to get the kiss of death. What he said was: "Henny. You saved my life!" Again I should have said, "And you saved dough on the Hartmans." But again I didn't. I was too steamed up over the reception they gave me.

After the place was closed and we were having a cup of coffee, he said to me, "Henny, if you can do that good, what do you need that band for? I'm losing my shirt on those musicians. All I really need is a piano player and you." So he kept his shirt, gave the band the sack, and I stayed on as house comedian.

I was glad. Being leader of the band makes you sound like a big shot. No way. Not only did I not know how to lead a band, but I had all the responsibilities. And I don't mean just for the sour notes. I had to take care of all the music and carry it around, set up the music stands and spread the books around, see that all the guys showed up, and, with all that, I didn't get any more dough than the others who did nothing but just read the notes and play them. Even this was too hard for some of them because they couldn't read music.

As soon as I closed the Nut Club, the word went around among "the boys" in Jersey, and I got an offer to play the Lido Venice. At first I didn't think I'd take the job because I'd have to pay my way across. But it turned out it was only across the Hudson, and that was only a nickel on the ferry and a twenty-five-cent train ride. The Lido Venice was in Paterson.

When I had the right audience in the room, I used to say, "As you are sitting here in the Lido Venice, there are people in Venice sitting sipping their grappa in a café called the Paterson." I don't know whether they thought the joke was funny or whether they laughed to show their appreciation that I knew about grappa, which is to Italians what pulque is to Mexicans. I'll bet you thought pulque was music by Lawrence Welk.

To make the whole thing more complicated, the stuff those Jersey joints sold the most of was applejack, sometimes known as Jersey lightning.

The Lido Club turned out to be a hangout for famous hoods like Waxie Gordon and Longie Zwillman. They were great to work for. If you made them laugh a lot, they'd slip you a fifty-dollar bill. If you made them mad, they'd slip you a hunk of lead.

Money meant nothing to those guys. Nothing meant anything to them. One night I was sitting at the table waiting to go on, and Gordon sat down with me.

"How's it going?" he asked.

"Okay."

"Listen," he said. "Want you to do me a favor. Hold this till I come back. There's a waitress in this place who has something I want."

He handed me an automatic I could barely lift, got up, and went out back through the kitchen door. When he returned, he handed me a hundred-dollar bill and took his gat back. "Thanks," he said. "She's a nice girl. You did a nice job. Have a drink."

That was one of my big problems with those guys. They'd ask me to drink with them. But it actually made me sick to drink. When I refused Waxie, he said, "What's the matter? You don't think it's good stuff?"

This was like telling him his father wasn't married to his mother. "It's not that," I said. "There's something about all booze that makes me feel like vomiting and I can't go on and tell jokes."

"Sure. Sure," he said. "And when you go on and tell the jokes, it makes everybody else feel like vomiting." But he laughed as he said it. The ice was broken. He got up and walked away, and I was afraid to go home for fear I'd wake up the next morning at the bottom of the Hudson with my feet in a block of cement.

The ice wasn't all that was broken. A jaw was also broken. It turned out that the waitress Waxie thought had something for him didn't want to give it to him, so he socked her in the jaw, rattled some of her teeth, tore her dress, and took it from her. For waitresses in those joints, rape was considered part of the tip. One of them said, "Around here when you see that rape is inevitable, the best thing to do is just lie back and enjoy it."

Being a headwaiter in one of those dives wasn't all hundred-dollar tips either. The guy at the door at the Lido Venice got a lot of arms and legs broken by "one of the boys." One night this torpedo happened to walk in with his wife, and the man at the door laughed and said, "Hey, how'd you get home last night?"

Joe Lefkowitz, the manager of the Regent Theater in Paterson, came in a couple of nights and then booked me for his theater. At first Nick Durante—no relation to Jimmy—who ran the Lido, wanted to cancel me. "Why should anyone come in our joint an' spend two, three bucks when they can catch you at the theater for fifty cents?" It was a good question.

Luckily I had a good answer. "They don't come here to see me. They come for that good Italian food and booze. Besides, all the time I'm up there on the stage at the Regent, I'm plugging the Lido. A guy's there with his dame. He wants to make it big with her. So after the show he brings her here for a drink."

"Yeah. You're right. You're pretty smart for a comic."

I was always arguing myself into jobs and talking myself out of tough spots. Some people used to say I ought to be a lawyer. Once I asked why and I was told, "Someday you gotta wind up in jail."

Lake Hopatcong, a little farther into New Jersey than Paterson, was a popular summer resort at that time for all comedians because one of the greatest of them all, Joe Cook, had a home there. People would do anything to get invited to Joe's because the place was filled with all kinds of gags.

You'd go into a bar that looked like a German beer garden. One of Joe's company, maybe Dave Chasen, would be serving beer and telling jokes with a German accent. Then you'd walk across the hall into Paddy's Irish Pub, and there was Dave in a red wig and a brogue singing a come-all-ye.

But the greatest attraction at Joe's was his golf course. It had a hole that everybody made in one. It was built so that you couldn't avoid it.

Well, a man named Walter Jacobs, whom I met one night at the Lido, booked me into his place, the Hotel Alamac at Lake Hopatcong. I was to be social director, a chance to use my Mountain experience.

The Alamac had a rule that none of the employees could be married to each other. It's that way in a lot of resort hotels. The help has to feel free to mingle with the guests and do anything that might make them happy. But I told Mr. Jacobs that I had a girlfriend who had worked in the Mountains taking care of guests' children. It struck him as a good idea, so he gave Sadie a job. So I managed to keep Sadie with me, at a time when we'd only been married for a little while and it was very important.

Because Joe Cook and other comics had places around the Lake Hopatcong area, a lot of agents used to come up and stay at the Alamac on weekends. And Mr. Jacobs would invite comedians to come up and be his guests. Berle was there a lot. Like all the other "guests," he paid off in entertainment. Every Saturday night the room was full of big-time vaudeville comics like Shaw and Lee, Joe Frisco, Joe E. Lewis, Bert and Betty Wheeler, and they'd all sit there and heckle me.

One night something went right, and I began to talk back to these hot comics who were giving me a hard time, and I was topping them. After the show a stockbroker who was staying at the hotel, a man named Toots Schnoor (that's right) asked me to come see him in his office in New York.

When I got there, he said he wanted to back me in an act and gave me a contract to sign. I didn't even read it. I signed it. Then he went to Richie Craig, Jr., who was one of the funniest monologists around, a little pale, skinny guy who used to fracture them at the Palace. He paid Craig five hundred to write an act for me.

It took Richie about three months to get the stuff together, and when I got it, I booked myself into a hideaway in Elizabeth, New Jersey, to try it out, using a stooge by the name of Sol Berry. (Incidentally, isn't that a laugh? "A hideaway in Elizabeth, New Jersey"? Elizabeth, New Jersey, is a hideaway.)

Everything was going great until, in the middle of the act, Berry suddenly decided he was the funny man, funnier than the script Richie Craig had written, funnier than me . . . and he was wrong. The result of his attempt to go into business for himself was a solid bust in front of all the bookers I'd invited to catch the act. Dagmar later made a success by having a solid bust in front of all the bookers but my case was different.

I had to do something quick, so I got myself booked as the comedian in a unit that starred Tommy Dorsey's band. Traveling with the band was a quartet. In the quartet were two people who became very famous. One of them was Jo Stafford, who at that time could have been half a quartet all by herself. She looked like twins when she was standing alone. The other quarter of the foursome was only about one-sixteenth of it, a skinny kid named Frank Sinatra.

Frank and I got very friendly, and I asked him how he happened to be with the Dorsey outfit. He told me it was his second choice out of two offers.

"Who was the other?" I asked.

"Paul Whiteman," said Frank with a straight face.

"Why didn't you go with him?"

"He didn't want me as just a singer. He wanted me to double."

"As what?"

"A baton."

I began doing jokes about him in my monologue. "Wait till you see the skinny kid in the quartet. He used to have a job modeling for the ham in bus stop sandwiches." Or "He's in danger if he doesn't get out of the bathtub before he pulls the plug." Or "When the wind blows, it makes his belly flap against his spine." Or "When he swallows watermelon seeds, they show." Or "Last night he climbed the drainpipe to his girl's room, on the inside."

Frank has given a lot of credit to Tommy for teaching him how to phrase a song, saying he'd sing the way Tommy played it on the 'bone. Maybe. But they didn't get along at all. I was constantly trying to get them to cool off and back away when they got into scraps.

Finally, the lid blew off everything in Youngstown, Ohio, and Frank said he quit. Dorsey said, ''You can't quit till I get a replacement for you.'' This started another fight, but it was finally settled that Frank would go on to the next date, which was in Akron, Ohio, and sing with the group till his replacement arrived.

A couple of days later in Akron, the new singer showed up. He'd come by bus from Chicago. His name was Dick Haymes. By this time Frank had cooled off on Dorsey and wanted to stay, so he threw Dick out of the theater.

There was a girl singer with the Dorsey band named Patti Palmer. I thought she was great. So did Jerry Lewis. But he couldn't get past the man at the Capitol stage door to see her. I got him in by saying he was visiting me. Lucky thing he wasn't. He *married* her. People would have talked.

Back in New York, finally, I saw Richie Craig's name on the marquee of the Palace and went backstage to tell him what had happened with the routine he'd written for me. When I knocked on the dressing room door, a doctor opened it and said Richie was very sick. So I went away.

Very soon after that Richie Craig, Jr., died of tuberculosis. It was too bad. He was still young and a very funny man. His routine about how he used to take his girl out in the evening and how they'd go and sit behind the bakery together and smell fresh bread is still quoted when old vaudevillians sit around a bottle and get dewy-eyed.

*I worked in spots that were too swell to serve
paper napkins. The waiters walked around with
roller towels.*

16

Off "The Street"

"THE Street" was the block between Fifth and Sixth
avenues on West Fifty-second Street in Manhattan. It was the place
where everybody in show business wanted to work because it was
the best place to be seen by the most people.

It was where the action was. Not being hip to what was happening
on the Street was like not keeping up with the late-night talk shows
in the seventies.

Every night the spots that lined both sides of the Street, from the
Onyx Club at one end to Jack and Charlie's, the famous 21, at the
other, were made noisy and nutty by the strange variety of types
who came to participate in the unique entertainment. There was
something for every taste.

Hot musicians, singers, comics of all kinds rubbed elbows with
society people from Park Avenue, new young talent from Harlem,
rich butter-'n'-egg men from upstate and points west and kruising
kollege kids on weekend jaunts from almost every East Coast
institution of higher football.

This strange assortment of characters all were attracted by the same thing, each other. They came to see and be seen. The informal attitude that prevailed in all the spots practically guaranteed that something unexpected would happen. It could be anything from the birth of a new star to the death of an old hood. It had some of the elements that are being seen in the experimental theater. In its confused and undisciplined way it brought people together who normally would never meet.

It let the public see some of the inside workings of show business. People felt free to mingle with the performers, to talk back to them, and often tried to get into the act. If a performer could handle this type of audience, he or she succeeded. If you couldn't handle a heckler, your chances on the Street were zilch.

I guess this informality grew out of the fact that the whole scene was born of Prohibition. Most spots started as speaks. All served about the same booze. All competed heavily trying to serve better food. But the real competition was in how much fun you could have in a place after you got high enough not to care what you were doing. It was quick and easy to do this on that Volstead-type booze. So the speakeasy became the great leveler.

Because of this Prohibition background, the Street was the frontier of "Godfather" country.

And I started on the frontier of this frontier in a spot that was sort of around the corner and up the block from the Street. It was called the 711 Club. Guess why.

The pay was forty dollars a week, and four dollars of that went to my agent. Went to him? *All* of it went to him. Then he took out his 10 percent and graciously paid me thirty-six dollars.

What you have to remember is this, at that time forty dollars was worth at least a hundred and sixty dollars by today's standards. Come to think of it, that still isn't very much. But then neither was my agent.

Those were the days when all we had to fear was fear itself, and we sure feared it. First, we were afraid every meal we had would be our last. Then, when we got a job, we were afraid it wouldn't last. And if it lasted a little while, we were afraid we were getting in a rut. A rut is nothing but a long grave. And if you worked on the Street, you also had every right to be afraid of a stray bullet. If one of the customers set off one of those party snappers with a paper hat in it, everyone in the joint, particularly the bosses, ducked under tables.

Not long ago I read a story in the New York *Times* about two policemen, both in plain clothes, who ran into each other one day. It happened on the Long Island Expressway. In the argument that followed over whose fault it was, one of the cops reached into his

mg. "tar," 0.7 mg. nicotine
v. per cigarette by FTC Method.

© Lorillard 1976

NEW

Famous Micronite Filter

KENT
Golden
Lights

Low Tar & Nicotine

8 Mgs. Tar. 07 Mgs. Nicotine

KENT GOLDEN LIGHTS
ONLY 8 MG TAR.
YET TASTES SO GOOD,
YOU WON'T BELIEVE THE NUMBERS.

Of All Brands Sold: Lowest tar: 2 mg. "tar," 0.2 mg. nicotine
av. per cigarette, FTC Report Apr. 1976.
Kent Golden Lights: 8 mg. "tar,"
0.7 mg. nicotine av. per cigarette by FTC Method.

NEW!
KENT GOLDEN LIGHTS
LOWER IN TAR
THAN ALL THESE BRANDS.

Non-menthol Filter Brands	Tar	Nicotine	Non-menthol Filter Brands	Tar	Nicotine
KENT GOLDEN LIGHTS	**8 mg.**	**0.7 mg.***	RALEIGH 100's	17 mg.	1.2 mg.
MERIT	9 mg.	0.7 mg.*	MARLBORO 100's	17 mg.	1.1 mg.
VANTAGE	11 mg.	0.7 mg.	BENSON & HEDGES 100's	18 mg.	1.1 mg.
MULTIFILTER	13 mg.	0.8 mg.	VICEROY 100's	18 mg.	1.2 mg.
WINSTON LIGHTS	13 mg.	0.9 mg.	MARLBORO KING SIZE	18 mg.	1.1 mg.
MARLBORO LIGHTS	13 mg.	0.8 mg.	LARK	18 mg.	1.2 mg.
RALEIGH EXTRA MILD	14 mg.	0.9 mg.	CAMEL FILTERS	18 mg.	1.2 mg.
VICEROY EXTRA MILD	14 mg.	0.9 mg.	EVE	18 mg.	1.2 mg.
PARLIAMENT BOX	14 mg.	0.8 mg.	WINSTON 100's	18 mg.	1.2 mg.
DORAL	15 mg.	1.0 mg.	WINSTON BOX	18 mg.	1.2 mg.
PARLIAMENT KING SIZE	16 mg.	0.9 mg.	CHESTERFIELD	19 mg.	1.2 mg.
VICEROY	16 mg.	1.1 mg.	LARK 100's	19 mg.	1.2 mg.
RALEIGH	16 mg.	1.1 mg.	L&M KING SIZE	19 mg.	1.2 mg.
VIRGINIA SLIMS	16 mg.	1.0 mg.	TAREYTON 100's	19 mg.	1.4 mg.
PARLIAMENT 100's	17 mg.	1.0 mg.	WINSTON KING SIZE	19 mg.	1.3 mg.
L&M BOX	17 mg.	1.1 mg.	L&M 100's	19 mg.	1.3 mg.
SILVA THINS	17 mg.	1.3 mg.	PALL MALL 100's	19 mg.	1.4 mg.
MARLBORO BOX	17 mg.	1.0 mg.	TAREYTON	21 mg.	1.4 mg.

Source: FTC Report Apr. 1976
*By FTC Method

Warning: The Surgeon General Has Determined
That Cigarette Smoking Is Dangerous to Your Health.

inside pocket to get a pencil. The other one thought he was going for a gun, pulled his own, and shot him. The cop who was shot didn't like this too much, so he pulled *his* gun and shot the other guy. They both died.

Something like that happened about thirty-five years ago at the 711 Club. At the time this happened the name of the club had been changed to Gallagher's. That was the name of the retired police captain who owned the joint. But it was run by a man named Pope. Pope's sister was one of Earl Carroll's *Vanities* beauties. She was going steady with a city detective whom she'd grown up with in Queens just as it says in the song, "I just adore the boy next door."

It's a well-known show business fact that a chorus girl doesn't have to starve. The really beautiful ones can do a whole lot better than a half share of a city policeman's pay. At least it was that way in those days. I haven't checked up lately. I'm true to Sadie . . . or she'd kill me. The way to do that gag is: "I've been in love with the same woman for twenty-seven years. If my wife ever finds out, she'll murder me."

Because of all the high rollers making plays for the Earl Carroll girls, the policeman began to feel a little insecure about his girl's affections. Something told him the chill was on. He was convinced of this when he called her about taking a walk one Sunday afternoon—there's a laugh, a cop taking a walk—and her mother told him she said to tell him she was out of town, and when she got back if ever, it'd be all right with her if he didn't call up anymore.

This didn't go down well with the dick. Like every other policeman, he had to have a victim, so he came to the club looking for Pope. Can you imagine how mad a Catholic cop must have been to come after a Pope?

When he got to the club, he rushed right upstairs to Pope's office. I was in a dressing room down the hall putting the makeup on my violin to make it look like a Stradivarius, and I heard a lot of hollering. When I went to find out what was going on, I saw the detective had a gun in Pope's belly. Luckily, he didn't see me.

I rushed downstairs and found another cop, Buck O'Neill, who was, at one time, one of Hearst's bodyguards. When I told Buck what I saw, he pulled his gun and rushed upstairs. I was waiting to hear some gunshots. I would have called the police, but the police were already there.

After a minute or so I began to hear talking. It's a miracle that no one got shot. But it's proof that there was a time when policemen weren't so gun-happy as they now seem to be.

Pope said to me, "Henny, you saved my life. I'm going to do

something big for you someday. Just wait and see."

I'm still waiting. And while I'm waiting, I'm reminded of the time I had *my* life saved. *One* of the times I know of. Like Pope, I said I'd never forget the guy who saved me. It was while I was playing a one-night-stand Sunday concert in a burlesque house in Brooklyn. They called them "concerts." That was just to get around the law that said there could be no regular theatrical performances on Sunday. Actually these concerts were merely vaudeville shows without scenery or costumes.

While I was taking a bow, some jerk backstage did something that caused the curtain to come crashing down. If a stagehand hadn't quickly pulled me back, it could have broken my neck. I promised that man I'd never forget him, and I want to tell you right now, I was never more wrong in my life. I can't even remember what he looked like, much less his name.

I said Pope never did anything for me. I was wrong about that too. He did. He fired me. And just for having a little fun.

One night I started a conga line. That was a popular dance that men liked because it gave them a chance to grab hold of women's hips. Women liked it for the same reason. So, hands on each other's hips, they formed a conga line. Then they'd weave around the dance floor to music. One, two, three, kick! One, two, three, kick! You kicked sideways. You didn't kick the person in front of you. It didn't make much sense, but it was easier to do than the rumba, which also came into popularity at that time.

The person to blame for all that South American dancing that had been limited up to that time to the Argentine tango, as introduced by the Italian Rudolph Valentino, was a Brazilian named Carmen Miranda. She was a little woman who made herself look tall by wearing platform shoes. She introduced them into this country. That never should have been allowed—they make women look stump-legged. But she was great for comedians. She wore high headdresses made of fruit. There were a million variations of the basic joke "Did you see Carmen Miranda's headdress?" "See it? I ate it." Another was: "Have you seen Carmen Miranda's rumba?" "No! She was facing me." Or "How did you like the way she uses her maracas?"

For some reason—maybe it was to make it look sexier and more suggestive—when a man and woman danced the rumba (and that was the usual sex mix), they stared at each other very intensely as if each were trying to figure out what the next step would be. This shouldn't have been hard because the next step was always exactly like the last step. It's a dumb dance.

Somebody said, "The dancers stare at each other as if they're psychoanalyzing each other." They might just as well have been doing that as dancing, for all the action there was.

But to get back. I started this conga line one night, and after a couple of turns on the dance floor I led everybody right out onto the street. The cop stopped traffic to let us cross. It made Mr. Pope awful sore, and he fired me. Just because when the people found themselves out on the street, they all went home without paying their checks. It's an example of the kind of do-whatever-comes-into-your-head attitude that made those Fifty-second Street spots fun.

Of course, when all the people who went home without paying their checks got home and sobered up, they remembered they'd left their coats and hats and handbags in the joint. So they all had to go back and get them and pay up. So I got my job back.

It just goes to show what kind of things the customers would do. The audiences were just as crazy as the entertainers. One night I was introducing a girl singer. I said, "Ladies and gentlemen, I'd like to have you meet Miss Helen Travis."

Was Helen surprised when she walked out on the floor! The whole audience rose just as if they'd rehearsed it and came up and shook her hand and said, "Pleased to meet you."

While I was working at Gallagher's, a comedian named Roy Sedley came to me with a proposition to do a double with him. I'd only worked double once before. It was with a dancer named Kay Hovell. I figured George Burns was doing all right with a girl. Try it. Kay was a sweet kid and a good dancer, but she was no Gracie Allen. That was because I was the Gracie Allen of the act. I got the laughs. She did George Burns. But she wasn't as pretty as George.

I go through all this, so you'll understand why I said no to Roy until he told me he had a solid booking at the State-Lake in Chicago. Roy was a smooth, Bob Hope type. His idea was that I be his straight man and heckle him. Heckling was what I was good at. The money was so much better than what I was getting that to say no to Roy's idea would have been like turning down a gas mask at a peace rally.

There was one little problem. Roy had a bad case of the shorts. He needed a hundred to get him to Chicago.

I called a man I knew named Harry Drucker, who made a business of lending money to people who couldn't establish enough credit to get it elsewhere. For this he got what the gangsters call vigorish and what the United States government calls usury. It was what Drucker called getting rich. And he had a way of collecting his debts that was really a killer.

He gave me the money, and I passed it on to Roy, who said he'd meet me in Chicago. At that time the fastest and easiest way to get there from New York was aboard the 20th Century Limited. It took about eighteen hours.

It took Roy three days. He had a way of traveling that gave him a layover in every bar along the way. He just made it for the first show. There was no time for rehearsal. There was no need for rehearsal. He was so lit the glare blinded the man who was running the spotlight. We were instantly canceled, and Roy started his bar-studded trip back to Manhattan, leaving me stranded in the Windy City with about ten bucks in my pants.

Faced with the necessity to get a job or starve and considering the alternative, I made the rounds of the Chicago clubs and agents and managed to talk myself into a spot called the Paramount Club. The manager told me that some of my New York friends had played the date, so I had him call a couple of them to give me a reference. Jack Carter said, ''He's very funny. Won't steal the tables. Keep an eye on everything else.'' He talked to a couple of others and then told me, ''They say you're great.''

''If another comic praises me, that ought to mean something, shouldn't it?''

Why should they lie when saying what they said was better for them even if they didn't mean it? They got what I had figured out. As long as I worked in Chicago, there was one less comic looking for a job around New York. There was only one hitch about the Paramount job. I had to have a tuxedo.

Right next door to the Chicago Theater there was a men's store run by the Cooper brothers. They did a lot of business with show people, and they were good enough to take a chance on me. They let me have the tuxedo and pants on credit. I promised to pay in full the minute I got my first week from the club.

Then a strange thing happened. The manager told me how good I was at the end of the first week, and then he fired me. He said I was too funny. No kidding.

The club had a gambling casino in back where they made their real money. I was keeping people in the front room listening to me instead of letting them drift back to play the wheel and shoot crap.

I was in great shape. Right back where Sedley left me. I paid the Coopers for the suit and wound up with about ten bucks left in my pocket. It began to feel too familiar. I suppose I could have looked for another spot in Chicago, but by this time I wasn't too crazy about the city. I had a big urge to get back to New York. Sadie was pregnant for the first time. For the first time I was beginning to understand what marriage was all about. I felt terrible.

I walked over to the Palmer House to see if there was anyone I knew sitting around the lobby. I took a chair that had a *Tribune* lying on it. I picked it up and started to read it so the house detective wouldn't get the idea I was just sitting there to keep out of the rain or to make some kind of score.

All of a sudden my eyes were grabbed by an ad that said: "Wanted—Passenger to New York. Male. All expenses paid. $10." Then there was a phone number.

I've never made such a quick decision in my life. It was to motor to New York. I called Sadie collect to tell her.

When I got to the place where I was to pick up my car and driver, there were five other people waiting. One was going to Detroit. One to Cleveland. One to Buffalo. One to Ithaca. One to Albany, and I was going to Brooklyn. I was the only one who got his full ten dollars' worth of ride.

But what a racket that guy worked out. He got fifty dollars and all expenses to drive that big Packard back to New York and ten dollars each from six people, plus whatever padding he put on the expenses. We drove day and night, and it took three days.

When I got to New York, I heard Sedley was looking for me. He was full of apologies. They didn't do me much good. But they were an improvement on what he was usually full of. He'd managed to get another booking. This time at the Academy Theater on East Fourteenth Street near the arcade where I used to have my printing booth.

I agreed to try again with him. This time, when I showed up at the theater, Sedley wasn't there. But two friends of the man who had lent him the hundred dollars were waiting for him at the stage door. They were obviously on their way to play baseball because each of them had his bat with him. They stopped me to ask when Sedley would show up. I asked them what they were doing with the bats.

One of them said, "We're taking them home to our kids as a present."

The other said, "But if Sedley shows up, first we'll let *him* have them."

All gangsters were wisecrackers in those days. They got their material from Jimmy Cagney movies. They used to hang around in the lobby of the Strand Theater on Broadway, where most of the gangster films had their first run, waiting for the doors to open for the first showing of a new one. It was like going to night school at noon.

I pleaded with these mugs to leave Roy alone, let him work for a week, and I'd see that he paid them the money he owed. I told them I needed the money for the week, that my wife was going to have a baby and that we were both broke, and that if they beat up Roy, neither of us would have any dough. Little by little I appealed to their better nature. It wasn't too good, but it was better than getting Roy killed. I would have been canceled.

All week I kept my eye on Roy every second to make sure he wouldn't hit the bottle again. When payday came, I was with him when he got his share. So were the boys with the bats. I saw to it that they got theirs while the bills still had damp spots where the treasurer wet his thumb counting them.

Not long after that Marilyn was born. It might have saved my life. If those thugs with the Louisville Sluggers found out I lied about my wife being pregnant, you couldn't tell what they'd do to me and to her.

A terrible thing happened to me on the subway. The paper I was reading got off at Fifty-ninth Street.

17

Taking a Cut

BY this time you've probably guessed that I was out of the printing racket. Longer and longer bookings, farther and farther away from New York killed the whole idea of being in both show business and the printing business. For one thing, I couldn't keep my hands clean. And when you're working in joints like I worked in, you've got to keep your hands cleaner than the customers.

I sold the whole layout to a guy for a small profit: press, lease, and goodwill. I sometimes wonder what he did with the goodwill. Every once in a while I find I could use a little of it. Almost as soon as I stopped competing with the Reuben H. Donnelly Company, I was booked into a spot called the Lynnbrook Club in Rhode Island, near Providence. Everything in Rhode Island is near Providence, just the way everything in Delaware is near Dupont.

It was a nice place. Things were great. The audiences loved me, but the management didn't. I couldn't collect my salary from them. They considered it a good week when they broke even. So I had to figure a way to get some cash out of the date. All I was getting was the privilege of signing for food and drinks.

What I did was, I told some of my friends in the area what was going on. They'd come in and have dinner. I'd sign, and they'd pay me. It wasn't the greatest way in the world to make a living, so I quit. But no night spots were doing much business in those days.

I remember a spot in Newark called the Blue Mirror Club. Well named. The place was doing so bad that every time I saw myself in the mirror I looked blue. And you should have seen how the owner looked. One night after closing I was on my way out, and he stopped me. "Where's your fiddle?" he asked.

"I left it in the dressing room. Why lug it back and forth?"

"Go get it," he said. "It won't hurt you to lug it back and forth. It's good exercise. And while you're getting it, you might as well get your clothes and your music. As long as you're lugging, you might as well make it a good lug."

"That's silly."

"Look, Mr. Youngman. Don't be silly. Don't talk silly. Lug!"

Later that night, by accident, the place caught fire and burned to the ground. To this day I think it's a miracle how that man's intuition told him there'd be trouble and to pass the information along to me without charge.

I finally got back into the Fifty-second Street area and was working at the Kentucky Club when Joe Lefkowitz, a cousin of Sy Fabian, if that means anything to you (I promised to get his name in the book), got me a regular job MC'ing the stage show at the Fox Theater in Brooklyn. The pay was a lot more than I was making at the club, but I didn't want to give the club up because two paychecks are better than one. Besides, I was going over great doing the same sort of thing that Don Rickles does now. So I had two jobs. It wasn't easy.

I did two shows in Brooklyn, then took the subway to New York to do two shows, and when they were over, I sat around a table at Lindy's, where all comics who were working, and could afford it, sat until four or five in the morning. Then I'd take the subway back to Brooklyn. That sitting around Lindy's was the most important part of the day's work.

Every night after closing, Jack Carter, Jerry Lester, Red Buttons, Milton Berle, Phil Silvers—everybody who was working—would sit around there smoking big cigars. None of us could afford them, and I didn't even like them. But they saved me money. After smoking a cigar, I didn't feel like eating.

We'd tell each other how great we were as loud as we could for the benefit of the other customers. And we'd try to top the waiters. Those Lindy waiters were comedians, critics, philosophers, and dieticians. "Don't eat the cheesecake, you're getting too fat."

The cigars we smoked gave us confidence, and occasionally Walter Winchell would stop at our table, pick up a few gags for his column, and give us a plug. It got to be a tough routine. But nobody was ever too tired to pull a good gag. One night, when we broke up and headed for home, Red Buttons said something about a friend of mine that I didn't like. I don't mean I didn't like the friend. I didn't like the crack.

So when I got home, I called Red at the Piccadilly Hotel, where he was living, and told him I was a reporter for the *Daily News*. I said I'd been trying to get to see him for an interview, but he was always so busy I finally had to call when I was sure he was home. He said, "Well, what do you want to know?"

I started asking questions and talked to him for about two hours. Red told me how great he'd been everywhere and what he wanted to do. It was beautiful. He got an ego boost. I got a laugh and a couple of good jokes. And he's still buying the *News* looking for the story. *Sayonara*, Red!

At the end of two weeks I was glad the Fox job was ending. Then they told me the picture was being held over another week. It was Grace Moore and Tullio Carminati in *One Night of Love* . . . and three weeks in Brooklyn. Of course, I had to be held over to tell some jokes while the projectionist rewound the film.

By the time it came to the weekend of the third week it turned out to be the weekend that weakened me. So I talked Milton Berle and some of my other Lindy pals into subbing for me at the theater. This meant that in Brooklyn I was just working for billing. My pals got the pay. They'll help you, but not for nothing. They had to eat, too.

Apparently it didn't matter to the Fox management who told the jokes while the projectionist rewound the film. I got the idea they figured they got a little better than they bargained for. But at the Kentucky Club I began to have problems.

When Grace and Tullio started charming the Brooklynites for a fourth week, I decided I'd better let the club slide a little and concentrate on the theater. But at the club I was the one the customers came to see, and when I didn't show, there was grumbling at the tables. This led to some grumbling in the office.

But nothing was actually said. There were just a lot of menacing looks from some guys who knew they didn't have to rely on looks to kill. Then the picture was held over for a fifth week, and by this time I was sloughing off both the theater and the club.

It was during this week, while I was resting in my dressing room between shows at the theater, that a couple of gentlemen with menacing looks and chests that bulged more on one side than the other came to call on me. They talked slanty English out of the sides of their mouths and made it clear that the management didn't like it too much that I wasn't giving them the best I had in me. They also said that if I knew what was good for me, I'd quit the theater job altogether and get back to some real solid work at the club unless I wanted the theater job to be my last. I told them I'd be there right after the next show.

But after the next show I couldn't get myself together to make the long trip to New York. Actually, I was as scared to go back as I was not to. So I went home. I figured if they wanted to get me, why should I go to them?

Sometimes you do things and you don't know why. Then you find out later that what you did was right. Well, I did right not to go back to the Kentucky Club. That night, according to the next morning's paper, a bunch of city detectives hit the club looking for some info on a gangland rubout. They pushed a lot of people around and beat up some innocent men in bulgy double-breasted suits who just came in from Detroit to have a little fun.

On the basis of what I heard I'm sure if I'd been there, I'd have been beaten up. I never went back, and I never was sent for. Grace and Tullio and I played a sixth week at the Fox. And I must have told the jokes better that last week. I was awake.

The whole experience of doubling between Brooklyn and New York made me feel lousy because it went on too long. I also had a feeling that if I knew anything about the gangsters who ran the clubs, it would be a good idea if I weren't seen around town to remind them of what had happened.

With all the places outside New York that I might have got a booking, I finally wound up in Fort Wayne, Indiana, and in pain.

Fort Wayne all by itself could be a pain in those days, but that wasn't what had me almost doubled up in agony. There was something very unpleasant going on on my right side. Finally, after three days of working in more pain than I was inflicting, they pulled me off the stage and rushed me to the hospital. They said I had a ruptured appendix.

The doctor in Fort Wayne couldn't have had much faith in himself because while I was still alive, he phoned my uncle, Dr. Chetkin, in New York to come and get the body. He must have figured that by the time the doctor got to Fort Wayne to pick me up, I'd be ready for him.

Things were pretty tough at our house around that time, and my father had to try to borrow some money from cousins who were doing all right to bring me home. Dead or alive he wanted me back. But the cousins were not that interested in me. Nobody even came to Fort Wayne to see me except, of course, my faithful Sadie.

Later, when I began to get some recognition and was all over radio, they kept bragging about how they were related to me. You know how people are. One Christmas I sent them a card saying, "Merry Christmas. Can I buy back my connection?"

It was extremely embarrassing for the Fort Wayne hospital that I didn't die and nobody showed up to get me. On top of that I was very sick and had to have private nurses around the clock. I kept asking if some of them couldn't hang around me a little.

Naturally I was broke. But there was one pretty nurse who said she didn't care. She'd take care of me no matter what happened. When I say she was pretty, I mean she was pretty fat. I used to kid her about her size. I said she was the only set of twins I ever saw in one package. But I promised that if I ever got out of Fort Wayne and really hit it big in show business, I'd have a job for her. I figured if I got sick only working sometimes, how sick would I get working steady?

Her name was Edith Drennan, and I kept my promise. When I got a steady job on the *Kate Smith Show*, I sent for Edith to take care of Marilyn and Gary. Between Kate at the studio and Edith at home I used to tell Sadie I was living off the fat of the land.

The whole time I was in the hospital I was worried about how I was going to get out without paying the bill, which I didn't have the dough to do. I thought I might have to raffle myself off to the highest bidder. But my agent, Jack Kalcheim, organized a benefit for me. He figured I'd played enough to be entitled to one. And the people in show business came through as they always do.

Acts playing in the various vaudeville and burlesque houses in and around Fort Wayne and from as far away as Chicago came and did the benefit. It was great.

But when they finally released me from the hospital, I was told they they hadn't taken out my appendix. They said they were afraid to. I had a chicken surgeon. They'd just drained off the poison and sewed me up again. They said I'd have to have another operation, later, to get rid of the appendix. This bothered me. My friends had paid for an appendectomy I didn't get. I felt I owed them my appendix.

When I got back to New York and got examined, every doctor I went to told me something else. One said have the appendix out right away. One said wait and see. One said, "Check with me every week." Another asked, "Did you ever have pain in that region before?'' When I told him I had, he said, ''Well, you got it again.''

There's nothing more depressing than going to a doctor who talks like that quack Dr. Kronkeit, which was the name Smith and Dale used in their doctor act.

While I was wondering what to do with whatever the problem was that I had inside me, I ran into some old friends who operated cigar stand concessions in Hi Mount and some other summer resort hotels I'd worked in.

Their name was Jack and Ida Mendes. Ida said she was working for one of the head men at Mount Sinai Hospital in New York and suggested I come and see him. The Mendeses were really great to me. They even offered to pay for any operation that might be necessary.

To show them how I appreciated it, I offered to pay for any operation either of them might need someday when I got going and had the dough.

Neither of us had to keep the bargain. When I went to Mount Sinai, they told me they couldn't find my appendix. There was nothing to operate for. I never found out what happened to it after it got through hurting me. Maybe it did so badly that the William Morris Office booked it somewhere in the Middle West, where it died and was never heard from again.

Business was so bad that when someone called and asked, "What time is the show?" I said, "What time can you make it?"

18

The Shirt off My Back

WHEN Paul Small booked me into the Yacht Club on the Street, things really began to move for me. The money was almost twice what I was getting. Of course, it was only half of what I was worth. And only one-tenth of what I wanted.

After Jack and Charlie's 21 Club, which was always very plush, the Yacht Club was really right up there with the Street's top spots. There was also Tony's, which got the intelligentsia, writers, publishers, and actors who could either read or write. Of a different kind but also a product of the Volstead era was a place started by a singer named Eddie Davis and a manager type named Leon Enken. For some reason, I'll never know why, they called their place Leon & Eddie's. I want you to get the fact that the guy that handled the money got top billing over the man with the talent it took to fill the joint.

I don't know whether it got started by accident or whether it was planned that way to get a lot of free talent, but every Sunday there used to be a sort of happening at Leon & Eddie's. Everybody who was working and, of course, all those who weren't would drop in to show off their stuff and catch the competition.

Bob Benchley at Tony's said, "They gang into Leon & Eddie's to peer at their peers," whatever that means.

With guys like Alan King, Jack E. Leonard, Jerry Lewis, Joey Adams, Milton Berle—you name him, he was there—all hanging around looking for a spot to zap in a yock, you can imagine the heckling that went on.

You didn't even have to be a pro to get in on the gab. You didn't have to sing, dance, or tell jokes. If you thought you had something to say, if you were drunk enough to make a speech, or if you wanted to get some gripe off your chest, all you needed to get up and do your stuff at L & E's was the guts to handle whatever the other customers felt like dishing out to you.

Sometimes I'd walk across the street between shows to get in on that action, maybe slip in a plug for the Yacht Club, and in general do a little toomling. One night I was sitting there at a little table in the back of the room, all by myself. Berle was on. He started talking about the personalities in the room and stopped in the middle of a sentence to say, "Light man. Put the spot on that gentleman all alone back there." When the light found me, he went on, "That's Henny Youngman surrounded by all his friends."

I stood up and took a bow. "That's Milton Berle, my friend," I said. "I'll trade him for two enemies." (Now you know where those two gags started.)

The show went on and on and on. Berle kept talking and talking and talking. It looked as if he planned to stay on the floor all night. I hollered, "What this place needs is a clock. It's already got the cuckoo."

Berle came back with: "What this place needs is a clock that will strike one, and you're the one." Then he went on and on again.

I got impatient. Clearly I'd have to go back and do my own show before I'd get a chance to try out some new material on a tough audience. I got up, rattled a bunch of keys so everyone would notice me, and then threw them on the floor in front of Berle, saying, "Sweep out and lock up!" And I left.

Outside, the regular mounted man on the beat was standing beside his horse gabbing with the doorman. "Do me a favor," I said, "and I'll buy this many tickets to the Policeman's Ball" and I handed him a twenty-dollar bill. "Get on this old gray mare of yours, and ride into Leon & Eddie's, and say to Berle, 'Come on, Milton. Time to lock up. I'll give you a ride home.'"

He did, and it broke up the joint, naturally.

Also, I know it sounds unbelievable, but nothing was out of the question on the Street. It was carnival time every night. And as far as the policeman was concerned, he looked upon the deal as public relations. I was a member of the public, and the twenty would help him support his relations.

Frances Faye was my co-star at the Yacht Club. She didn't like that too much, and we didn't get along very well. She figured every minute I was on the floor was just another minute she wasn't. She even tried to get me fired. But she was good. Very good. And she brought in a lot of business. What she forgot was that we both did.

She was a torch singer. It was wonderful to watch the hardboiled thugs that always used to fill joints like that, sitting around trying to keep from crying so they wouldn't wet their ammunition.

My two shows at the Yacht Club were at eight and midnight. This gave me plenty of time between shows to play another date in the area. Every time I did, it reminded me of when I was a kid and used to bicycle movie reels from one Brooklyn theater to another. Now I was bicycling myself.

I'll never forget one of those extra shows. It was at the Manhattan Opera House on West Thirty-fourth Street. Some labor organization was running a benefit. The president was probably trying to raise money to send himself and his wife and family to Miami for two weeks.

I got to the opera house a few minutes after nine and started shaking hands. Those affairs have more committee members than a politician has alibis. And that was what I spent the next three-quarters of an hour doing, shaking hands. But then, I'd rather have people shake hands with me than fists at me.

By about ten o'clock I was onstage working, and everything was going pretty good. The people were laughing and my violin string hadn't broken. But there was so much noise backstage I was surprised the audience could hear me. There was loud talking and banging. I was sure the audience could hear *that*, so I looked offstage and said, "They promised me the theater would be finished before I went on."

Then the talking got so loud I said, "Maybe I'd better shut up. There seems to be a better show going on backstage."

Finally I finished, shook hands with a few more people backstage, grabbed a cab, and dashed back to the Yacht Club for my midnight show. While the cab was going across town, I heard newsboys hollering, "Extra! Extra! Read all about it!" Then, of course, you couldn't understand what it was you were supposed to read all about. They still had "extras" in those days. Newspapers were still trying to beat each other to the street with a piece of fast-breaking news.

I asked the cabdriver if he knew what the kid was squawking about and got the usual cabdriver answer: "He's probably stuck with a few papers he wants to get rid of so he can go home."

When I arrived at the club, the doorman said, "Hey, Henny. Did you hear what happened at the Manhattan Opera House?"

"Yeah. I killed 'em!"

He said, "Oh, it was you?"

Something told me he wasn't trying to be funny. I asked what he meant.

He told me there'd been a fatal stabbing backstage. Suddenly I realized what the noise was while I was onstage. At least they couldn't say that *I* was getting away with murder. It was like the not too distant speakeasy days when the gangs were fighting each other, just as they're still doing.

But in those days a hood would come into a joint with a few well-armed friends, slip the bandleader a C-note, and tell him to play very loud. That way nobody knew anything happened till some guy would fall out of his chair not dead drunk, just dead.

When I got to my dressing room, was I surprised! There were two men waiting for me. I recognized one of them as a guy who had been introducing me to people backstage at the opera house. I never did hear his name.

I said, "Come to see the show?"

The guy I didn't know said, "Quit kidding. We're not. We came here because nobody knows we know you. If we went anywhere where people know us, they'd look there. So we came here." I knew right away he was from Brooklyn. Who else would talk like that? And I understood him.

"I don't get you," I said.

"Didn't you hear the noise backstage when you were on?"

"Was that you?"

"Yeah. We had a little misunderstanding with a guy, and we cut him."

"Seriously?"

"I think so. He's dead." The man opened his coat. His shirt was full of bloodstains.

"You're bleeding," I said. "I'll get a doctor."

"I'm not bleeding! *He* was bleeding."

By this time the other man was showing me *his* bloodstained shirt. They were two of the sloppiest murderers that ever came to visit me in my dressing room. I didn't know what to say. I never drink, but I always had a bottle of something in the dressing room for friends. So I said, "Have a drink."

"We drank it all while we were waiting for you."

As he said that, a funny thought flashed through my mind. I thought to myself, "As long as they were coming over to use my dressing room as a hideout, it was kind of thoughtless of them not to offer me a lift over in their car." Nonsense.

Writing such thoughts and knowing what's coming, I find it hard to continue. The whole incident was, in some way, like an incident in some British gangster film starring Alec Guinness.

I looked at my watch and saw I had to go on in a few minutes, so I said as politely as I could, "Would you mind if I changed my shirt?" That was all the makeup I ever used—a clean shirt.

"That's what we dropped by for," one of my friends said, "a couple of clean shirts." They had finished off my scotch; now they were going to polish off my haberdashery.

Luckily I'd just got a dozen new ones from Al Lewis, I pulled out two and tossed them over to my guests.

They started to take the pins out and were ripping off their own bloodstained shirts when one of them said, "Hey! We can't use these. They got your initials on them." I apologized.

"I'm sorry. I didn't know you were coming or I'd have ordered some with your initials on them . . . if I knew what they were."

"Never mind getting nosy," one of them said. "No names, see."

I said I saw. I didn't tell them I had no idea what their names were, and I was glad. They acted like big shots who were used to being recognized immediately in whatever world it was they lived in.

"Well. That's that. This ain't our night," said one of them. "Let's get moving out of here."

As they were leaving, one of them said, "Thanks, anyway, for everything. I'll be back with the old lady some night to see the show. You got good jokes."

Naturally I called the police as soon as I could get my hand to stop trembling enough to pick up the phone. Naturally the cops found it as hard, as you must find it, to believe my story. The only thing that convinced them that I was telling the truth was this: If I weren't why would I have called them?

The cops told me the names of the two guys, whom, incidentally, they caught and sent to jail. A few years later the one who told me I had some good jokes did just what he said he was going to do. He came to see me and brought his old lady. I didn't recognize him till he introduced himself. Today he's a big man in one of the unions, and I'd rather not mention his name.

I hadn't been working in the Yacht Club very long before I became aware of what Jimmy Durante would call "a revoltin' development." We were getting repeat customers. I didn't figure they were coming back to hear the jokes again. They weren't that hard to understand. I knew they were coming back to hear Frances Faye. But if they didn't hear new jokes while waiting for Faye, they might get restless and not wait. So I had to find a steady source of new material in a hurry.

If I'd told Momma about my problem, she would have said, "God will provide." And as another of Momma's old sayings goes: "Mother knows best." She did.

One night after the first show I was sitting in my dressing room trying to work out a new routine when a young man came in and introduced himself as Al Schwartz. He said he was an attorney just out of law school.

I said I was glad to meet him, but with the kind of trouble I was apt to get into, I needed an old lawyer with a lot of savvy.

"I'm not soliciting your legal business," said Schwartz, talking exactly like someone who'd just got out of law school. "I caught your act. I like that machine-gun delivery you have."

"This is machine-gun territory," I told him.

"That's it," he said. "Take a cliché, and turn it into a laugh in one line. It must use up material awfully fast."

I told him how smart he was and that I'd just been thinking that I needed some writing help.

Like a good young attorney leading a witness, he'd led me right into saying what he wanted me to say. But when he got around to the line, "I like the way you sell jokes," I got wise and said, "And you're here to sell some to *me*."

He just smiled and said, "Have I got a writer for you!"

"Got any samples?" I asked.

He did. I read them and hired him on the spot. "Shall I go to work right away?" he asked.

"Why not?"

"Okay. But you have to wait till I go around front for a minute. I have to get something."

"What?"

"My typewriter. I checked it."

When it was decided that I'd write this book, I wrote to Al asking him if he had any recollections of our association. Recalling our first meeting as I just described it, he said, "That moment started a warm, pleasant relationship that has lasted to this very day.

Although it was thirty-five years ago, I can still see myself sitting at an old battered typewriter.

"Hot off the assembly line you'd select the jokes you liked, and twenty minutes later you'd be regaling the customers who frequented the club with them. It was great training for me and was to come in handy in the near future."

More about "the near future" in the near future.

Not even my experience with the backstage stabbing at the Manhattan Opera House soured me on doing quick dates between shows at the Yacht Club. One day Sidney Piermont, who was a big-time vaudeville booker, came to me after the last show one night and asked if I'd like to play a benefit at the Actors Synagogue. I don't know why. I don't look Jewish.

Anyway, what happened when I played the benefit should have made me a religious man.

Many, many years later—in 1972, in fact—I was appearing on the same *Dick Cavett Show* with Bob Hope. He walked into the Green Room, saw me waiting there, and said, "I hope I don't have to follow you." Then he recalled what happened at that Actors Synagogue benefit.

I was the new boy in the neighborhood, so naturally I was scheduled to go on last. But I'd got there early because in show business anything can happen. It did. As always, someone didn't show up. So they ran me on earlier. People heard my name announced, didn't know who I was, and started getting up to go out for a smoke. I began to understand how Power's Elephants must have felt. They always closed the show because with a stage full of elephants you never know how long it might take to clean up.

Telling the story, Bob turned to the other people in the Green Room and said, "It was marvelous. I was just leaving and I heard some scuffling. So I went back and saw people walking up the aisles like a bunch of refugees fleeing from a bombing. And I knew who was doing the bombing.

"It's no fun to stand up there on the stage and see nothing but departing backs. I was feeling sorry for Henny when suddenly the people seemed to stop automatically. They listened for a second and then started returning to their seats. Man, that was getting them when they're almost gone!"

By luck Ted Collins who was Kate Smith's manager happened to hear the radio broadcast. He called up and signed me sight unseen. It was the first contract signed on the telephone. Well, it wasn't exactly a contract; it was a handshake.

The salary was to be two hundred and fifty dollars a week. When I called up to tell Momma, she said, "I still don't think you're *that* funny!" I was glad my mother wasn't booking the *Kate Smith Show*.

Here's some more from Al Schwartz's letter. It's about the first spot we did on the *Kate Smith Show*. "Six minutes crammed with sixty one-liners which averages out ten jokes a minute."

What Al didn't remember is that six minutes was all I was supposed to do. But the spot got rolling so good Ted gave me the sign to keep going. I did a little over ten minutes. I don't know to this day what they cut out of the rest of the show to get off the air on time. But, according to Al Schwartz's figures, in that one broadcast I used up about a hundred jokes.

"After every performance," Al goes on, "I had to fan your gums to keep your bridgework from melting. And, of course, we were eating up a lot of material." What was more important, Al forgot to add, we were eating.

Immediately after the first broadcast Ted came to me with a contract to be a regular on the show. Then and there Al and I realized we needed more help. So I rented a suite of offices in the Piccadilly Hotel on Forty-fifth Street only a few doors from what is now a garage. Before that it was CBS Playhouse 2, formerly the Avon Theater. CBS Playhouse 2 was where the broadcast originated.

When we sent out word that we were in the market for joke writers, as if by magic they seemed to come from all directions. Radio at that time was getting hotter and hotter with a heavy accent on comedy, and it looked as if every kid who got out of college wanted to get into radio, writing jokes.

One evening I was sitting alone having a bowl of soup in Dave's Blue Room, a delicatessen-type restaurant where show people liked to eat. A little man half staggered and half slouched up to my table and said he had some terrific jokes he'd like to have me read. I asked him what made him think they were so terrific.

"Because I wrote them," he said in his drunken logic. "And I'll tell you what I'll do. I'll bet you five hundred dollars you'll like them."

In my sober logic I said, "It's a bet. I don't like them. Pay up."

"Very funny," he said. Then he laid his sheets on the table and wobbled off toward the bar. I put the papers in my pocket and a little while later I had to make a visit to Portnoy's reading room. While sitting there with nothing to do, which was why I was sitting there, I started to read the drunk's stuff. It was great. Right down my alley.

Now I had a problem. I hate drunks, and the little man didn't look as if the load he was carrying was just some casual bender. But I needed all the material I could lay my hands on. So I made the kind of quick decision everybody makes. When in doubt do what's best for you.

I found my would-be writer at the bar and I hired him. His name was Joe Quillen. He was about as dependable as a Mexican jumping bean. But he was funny. And Joe worked for me and Seagram's until he died.

I heard a story that he and his wife were going to a dinner party in some friend's station wagon and she'd been lecturing him because he'd taken on quite a cargo before they left home. On the way they passed a distillery and Mrs. Q. took the opportunity to point out to Joe a terrifying fact. She said, "They can make it faster than you can drink it." Her words cast a pall over Joe for the whole evening.

On the way home they passed the place again. It was all lit up, and smoke was pouring from the chimney. Joe brightened immediately. "See," he said, "I've got them working nights."

You could buy a lot of booze in those days for the twenty dollars I paid Joe as a starting salary. I'd probably have done him a favor if I'd paid him less. He might still be with us.

Among the other writers who got their start making up one-liners for me were Bill Manhoff, who wrote the Broadway hit *The Owl and the Pussycat*; Harry Crane, who is now head writer on the Dean Martin TV show; Ray Singer, who went from me to the Joan Davis radio show and then on to do a lot of the top radio comedy shows; Bobby O'Brien, who's written for every comedy show on any network and who is now writing the Lucy show.

Snag Werris, Izzy Ellinson, and Danny Shapiro all started with me, and I still owe Danny more than money can pay for all he's done to help me. Al Schwartz's letter closes, "You discovered and launched the careers of more comedy writers than any other comedian in the business."

I like to think Al's right. Even Morey Amsterdam used to give me jokes.

When he heard me doing them and playing violin, he figured to top me by getting a bigger fiddle and starting to work with a cello. He couldn't get it under his chin, so he stuck it between his legs. When he played, he got bigger laughs than he ever got before.

I figured if he could top a violin with a cello, I'd top him with a bass. But when I asked a musician how long it would take me to become a bass player he said, "You already are."

As soon as things got good, my wife said she wanted a mink. I got her a mink. Then she wanted a sable. I got her a sable. Then she wanted a chinchilla. I bought her a chinchilla. The house was full of animals.

19

. . . And I Went over the Hill

THINGS were going great and I was perfectly happy on the *Kate Smith Show* till I picked up a piece of gossip that made me mad. When I think back on it now, I've lost an awful lot of work, maybe some great chances, because I got mad and sounded off before I really figured out what I ought to do.

Take, for instance, what happened in Las Vegas.

I was playing at the Sands Hotel with Billy Eckstine. Across the street at the New Frontier, but it was still the Old New Frontier, Mario Lanza was going to open. He had just hit it big on radio and records. But the bigger you are, the more you worry, and Lanza developed a classic case of flop sweat.

"Flop sweat" is what an actor gets when he's up on a stage laying an egg. A hen cackles. An actor gets flop sweat. It's a terrible thing, and no one has yet found a cure for it.

The trouble with Lanza's flop sweat was, he had it *before* he went on. In plain English he was scared. He had an acute case of stage fright. My uncle, the doctor, tells me this is called, in the medical profession psychosophlopswet. When it attacks singers, it generally hits them right where they're most vulnerable, in the vocal chords. That's why so many singers cancel because of laryngitis. Actually, in most cases, it's psychosophlopswet.

With a "sick" Lanza, the New Frontier had no show. So Jack Entratter of the Sands, in a grand gesture of unselfish understanding, asked if I'd do his competition a favor and go across the street and fill in for Mario. I did.

This meant four shows in one night, two at the Sands and two at the New Frontier. The next night Lanza hadn't improved. Four more shows.

The next morning I went to see Entratter and asked who was paying me for the four shows I did at the New Frontier, them or him?

Jack said, "What do you mean, paying?"

I explained about money and how people who get up on a stage and make other people laugh expect to get it in exchange for their services.

He said, "Don't be silly. We hotel people have a reciprocal agreement to exchange talent in case of an emergency."

"Great idea," I said. "Why don't you hire a very sick act and run for a couple of weeks on the exchange talent you get from the other hotels?"

He said, "Very funny."

"I'll tell you something else funny. We actors have an agreement, too. It's called a contract. I have one with you. Do you pay me or does the New Frontier? Or does the New Frontier pay you and you tell me about your reciprocal agreement?"

"Don't be silly," said Jack. "If you were sick, Lanza would go on and play for you."

"Great. Then you'd have two cases of stage fright, and you'd have to borrow Sinatra from the Riviera or wherever he's fighting. And you'd sure pay *him*."

What I didn't tell Entratter was that after my second show at the New Frontier, Sammy Lewis said he'd give me a thousand dollars a week more if I'd come to work for him. So I got madder and madder, and finally Jack said, "Okay, if you don't like it here, quit!"

I quit.

I walked across the street to the New Frontier and told Sammy I was taking him up on the offer he made me. He said, "What offer?"

I reminded him. "Impossible," he said, "I couldn't have said that. We hotel people have an agreement among ourselves not to boost salaries by trying to steal acts from one another."

Final score: Hotel men—two agreements. Youngman—out of two jobs.

When I got back to New York, I told the story to my financial adviser, Sam Mitchell. He's a pretty good businessman, and he gave me a great piece of advice: "Never talk business when you're angry."

I said, "*Now* you tell me!"

Ever since then I have consistently ignored his good advice.

But I'm getting a few years ahead of my story. About the same time Ted Collins discovered me, somebody discovered an act called Edgar Bergen and Charlie McCarthy. He was a ventriloquist, and McCarthy was the name of his dummy. And it was a good act. Bergen wasn't the best ventriloquist in the world, but he had the wittiest dummy. Technically he couldn't come close to a man like Señor Wences or Paul Winchell. But Charlie McCarthy was funnier than any of them.

It was one of the big laughs of radio that one of its star attractions was a dummy and the ventriloquist who made it work. No matter how you look at it, the ventriloquial act is a visual one. On the radio you couldn't see the trick. And that was great for Bergen because even his best friends said that he moved his lips more than the dummy.

Well, I heard Bergen was getting five hundred dollars on Rudy Vallee's *Fleischmann's Yeast Hour*. So I went hollering to Ted Collins, screaming that I was worth as much as Bergen, who was getting twice what I was being paid.

Collins said, "I don't understand you. You're getting penny for penny what Bergen's getting."

"Don't try to lie to me," I protested. "I happen to know for a fact that Edgar Bergen and Charlie McCarthy are getting five hundred dollars."

"Sure. But there's *two* of them." Then he laughed. I didn't. We argued for a while; then Ted finally agreed to give me the raise if I took him on as my personal manager at 20 percent of my salary. So instead of getting five hundred dollars, I got four hundred dollars, but it was still one hundred and fifty dollars more than Edgar's share of what the team got.

Also, I was getting some vaudeville offers that were better than anything I'd had before, so I figured being on the *Kate Smith Show* would even everything out. I didn't know Ted was against my doing anything that could possibly take my mind off his show. Every date I got I had to hassle Ted into letting me take and I didn't often win.

I should have got the idea quicker about how possessive he was of his talent. Only a couple of days after he became my manager, he said I ought to change my name. He said Henny wasn't classy enough. I said I knew of a very classy singer named Bing, and that didn't sound too stylish.

Ted said, "He won't last. He's trying to be too many things."

At that time Bing had made his first feature picture for Paramount and his NBC radio show called *The Kraft Music Hall* was getting more publicity for its class and style than any show on any network.

"We'll just change it to Henry," Ted decided. "That's easy. Now about Youngman. What'll we do about that?"

"What's wrong with Youngman?"

"It sounds too Jewish."

"Bernard Baruch sounds Jewish, too, and he's doing all right."

"Not in show business," said Ted.

You've got to believe me this was a perfectly serious conversation, stupid as it sounds. As we're talking, we're walking up the east side of Broadway toward the Capitol Theater, which was then on the corner of Broadway and Fifty-first Street. On the marquee of the Capitol, in lights, it said MAE WEST IN GO WEST YOUNG MAN.

"Look!" I pointed my finger. "There's my name in lights, and it doesn't look Jewish." Collins never brought up the subject again.

But, like a nut, I tried out the name Henry—why not, it was my real name. Here's what the show business bible *Variety* said about me when I played Loew's State as Henry Youngman after I'd been on Kate's show only a few months.

HENRY YOUNGMAN
Comedy
20 Min: One
State, N.Y.
   Henry Youngman is not a new act. As Henny Youngman, he was m.c. and life-of-the-party in tank theaters and Catskill resorts and recently was conferencier at the Yacht Club in New York. He's listed in the radio reports, however, and it is radio (Kate Smith's A&P Program) that is chiefly responsible for his Broadway vaude booking.

Translation from Henny to Henry also comes through radio. The former not being considered classy enough for the air. But that's the only major change so far as Youngman, himself, is concerned. Tall, skinny comedian whose flair for gag switching and ad libbing is bringing him favorable comparison with Milton Berle, hasn't altered his intimate style of working. At times that style is too intimate but Youngman will learn as he goes along that customers further back in the theater count much more than the fiddlers in the pit. Laughs from the latter won't add to his pay check which, incidentally, has grown considerably since his knock around days of six months ago.

At the State, besides m.c.ing, Youngman holds down two solo spots. First is what is nominally the deuce and the second is next-to-closing. Does close to ten minutes in each frame and his laugh average is high. Not all his gags are new nor are all these given a new twist but his original material is tops. Delivery makes almost everything sound ad-lib.

With Berle now in pictures (RKO) Broadway has need for a comic like Youngman. How far he can go depends almost wholly upon himself. He's getting the necessary breaks.

Scho.

For those who would like a translation, here's what some of that means:

(1) Where it says at the top "20 Min: One," it means that I was on stage for twenty minutes and that I worked in "One." Vaudeville divides a stage into "one," "two," and "full stage." "One" is just the very front of the stage, the apron. "two" is about half the stage. If you use the stage full, you're drunk.

(2) Tank theaters are those in small or tank towns. They got to be called that because the only reason trains stopped at them was the tank from which they filled the tender with water.

(3) "Deuce spot" is "*Varietyese*" for the number two spot, which was the second act to come on. It wasn't a very important spot on the bill and was generally filled with some fast-talking comedy or dancing act, generally two men or a man and a woman.

(4) "Next to closing" was the star spot. The reason I also had the "deuce spot" was that I was the master of ceremonies and had to work right at the beginning of the show to establish myself so that when I came on between acts to introduce the next one, people would know me and accept me.

(5) The signature "Scho" is the way most stuff in "Variety" is

signed. Just part of the writer's name. It stood for Joe Schonfield, later with the William Morris Office and also later editor of *Hollywood Daily Variety*.

(6) That bit about "with Berle now in pictures (RKO)" needs some explaining. He did make some movies. But hardly anyone ever knew about them. His movie career and the pictures he made would make Jack Benny's screen career look like a rival to Clark Gable's.

Another guy who came to sell me jokes while I was doing the *Kate Smith Show* was a label salesman named Abe Burrows. At that time he was teamed up with a guy named Frank Galen, who was working for nothing at a Brooklyn radio station. The radio station was also working for nothing because no one ever listened to it.

Frank later became head writer for Burns and Allen's TV show and created one of the hit series in the early days of television, *Meet Millie*. He died of a heart attack while playing tennis at the Beverly Hills Hotel.

Abe Burrows is one of the biggest names in the Broadway theater with sensational credits for both writing and directing, starting with the smash success of Frank Loesser's *Guys and Dolls*.

From this you can gather that these guys were good. So I bought six jokes from them for three dollars. It was only fifty cents a joke, but it was more than they had. Then a little success made them greedy. The next time they showed up they said they had to have a dollar a joke. I wouldn't argue with them over such a small amount of money. I bought three jokes.

The next thing I knew they got mixed up with a young lawyer who later became one of show business' top agents—a man named Irving Lazar. Lazar told them that the type of grade-A material they produced was worth more than they were getting. And he was right. He made them raise their price to a dollar fifty a joke.

I bought two jokes. Any good businessman will tell you, you can't fool around with the budget.

Actually, I didn't know it was Irving Lazar who got the guys to raise their price until I met him one night at Ted Lewis' home. I happened to mention that Ted Collins was grabbing 20 percent of my salary. Lazar got mad. "That's too much," he said. "He's not entitled to that much. Let me handle the matter and I'll get it down to fifteen percent."

I let him handle it. What could I lose?

I'll admit I was surprised when a few days later he called me to say that he'd got Collins to agree to the 5 percent cut. I was even more surprised when he told me that his fee for handling the matter would be 5 percent of my salary. I didn't have anything to lose. I didn't exactly win either. I didn't even have to fool around with the budget.

What you've forgotten is that while I'm still doing great on Kate's show and at Loew's State, I'm also still at the Yacht Club for two shows every night. I kept asking for release from my contract, but they wouldn't let me go. It was a crazy circle. I got the Smith show because of a benefit I played. I wouldn't have been asked to play the benefit if I hadn't been seen at the Yacht Club. Now the club was benefiting from my weekly radio appearances and the local vaudeville dates. So that's why they didn't want to give me back my contract.

Then one day a guy in a black fedora, a long black overcoat, and a cigar to match walks into my dressing room at the club, sits down and asks, "How are things?"

I asked, "What things?"

Ask a foolish question, you get a foolish answer. He said, "Things."

"Oh," I said, "those things? Fine."

"You're good," he said. "You're funny. You make me laugh."

I said, "Thanks." I didn't know what the man wanted, and I was afraid to guess. Comedians in nightclubs had got hurt when men like him came to see them.

Then he said, changing the subject, "You don't dress like a star. You're sloppy. To succeed, you gotta be neat. Look. You got a torn collar. It don't look good." He reached over and grabbed my shirt collar, which was open, and ripped my shirt off. "Here," he said, throwing a twenty-dollar bill on the dressing shelf, "take this and buy yourself a decent shirt. It's a present from a fan."

I left it lying there and got a fresh shirt out of my bag.

"Are you happy here?" he asked.

"Sure," I answered, "but I'd like to get out of my contract. I don't have enough time to devote to my broadcasts, and it's beginning to affect my health."

"Yeah," he said, thoughtfully. "You're funny on the air. Come with me." I followed him out of the room, and we went to see the guys who owned the Yacht Club, Irving Felchun and Jerry Brooks. Before even saying hello or anything, he opened up with: "Why don't you let my friend Henny out of his contract like he wants? It's hurting his health."

"Anything you say, Frankie," said my bosses. And that's how I got excused from the Yacht Club contract. Later I found out that my fan, Frankie, was one of "the boys' " most efficient "enforcers." Any friend of his got what he wanted. I wondered what would have happened if he hadn't liked me.

Just for the record, here's the kind of monologue I did on the Smith show. It was sent to me by Al Schwartz. As I've already said, all this sort of junk was thrown away when we sold the house in Brooklyn.

Good evening, ladies and gentlemen, it's nice to see a crowd in front of me for a change. I just played a theater last week, and things were so bad the ushers had to pay to get in. The band played "Tea for One." After one show I sent the whole audience home in a cab. A little kid came down from the balcony crying. He said he was afraid to stay up there all alone. It's different here in New York. Nobody's alone. Everyplace is crowded. The subway's so crowded even the men are standing. I saw an empty seat. I'm a gentleman. I pointed it out to a lady. Then I raced her for it. That's one thing I hate. To see a lady standing in the subway. So I shut my eyes. I finally gave the lady my seat, and she fainted. When she woke up, she thanked me. Then I fainted. It was raining when I got out, so I hailed a cab. When I got in, there were four musicians, playing. I said to the driver, "What's the idea?" He said, "I can't afford a radio." I usually drive my own car. It's the most unusual car you ever saw. It's paid for. It's not exactly new. In fact it's so old the insurance covers fire, theft, and Indian raids. The tires are so worn out the air is starting to show through. I like it because it's less expensive to keep. You don't have to pay a dollar to have it washed. You can have it dunked for fifty cents. I've been teaching my wife to drive. She's doing great. Yesterday she learned how to aim it. She's really overcautious. She never lets her right hand know what her left foot is doing. She's so careful she always honks before going through a red light. One thing I've noticed since driving. The Motor Vehicle Bureau is always making improvements in the laws. They're now thinking of putting the license plate under the car. So while you're lying there waiting for the ambulance, you can take the guy's license number without getting up. While I'm at it, I'd like to explain the traffic signals. Green light is for pedestrians to cross the street. Red light is for automobiles to cross the pedestrians. But I must say

I've never been able to understand some of our traffic laws. You get a ticket for speeding, and what does the government do with the money? It builds faster roads! Thank you.

After I'd been doing the show for a while Ted Collins decided I should do some work with a stooge instead of just a monologue. He got this idea because all the other hit radio shows were using stooges. So I created a character I named Uncle Max. The part was played by that great little guy, a very funny comedian, Charlie Cantor. For readers who remember he was the one who played Clifton Finnegan in Ed Gardner's *Duffy's Tavern* show.

Here's a little sample of what we did.

MAX: Hello, buddies. I'm very angry on you, Henny. Why didn't you come to my twenty-fifth wedding anniversary?

HENNY: Your twenty-fifth wedding anniversary? You're not married twenty-five years.

MAX: I know. But we needed the silver.

HENNY: Where have you been all day, Uncle Max?

MAX: I was with my wife.

HENNY: How is Aunt Chiquita?

MAX: She's having trouble with her face.

HENNY: If you had her face, you'd have trouble too.

MAX: Joking all the time. This is serious. I took her to a beauty parlor to find out what to do about her complexion.

HENNY: What did the beauty expert tell her?

MAX: Wear a heavy veil. I also got trouble with mine boy.

HENNY: You mean Cousin Tyrone.

MAX: He goes to college, and he does nothing but go to shows, ride around in fast cars, and date pretty girls.

HENNY: So you regret sending him to college?

MAX: Definitely. I should have gone myself. You want to make me happy, Henny, boy?

HENNY: Sure, Uncle Max.

MAX: Play something for me on your violin.

HENNY: What would you like to hear?

MAX: "Heartaches."

HENNY: What makes you ask for that?

MAX: There's no song called "Earaches."

That's enough of that. I chose the name Uncle Max because I

really had an Uncle Max. He was very fond of me. He was the one person in the family who encouraged me to go into show business and stay in it. No wonder I loved him.

Just to who you what kind of a man Uncle Max was and how much he thought of me: Shortly before he died, he was in a hospital. Of course, that's where lots of people are before they die. But very few, if any, do what Uncle Max did.

He was very sick, but when the nurse took a few minutes off while he was supposed to be taking a nap, he sneaked down the hall to a phone booth, called the hospital, and asked about the condition of Max Chetkin. He was told that Mr. Chetkin was in critical condition.

When he heard this, Uncle Max hurried back to the room, put on some clothes, sneaked out, and took a plane to Cleveland, where I was playing. He said he'd got such a kick out of hearing his name on the show and hearing me being a success that he wanted to come and see me once again before he died. Of course, he didn't tell me at the time what he'd done. So we had a helluva time together.

The next day he said he had to go and I took him to the train. He stood on the steps of the Pullman car, and I stood on the platform, and we talked until the train started to move. Then he handed me a letter. It told me what he'd done to visit me. I felt sick.

He got back to the hospital safely, if it's possible to be safe in a hospital. But a few days later he died. To this day I keep wondering if it wasn't that sneak trip to Cleveland that caused his death. Or maybe he wanted it that way.

But to get back to the *Kate Smith Show*.

From time to time Kate would have guest celebrities on the show and I'd be introduced to them. I was supposed to break the ice with something funny. (Something funny to break the ice with is a rubber duck. But it's easier to use an ice pick.)

Here's how it worked. When Alice Marble, the tennis champion, was on the show the dialogue went something like this:

KATE: Miss Marble, this is Henny Youngman, our comedian.
MARBLE: Yes. I could tell by the funny mask he's wearing.

(An unexpected crack like that from a straight personality never failed to get a laugh.)

YOUNGMAN: I'm not wearing a mask.
MARBLE: Well, there's always got to be a loser.

YOUNGMAN: What did you say your name is?
KATE: This is Alice Marble, the tennis champion.
YOUNGMAN: Oh, yes. That's my game.
MARBLE: Tennis?
YOUNGMAN: No. Marbles.

I can't imagine why that one gag has stayed in my mind all these years. I know why I remember hundreds of other jokes. They fit in; they can be used from time to time. But how many times do you meet a tennis champion named Marble? It's a one-shot gag.

On the other hand, I can switch it someday if I ever meet a golf pro named Herman Basketball.

There was a guy named Sammy Shiff who was Ted Collins' right-hand man. He was always giving me advice and guidance on what material he thought was funny. As I read those thirty-five-year-old routines, I now wonder whose side Sammy was on. Ted's naturally. On the other hand, it *was* thirty-five years ago, and that was the stuff that killed the radio listeners. It may even have killed radio.

Ted was very protective of Kate's obvious dominance of the show. If a comedian or any guest star seemed to be getting too much attention, Ted would come onto the stage, diverting the audience's attention, to adjust a mike or something and accidentally bump into whoever was working in front of it, throwing off his timing. It's a wonderful way to turn a great routine into garbage.

Kate, on the other hand, was a great lady. She didn't bother with any petty show business nonsense like that. She just stayed in her dressing room until it was time for her to come to the microphone and say, "HEL-lo, everybody." But you can't write it like she said it. She closed every show with "Thanks for listenin' and good night, folks." She said that in such a way that diabetics were warned by their doctors not to listen to her.

The show was always very orderly and polite. Very formal. The only time I ever even ate a meal with Kate was when we did an Army show, and we ate wherever they put us. I found it awfully hard, working hospitals. I guess I'm just chickenhearted. When I go to see a friend who's convalescing in a hospital, I look so sad he has a relapse. I can't even stand the smell of hospitals. I don't feel safe in them. How can you? All those sick people. I want to holler at them, "Get out of here and get well!"

I guess the most vivid memory I have of playing a military base with Kate was when we went to Catalina Island off the coast of Southern California. I made the trip with a mezuzah in one hand and a crucifix in the other. The Catholics were so scared they were telling their beads, and I was so scared I was telling the Catholics to put in a good word for me. The reason for all this fright was that the waters all around Catalina Island were mined. That was because the island had so many antiaircraft guns on it that if they were all fired at once, the recoil would have pushed the island right down to the bottom of the Pacific.

We made it safely, but there was a terrible tragedy while we were there. Word came that President Roosevelt had died. The depression that hung over that place was so heavy it was unbearable. Doctors, nurses, soldiers walked around as if in a daze, tears in their eyes and their heads hung low so no one would notice how emotionally upset they were. We cancelled our shows and went back home through the minefields. But this time we didn't make it. Ladies and gentlemen, this whole book is a recording.

The itching feet that I inherited from my grandfather and my father began to bother me. I'd got a good look at California, and I wanted to go out there and work in pictures. I talked the whole thing over with Collins, who said he'd let me out of my contract if I could get a satisfactory replacement acceptable to him.

As it turned out, this wasn't easy. The first person I suggested, after checking with him to see if he'd do it, was Bob Hope. Bob said he was coming to New York and would do the show for two weeks. Collins turned that down unless Hope would come for two years. Paramount, who had Hope under contract, turned that down because they were making pictures in Hollywood and the *Kate Smith Show* was broadcast from New York. It was all very discouraging. Then one of those things happened.

A musician friend of mine named Pat Cristello, the leader at the Lido Venice in Paterson, asked me one afternoon to go with him to see his brother, who was working in a burlesque house in New Jersey. So we went out there, and that's where I first saw and met Abbott and Costello. Because they were working in burlesque and because burlesque comedy had by that time become filthy to keep up with the stripteasers, Bud and Lou were working very dirty. And they were using spluttering routines that got laughs because every time Lou spluttered he splattered spit in Bud's face. Never in a million years would it have occurred to me to suggest them to Ted for the *Kate Smith Show*.

In the second place, if the show would have had them, the network wouldn't have let them do what they were doing or say what they were saying. Radio was so antiseptic you had to wear a gauze surgical mask before you could get near a microphone.

Then I saw Abbott & Costello billed at the Loew's State. I knew they couldn't be doing what I saw them doing in Jersey, so I went to catch the act to see how they'd changed their material. They were working clean and absolutely killing the people with ''Who's on First?'' I called Ted Collins, made a date, and took him to see them. He booked them immediately and let me go. Nobody ever worked so hard to get out of a job as I did, a good job.

*I invested in a Broadway show. Opening night a
terrible thing happened. The curtain went up.*

20

Only a Rose

AFTER I left the *Kate Smith Show*, a funny thing happened to me on the way to California. I stopped off for a while at
Billy Rose's Casa Mañana on Broadway.

Billy was a little man with some of the biggest ideas in the world.
But there was no truth in the rumor about him that was circulated in
1947. People were saying he had plans for sending World War II on
the road with an augmented company.

It's hard to believe that Billy started his career as a male secretary. I think he wanted to be a court stenographer. Those were the
days before stenotype machines, and the court stenos had to be very
accurate and very fast. Billy won a national contest for shorthand
speed and accuracy, and the next thing he knew he was secretary to
the adviser of Presidents, Bernard Baruch.

Billy could take dictation so fast he had to carry a little atomizer
full of water in his pocket to spray down his pad when it got too hot.
He was a short man but liked to marry tall women. Some say it was
for protection. Some say he needed a lot of it.

From Baruch he learned the secret formula for success in the
stock market: ''Buy when it's low; sell when it's high.'' From this

Billy developed his own advice on how to become a wealthy man. "The only way to get rich is to make money . . . make money." He eventually backed up this advice to himself by accumulating a very large amount of AT&T stock.

Billy got into show business writing popular song lyrics. His very first stab at this kind of work was one of the biggest hits of its day. It was about the era's most popular comic strip, "Barney Google." The song was tailored for success. Billy carefully analyzed the ingredients of hit songs of the past and then created "Barney Google" to fit the pattern that emerged. I've often wondered if there wasn't some screwy relation, in Billy's mind, between Barney Google and Barney Baruch. It was a beautiful song. I'll never forget the first line, "Barney Google, with his goo-goo-gooogley eyes." Gets you right here, doesn't it?

But before I got mixed up with Billy Rose, there was a long period of disappointment. I'd been led to think that as soon as I no longer had to be in New York every week to do a broadcast, Hollywood would send for me and welcome me with open arms. I figured with their open arms and my itching feet it looked like a great year ahead. But before they got to carry me anywhere, I sat around Lindy's so long I began to itch someplace else.

I was so dragged down I had to look up to Billy Rose. I cried a lot. Late one night I was in Lindy's having cheesecake and coffee. I preferred to blame my nervous stomach on something I ate. I was sitting with a friend named Chuck Green. I was sitting with him because he was going to pick up the check. He was in the jewelry business and sold a lot of stuff to show business people, so it was in his best interest to keep everybody working.

In those days actors, as well as actresses, bought diamonds as an investment and as sort of a hedge against disaster. Almost every actor on the road had a great big diamond pinkie ring. It made a good flash in the act, and if the act didn't make much of a flash, he could hock the ring to get back to Broadway.

Chuck listened to me grumbling about my troubles as long as he could stand it. Then he interrupted me, and I was glad. I couldn't stand it either.

He said, "You ought to be working somewhere instead of sitting around here sponging sponge cake and coffee and bending my ear."

"I'd work," I said, "but I can't get the money I'm worth."

"You're never worth more than the money you can get," Chuck said. I've remembered that all my life. Then he asked how much I was asking.

"A grand a week."

He stood up in amazement. "A thousand dollars," he repeated in astonishment. "Who the hell do you think you are, Rin Tin Tin? How long have you been out of work?"

I figured it out and said it was ten weeks. "Can you imagine?" I said. "I've already lost ten thousand dollars."

"Why be such a piker?" Chuck asked. "As long as you're making mind bets, why not be out of work ten weeks at ten thousand dollars a week? Then you'd have lost a hundred thousand dollars. That would put you in the really big spenders' bracket. But if you want to come down to earth, what you've really lost is about three hundred and fifty dollars a week, which you might have been making if you didn't have such a swelled head."

When I got up to go and put my hat on, it came way down over my ears—Chuck had made me feel so small. I got sore at him because I knew what he said was the truth. A couple of weeks later I went to work at Billy Rose's Casa Mañana at three hundred and fifty dollars a week.

It was a great show. Vincent Lopez was the music, and Betty Hutton was just on the verge of being discovered by the movies as a gal who could belt out a tune without looking as if someone had given her the buckle right across the face. Bert Wheeler was the other comic on the bill. He did a routine called Baby Elephants that used to dissolve the people. He was a very tough act to follow. To top off the bill, the master of ceremonies was a suave, sophisticated darling of the society set, a smart son of a bitch named Frank Fay. He later made a smash hit in a play called *Harvey*. It was about a drunk, and he knew everything there was to know about playing such a part.

I called him what I did only because a lot of other people said the same thing about him. Besides, he obviously didn't like me, and I don't think he cared much for my people either. And when the show got started, he did everything in the world to make it tough on me.

Billy must have sensed that there might be trouble between us. I'd earned a reputation as a heckler when I was working on the Street. Fay was more polished and subtle than I was, but he did the same thing.

So before the opening show Billy warned us that he didn't want any onstage battle of wits to louse up the smooth routining of the whole thing. At the time, I think, Fay read Billy wrong. I think he took what Billy said to mean just the opposite. He thought that Billy wanted him to attack me, knowing that I'd come back with something and that Billy just said what he did to warn me to be ready. Naturally, Fay figured himself as the winner in any mortal chitchat that might go on between us.

I, on the other hand, didn't give it a second thought. I missed the boat on the whole thing. All I knew was that I wasn't hired to have anything to do with Fay. My job was just to come out, tell some jokes, make a few funny sounds on my fiddle, and that was it.

On the first show, when it came time for Fay as master of ceremonies to introduce me he said, "In a couple of seconds two shoes will walk onto this stage. Sticking out of them will be something called Henny Youngman."

I was thin then, tall and thin, and what Fay said became funny when they saw me. It made the audience think of a walking beanpole or something, and they laughed.

I just stood there and waited for his laugh to die down and said, "Look! I'm a success, and I haven't said a word yet."

There was more laughter. Fay said, "Don't say another word, or you'll kill you whole act."

I made a noise on the fiddle as if I were crying and bowed. This broke everybody up. Putting my fiddle back under my chin with great dignity and then, as a second thought, taking it down again, I asked "How do you like me so far?"

Fay said, "The trouble is you're not far enough."

I said, "He's such a nice man and never been sick a day in his life. Germs can't stand him."

Fay said, "Turn around. Your act's dying because people can see your face."

"I like your face, too . . . both of them." I quickly put my fiddle to my chin, and glancing sideways at the handsomely turned out, beautifully poised and precise Fay, I said, "For my next number I will play 'Sex Takes a Holiday.'"

Before I could start my routine, Fay said, "Will someone please send those shoes out and get them refilled?"

He walked off on the laugh. When it died down, I looked after him and said, "That's the first pair of shoes I've ever seen with three heels." On top of the following laugh, I threw in, "Some people bring happiness wherever they go." Again I paused to look in the direction Fay had gone. This brought a light laugh. Then I said, "He brings happiness *when*ever he goes."

From then on, all through the show, he kept making cracks about me, and I'd stick my head out from the wings and answer him. I can't remember all of them, but one thing sticks with me. When I'd finished my act, Fay came on to introduce the next act. But before he did, he said, "God giveth and God taketh away but sometimes not soon enough."

I stuck my head out and said, "If Moses had seen you, there'd have been one more commandment." It got a howl. People later asked me exactly what I meant. I didn't know, exactly. Sometimes something pops into your head to say, and you say it, and it gets a big reaction, and you really don't know why. You're just glad it worked.

Naturally, we both got hell from Rose. And if you think some people can raise hell, you should have heard Rose hell. But now we really couldn't believe he was serious. Even though we'd both meant what we'd been saying, we knew we were not only helping the show but helping each other to be successful. So we kept right on heckling every show and getting bawled out by Billy, who simply didn't like to have his orders disobeyed, even if he benefited by it.

I think the thing that really made Billy sore was that the ad-lib heckling loused up the tight timing of the show. He had everything timed to the second. If you were running over, you'd hear a buzzer, which meant that if you were doing a musical number you segued right into the closing eight bars. If you were doing a routine, you'd jump to the closing gag and get off. He did this to avoid running into overtime for the musicians.

He economized in many other little ways. The butter used to be shaved to a scant eighth of an inch, a slightly smaller than normal portion. And if a customer happened to ask for another napkin, the waiter would always conveniently forget to bring it. It figures. By skimping on the laundry, he kept from being taken to the cleaners.

The guy who made up the crack "One thing always leads to another" must have had me in mind. It's the story of my life. I hadn't been at Casa Mañana very long when I found myself doing a radio show every week for Trommer's Beer—Trommer's White Label. It was a local New York show because the beer was only distributed locally. But it was easy and relaxed after the tension of network broadcasting and the attention of Ted Collins.

The rest of the show was a band led by a man who always seemed more interested in doing sleight-of-hand tricks than in his music. It reminded me of a musical comedy I saw by Gilbert and Sullivan. A young man was supposed to be apprenticed to a pilot. Someone goofed, and he was apprenticed to a pirate. Something like that must have happened to Dick Himber. He wanted to go to a school for magicians but accidentally wound up in one for musicians.

Whatever it was, he wasn't an easy guy to get along with. He wasn't even trying to make his music make magic, and his big problem was that he wasn't good enough at it to make his magic make music.

If a guy was late for rehearsal—namely, me—Dick would do all kinds of things to embarrass him or louse him up while he was working at the mike. Nobody appreciates that kind of fooling around. I've played plenty of practical jokes on people, but I've never done anything that might make a man look bad in front of an audience.

One broadcast I got even with Dick for everything he'd ever done to everyone in the band, as well as me. I got to the studio early one day because I wanted a little time to practice the fiddle. Oh, yes. I used to do that. So I'm there, fiddling away, when the station manager comes in. I'm the only one around, so he tells me, "We just got the word that the President is going on the air tonight and will run into some of our time. But this show will go on right after the President is finished. So will you please tell everyone when they show up what's going to happen and to stand by and be ready to start on about five minutes' notice?"

I told him I'd pass the word along to Dick when he came in. When the program producer and the engineer showed up a little later, they asked if I knew about the delay, and I told them I did. Then I asked them to go along with a gag I had. They said they would. As each musician came in, we told him what I wanted done.

At the last minute Himber showed up. There was really only about ten minutes to air time. He shuffled through the arrangements and the routine of the show, asked the contractor if the band had been rehearsed, made a couple of quick phone calls and was waiting on the stand to start when the director said, "Thirty seconds to air time."

Dick picked up his baton, raised his arm, his eyes on the control room. He got his cue, gave the band the downbeat, and you never heard such a collection of sour notes in your life.

Dick was a short, chunky man with a red face. It turned dark purple when he heard that noise. He almost exploded. He couldn't say anything because he thought he was on the air. So he just rapped very hard and indicated that everyone should start the theme again. This time, when he gave the downbeat, not a sound came out of the orchestra. Dick just stood there, numbed by disbelief.

Then everyone broke out laughing and told him what was going on. Or rather, that the broadcast *wasn't* going on. He was so relieved to find out that nothing had happened to his musical reputation that he laughed, too. But, believe me, it was a tight, vindictive little laugh.

Dick Himber, who had worked for Rudy Vallee, was doubling as the band at the Hurricane Club in the Brill Building on Broadway. The management must have heard me with him on the broadcast and invited me to do a Sunday night guest shot at the club. They had regular Sunday night guest nights, and it was the first chance I had to play the spot because while I was with Kate, Collins wouldn't let me take dates like that.

I wanted to get a chance on Rudy Vallee's radio show, so I invited him over to the Hurricane to catch my act. I didn't know, at that time, that Rudy's entire show was booked by the advertising agency that produced it. Maybe it was because Rudy knew this that he insisted he'd only show up if he could pay his own way. It perplexed me. It wasn't like Rudy. But I agreed, and he arrived with his own champagne, his own whiskey, and his own soda. All the evening cost him was the minimum, which included glasses and ice.

After I'd done my stuff, I went to the men's room, and as I passed the club's office, I heard a terrific argument going on between Dick Himber and Nicky Blair, who owned the club. I listened a minute and then went back to my table to wait and see what was going to happen. From the sounds I'd heard I thought maybe the music for the rest of the evening would be supplied by Henny Youngman and his Velvet Violin.

Finally, Dick, looking redder than he did the evening we pulled the trick on him, came rushing out and went on the stand. It was very funny to watch. Try to imagine a mad director who isn't just waving his wand—he's hitting imaginary people with it. While he was going through the first number of a set in this angry way, I wrote a note and asked the waiter to give it to Mr. Himber when the set ended.

When Dick got the note and read it and started the next number, he brought his stick down so hard he hit the corner of the bandstand and broke the baton. Everybody in the joint laughed. They thought it was done on purpose. My note said, "This is your cancellation notice." I signed it Nicky Blair.

As a result of that Sunday night guest shot, I got booked into the Hurricane regularly, and things started going great, even if it wasn't in the direction of California. I did so well at the club that I got booked into the Paramount Theater, and even if I didn't see a lot of Sadie and the kids, there was plenty of money coming in to make missing me more comfortable.

A young clown by the name of Red Skelton and his wife, Edna, used to come into the Hurricane a lot. I'd sit with them, and we'd trade gags, and I'd sometimes give them some jokes that didn't fit my delivery because I liked him and I liked the way he worked on his radio show for Raleigh cigarettes. I don't know whether it was my generosity with my jokes that made Red suggest me or whether the Raleigh people saw me work at the Hurricane or the Paramount, but they came to me and told me Red had a contract to go West and make a picture. I wondered if it was the one I didn't get. Anyway, they asked me to take Red's place on the show, which also starred Carol Bruce, who was big in musical comedy on Broadway, and a bandleader named Frankie Howard. The show was produced by a man named Lee Segal, who was the one who created a quiz show called *Dr. I. Q.* Remember? ''I have a lady in the balcony, Doctor''? That lady always won. I think Lee had a piece of her.

I was constantly fighting with Segal because of the type of writer he'd hire for the show. He wouldn't give me the money and let me hire the men I liked, the ones I knew were good. Even if he had, I guess it wouldn't have made much improvement because it wouldn't have been enough to pay what they asked. The ones Lee bought were coming in week after week with joke routines that I'd heard a couple of nights before on other radio shows. I kept complaining about this, and Lee kept telling me to just tell the jokes and not try to be a producer. I told him I was just trying to be a comedian. It was a tough six months.

*By the time you learn to make the most of life,
most of it's gone!*

21

Fun and Games

AFTER you've written everything you can remember, you have to sit back and try to think of what you've forgotten. It's hard. Hard? It's ridiculous! How can you remember something you've forgotten? If there's a way, I've forgotten it.

What's even worse, some of the things you do remember really never happened. They're about places and people and things you've passed while riding a train of thought on the way to a punch line. Comedians always have a lot of silly things running through their minds. Those who haven't aren't comedians.

So, trying to recall all the different theaters, nightclubs, and hotels I've worked in, I sometimes can't separate the real from the imaginary. Many of the theaters are now supermarkets or skating rinks. Many of the nightclubs don't exist anymore. Many of the hotels don't exist anymore. It's possible that some of the cities don't exist anymore. I say, "It's possible." If I'd ever played in Vietnam, I'd say it's probable.

I'm dead sure that one city where I did a show can't be found. I got a thousand dollars for one night to work in a show called "Your

Future Lies in Sycamore City.'' There were also a lot of other lies in Sycamore City. One of them was that there was a city. Another was that there was a show. Unless you can call ten minutes of me, my violin, and one-liners a show.

Sycamore City, what a name. They must have called it that to attract dogs. Actually it was a dog, a dog real estate development.

The promoters had some land. They laid out a few streets, curbing, sidewalks, and everything except pavement. They said that wasn't down yet because first they had to put in the water and sewer pipes. To show you where these were going to be, there was a long ditch. Alongside it was a pile of pipes. It looked as if the sewer pipes and the water pipes were going to be the same pipes. Saves money.

They even had a few stakes stuck in the ground every few feet to show where trees were going to be planted. It was all very impressive and well thought out.

The guests at the dinner at which I was the main and only act were all people who had accepted engraved invitations to enjoy free transportation, a free dinner, and a free show in "Beautiful Sycamore City—A Good Place to Raise a Family." By the time they'd had a ride in a limousine, the booze at the bar, the dinner in a big air-conditioned tent and the jokes, all free, they were not only obligated but softened up for the hard sell that was to follow when we toured the city.

Most people found it impossible to resist. The down payments weren't much. Maybe three hundred and fifty dollars on a lot. But that was a lot of dough to pay for a ride in the country, a few drinks, a cold dinner, and some one-liners. If I'd known what kind of swindle it was, I never would have taken the job. I'm sorry to say Sycamore City does not exist anymore. I'm sorry to say it because I'm having a terrible time selling my lots there.

They talked me into taking them instead of cash. They said, "They'll be someting to have when you get old." They were right. I still have them. If I'd taken the cash, I would have spent it by now. The big trouble is, I haven't even got the lots. What I have is three hundred shares of common and fifty shares of first preference stock in the Sycamore City Corporation.

They told me this paper could be redeemed at any time on the basis of one hundred shares of common and fifteen shares of preferred stock per lot, with any small balance payable in cash. I keep trying to tell them I'll settle for the small cash balance.

The address on the stock certificates is a Wilmington, Delaware, PO box. And my letters keep coming back marked "No Key!"

The Capitol is one of the theaters I played many times that no longer exists. It's now an office building. But people who remember the big hits of radio will remember that the Capitol Theater was the home of Major Bowes' fantastic *Amateur Hour*. The major was such a nice, kindly man. He sat in a great, big leather chair, giving the poor struggling amateurs the gong and saying, "All right. All right." This meant all wrong, all wrong. Then he'd turn his head away and sluice some tobacco juice into a big brass spittoon.

I played the Capitol once in a unit with Les Brown and his Band of Renown. Les has been with Bob Hope so long, now, his is the only band that's 100 percent on Social Security. At that time he had a cute little blond singer. I told her to get herself a good agent because I thought she could do a lot better than just being the band vocalist with an outfit like Les'. She must have taken my advice. I've seen her in some movies and on TV. Her name is Doris Day.

And that reminds me of another girl singer who was with Charlie Barnett's band when it came into the Flatbush Theater in Brooklyn where I was the house MC. On the first show, when this girl got up to do a chorus of a number, the Brooklyn audience began to whistle and stamp and clap and carry on so much that the show had to stop. They brought the house curtain down and kept it down till the audience cut out the racket. Then they took it up again, and the band started another number. This time the girl came out to sing wearing a white sweater instead of a pink one.

Again all hell broke loose. There were two reasons why this same thing happened twice. The girl's name was Marie McDonald. Remember Marie "The Body" McDonald? She, too, went into pictures.

Getting back, now, to the day Les Brown opened at the Capitol: The rehearsal call was for 7 A.M. so they could run through their cues with all the acts and be ready for the first early show. I came in at seven, but there was no band. So I stuck my music under my arm and strolled down Broadway to the Paramount Theater, where Harry James and his band were scheduled to open. Naturally, they, too would be rehearsing for an early show. All the presentation houses ran on practically the same schedule. I got to the Paramount just as Harry's men were setting up. So I spread my music around on the stand and asked them to run through it with me.

They thought I was on the bill, so they did. When they were finished, I went around and gathered up my music. Harry said, "What's the idea? You think we memorize this crap? We'll need that for the first show."

I said, "My first show's at the Capitol with Les Brown. I just wanted to hear it to find out if Les' men played it right."

I thought Harry would blow his trumpet.

You think that's crazy? I was closing at the Holiday Inn in Evansville, Indiana, the day before Yom Kippur. So, as I was leaving early to catch a plane to be home by sundown for the High Holy Day, I saw some men on a ladder putting up a sign in lights that said, "Holiday Inn Welcomes West Indiana Dental Society."

There were two guys. I offered them five bucks each to put the one word "Jewish" in front of the name of the motel. As I drove off in a cab to catch my plane, the sign read: JEWISH HOLIDAY INN WELCOMES WEST INDIANA DENTAL SOCIETY. Sometimes I wonder how long it was before those two guys who changed the sign got another job. I'll bet it wasn't in Evansville.

I did some of that sign business in Vegas, too. Bing Crosby's four sons had formed a quartet and were singing in the lounge at the Sahara, where I was working in the main room. Naturally, I got talking to them one day about their famous father. They said they didn't want people to think they were trying to trade on his name.

"Then how come," I asked, "that the card in the lobby says, 'Bing Crosby's Four Sons—Gary, Dennis, Philip, and Lindsay—Now in the Lounge'?"

"That's just the hotel's idea," they said. "We don't like it."

So I looked up the man who painted the cards for the lobby and got him to make one that said, "Bob Crosby's Nephews—Gary, Dennis, Philip, and Lindsay—Now in the Lounge."

The next day the sign started "Cathy Crosby's Cousins. . . ."

I love to have fun with signs, maybe because my father was a sign painter. A comedy writer friend of mine named Lee Sands was one of the original owners of the Gaiety Delicatessen on the Strip, near Doheny Drive, in Hollywood. It was in the days when Mike Todd was romancing Elizabeth Taylor.

I had a big sign painted and got Lee to put it in the window of the Gaiety. It said: "Mike! Bring home two corned beef sandwiches! Don't forget pickels and mustard! Liz." That's the nearest I ever came to becoming a sandwich man.

If you stand in Times Square and look north, you'll see a big square sign on top of the building in the short block between Seventh Avenue and Broadway on Forty-seventh Street. For years it's been one of the most-sought-after advertising spots on the Great White Way.

I once made a deal to lease that space for a few days and have painted on it in light outline that couldn't be seen from the street:

"Henny Youngman—Available." Then I planned to stand on a scaffold, fill in the letters, and tell jokes through a public address system as I "painted" the sign.

It would have been a sensation. I got permission from the sign painters union to do it. But I couldn't get permission from the New York City Police Department.

They felt it would tie up traffic and that people standing around or walking along and looking up at the sign, or motorists doing the same, might get hurt. They didn't seem to care that by not allowing me to do it, my business got hurt.

I finally used a much cheaper version of the idea when the William Morris agency moved into an office building across the street from the apartment in which Sadie and I were living.

I put a big sign in our window facing William Morris, saying, "Book Thy Neighbor!"

Speaking of agents, after hearing week after week from one of them who was supposed to be working for me that he couldn't find any bookings, I got on the telephone and called a few people I knew around the country, and in an afternoon I'd booked seventy-five thousand dollars' worth of appearances.

Is it any wonder that I have telephonitis and a strong feeling that you can have an agent, but does he know he has you?

One day while sitting in the Stage Delicatessen waiting for my *matzoh brei*, I heard a customer come up with that old wheeze "Bring me a small check, please."

So I had some printed. They were about three inches by one inch, printed on regular safety paper, and are perfectly negotiable if properly made out and signed the way any check should be. I tried to interest my bank in using them as promotional material for small accounts. They said they didn't like small accounts. I said I didn't either, but I had one.

Speaking of the Stage Delicatessen, it's the greatest on Broadway and the place where all the show biz people drop in to stoke up on cream cheese and lox on a bagel. Incidentally, Fred Allen, who was about as Jewish as a Maine lobster, used to love the food at the Stage. One Sunday morning Fred and I left there together and were walking uptown on Seventh Avenue when a man stopped us and asked Fred if he had a pencil.

"Do I look to you like a blind mendicant, my friend?" Fred said. Then, of course, thinking the man wanted an autograph, he handed him a pencil. The man said, "Thank you very much, sir." Then he turned to me and said, "Can I have your autograph, Mr. Youngman?"

I signed my name, handed the paper to the man and the pencil to Fred. He said, "Well, that does it. That finally convinces me that anybody who stops you on the street and asks for an autograph is an idiot."

Fred never found out that the idiot he was talking about was my brother.

But to get back to the Stage Delicatessen. It was run by the late Max Asnas, a very funny and lovable character. He was a real, natural wit. I think Jack Paar was the first TV talk show host to try to use him on the air. But it never worked. It was strange but Max, from the Stage, always got stage fright and froze. I figured he couldn't work anywhere he couldn't smell corned beef and pastrami.

One day I stopped in at the Carnegie, another delicatessen in the neighborhood, and bought half a pound of corned beef to go. Then I walked into the Stage and ordered a corned beef sandwich. When it came, I added my half a pound to the generous amount the Stage always put in their sandwiches. Then I waved to Max.

As he came over to say hello, I said, "Congratulations, Max, you're finally putting some meat in your sandwiches." When he saw what I had in front of me, he said, "Either that new counterman is your brother-in-law or I fire him."

I once went to Washington to play a date at the Alfalfa Club. Every important politician came to their affairs, from the President right on down to Senators and Congressmen. I did my usual routine and got the kind of response Congress generally gives to a President who's asking them to raise taxes. The act that was following me was a very funny vaudevillian who billed himself as Senator Ford.

As I came off, he was standing in the wings. "They're tough."

He said, "Not for me!" He was right. They couldn't get enough of this man who was making fun of them, the way they talk and the things they do. I tried to figure out why I had failed. It finally came to me. Congressmen and Senators can't understand anyone who can get to the point in one line.

I used to send mail out to get people to come to see me wherever I was playing. I still do. But now it's mostly for TV appearances.

Not long ago I did a Friars' Roastmaster Dinner for Sammy Davis, Jr., that was telecast by Kraft. We taped the show weeks ahead, but it went on the air on Passover. Fine thing to do to a Jew like Sammy.

I sent out a flier saying, "Why is this night different from all other nights? It's the only one on which you can see Henny Youngman and Sammy Davis, Jr., on the *Kraft Music Hall*." Then I gave the date and time and so forth. When they reran the show some months later, I sent out the same card, adding, "If you missed it before, here's your chance to miss it again."

I sent out a letter with a picture of Sadie at the top. There's a balloon coming out of her mouth, like the ones in cartoons. She's saying:

One of the delights of New York this season is the musical comedy, "My Fair Lady." And if you haven't seen it, you're missing a real treat. I know tickets are hard to get. But until you're lucky enough to get a pair, take a trip to Ben Maksik's Town and Country Club in Brooklyn where my fair man, Henny Youngman, opens on October 24.

He isn't exactly as sexy as Rex Harrison, but he's taller, and besides he plays the fiddle. Thank goodness he's got a job, so I don't have to listen to him play around the house.

So hop into a cab and ride out to Brooklyn to see Henny. Even if you don't like him, the ride will do you a lot of good. Who knows, maybe you'll be lucky and hail my brother's cab and the money will still wind up in the family?

Desperately yours,
Mrs. Henny Youngman
(Herself)

Once when I was in Las Vegas I mailed out a lot of little packages containing three lemons each. The card said, "Playing in Las Vegas. This is what I won. Henny"

A friend of mine named Alexander Rose gave me an idea, a little pocket gadget that looks like a pullout tape measure with a button you press to snap it back. Only instead of inches, my measure gives you laughs. It's called Henny Youngman's Pocket Jester, and if you haven't seen any of them around, I really am surprised.

When you pull out the tape, the gags begin. The first one on one side is: "A drunk puts a dime in a parking meter. The arrow goes to 60. He says, 'Gee, I lost a hundred pounds.'"

On the other side of the tape the opening joke is: "My timing is off lately. When I sit down to eat, I feel sexy. When I go to bed, I feel hungry." There are forty-two jokes in all, twenty-one on each side of the tape.

Now then, ladies and gentlemen, you've heard all about this little article, and this is what I'm going to do. For the insignificant little sum of four hundred dollars (in small bills, please), plus the cost of wrapping and mailing, which may vary according to the state of the nation and the state of my finances, I will send you this handy little gadget. And I send it to you with the clear and distinct understanding that if, after you receive it, you should find that for any reason you don't like it and have memorized all forty-two of the jokes, if you feel I have misrepresented the merchandise in any way, you are free to return it to me, postpaid. Immediately upon receiving it from you, I will offer it for sale to someone else. Could anything be fairer and more aboveboard than that? What's more, this is the only offer of this kind to be made anywhere in this book.

Unless, of course, you're interested in my game plan. I mean the game I planned. It's "Now! It's Wow! It's with it!"

I figured that with unisex, boys wearing their hair like girls and girls taking off their pants like boys and wife swapping . . . I tried that. The best offer I got was an Edsel.

But to get back, with everyone talking and acting as if sex were something new, I had this idea for a game:

It's played on a board like Parcheesi or Monopoly, and any number can play. I took it to every one of the houses that make and market games, and not one could see it. I even had a whole ad campaign laid out to open with a full page that said: "A Game the Whole Family Can Play . . . INCEST!"

During the war, when food was scarce, Danny Shapiro wrote a parody for me that started "I love polly seeds/Polly seeds fill all my needs." I must have also sung the song in the Mountains because polly seeds are very big with the Jews. If they weren't always cracking Indian nuts and polly seeds, all the Jews would have teeth like Raquel Welch (she *has* them) and all the Jewish dentists would be out of business.

I was playing in Baltimore when I sent a letter enclosing a little envelope full of polly seeds to a lot of people. One of them was Georgie Jessel, who at that time was one of the top musical comedy producers at Twentieth Century-Fox. He sent me this letter in reply:

DEAR HENNY,

Your letter and polly seeds received, and food conditions being the way they are out here, I immediately ate them. I hope they will have no ill effects as I hate to pick up the phone and start talking to my mother and suddenly start saying, "Polly want a cracker." Her name isn't Polly.

Am hard at work preparing a picture which should take at least five months of preparation and four months more to get out. Between you and me, making pictures isn't as easy as we used to think it was early in the morning at Lindy's.

If I hear of any spot in any picture where they need such a stylish monologist as you, you may be assured I will scream your praises from the housetops, for not only do I think you're good onstage, but I like you very much personally, and, incidentally, your burlesque of my book was one of the funniest things I ever read.

LOVE,
JESSEL

He screamed my praises from the housetops, but in Los Angeles, in those days, the houses were only two stories high.

In the same file with Georgie's letter was one that really scared me when I got it. It was from the Federal Bureau of Investigation which is just about as much fun to hear from as the Department of Internal Revenue. But it was to thank me for a show I did for the bureau, and it was signed Edgar.

I was very happy to do the show for them. Can you imagine what would happen if one of those neatly dressed FBI men came and asked me to appear at a benefit and I said no? They might start investigating my jokes and find they were subversive, and then they'd really bug me.

I hear from all kinds of people. I once got a call from a company asking me if I'd mind if they used one of my jokes in their business procedure.

When I heard what their business was, I said I wouldn't mind if they'd promise to stay out of my business. It was a collection agency.

They had a lot of people they couldn't reach by phone. They'd either get no answer or be told there was no one by that name at the number. In any case, it was a waste of money to send a man around to people who were so clearly trying to avoid them.

The piece of material I had that they wanted to use was a gag telegram I used to send. Everybody's used it since. It said: "Ignore first wire." It drove people crazy. They couldn't resist calling to find out what the first wire said. It gave the company a chance to talk to them.

A cute note says: "Dear Henny, it was a pleasure to have you on the dais. [Signed] The Barber." The letterhead said Perry Como. He used to have his own TV show. Now he has his own camera company. For what Polaroid must pay him for those commercials, I figure they gave him the business.

Then there's another note from someone signed "Hubert" who blew being President of the United States three times. It says: "I'll be looking forward to that good speech material.''

Funny, that's the same thing the voters of this country are looking forward to.

But maybe my most treasured letter is one dated 1968 which says: ''Dear Henny, damned if I don't think you're getting better all the time, which must be impossible because you always were great. How about that! With all good wishes, [Signed] Brooks Atkinson.''

In case a few illiterates don't know who he is, Brooks was the best drama critic the New York *Times* ever had. If you don't believe it, just reread his letter. It's clearly the work of a very wise man.

I was working at the Barcelona Hotel in Miami Beach when Jerry Lewis was shooting his picture *The Bellboy*. When they broke for lunch, Jerry came in and joined me in the dining room. In a second our table was surrounded by people asking Jerry for his autograph, ruining any chance we had for a quiet conversation.

I sat there for a minute; then I went out to the lobby where there was a telegraph office. Remember them? I gave the girl two bucks and asked her to type out a message for me on a telegraph blank. Then I got a bellboy to go into the dining room paging Jerry Lewis, while I walked back to the table and sat down.

Jerry said, ''Over here, boy. What is it?''

''Telegram, sir. Sign here.''

Jerry signed with a flourish, tipped the kid a dollar, said ''excuse me'' to the crowd of autograph seekers, and opened the wire. It said: ''Dear Jerry, Please pass the salt. Henny.''

Everything that could happen has happened to me in nightclubs. Once a couple of drunken sailors thought they were being gypped, which was right. And they thought I was the manager, which was wrong. They started to beat up on me, and I would have been turned into rice pudding if a couple of Filipino waiters hadn't jumped in and saved me.

Those two guys made up—as far as I'm concerned—for the way all waiters kill jokes. If you're working on the floor, they're in the back rattling the ice and glasses. If you're at a table with some friends, just as you come to the punch line they interrupt for some reason. But try to catch a waiter's eye to get a glass of water when you're choking to death. It isn't his table.

One thing I'll never forget happened when I was working at Lou Walter's Latin Quarter on Palm Island in Miami. It was three weeks before my thirty-eighth birthday. Sadie and the two kids were living at the Angler's Hotel. It was during the war, and I'd been deferred because of a bad back. Just being a coward wasn't enough.

My draft board in Brooklyn was made up of three undertakers

(honestly, no kidding) who didn't like Jewish comedians and were very anxious to get me into the Army. At that time, thirty-eight was the cutoff age, after which men couldn't be drafted unless Hitler was standing in line to get in at the Roxy. This applied especially to men with two kids and a bad back. So what do I get? I get a thing that opens with "Greetings" and tells me to report at an induction center in Jacksonville, Florida, for a physical.

So there was a big farewell scene, like in *Gone with the Wind*. I said good-bye to Sadie and the kids and took the bus to Jacksonville. I told them not to worry, that I was too old and all that, but they didn't believe what I was saying, and neither did I. I've never felt so awful in my life. But just in case I got lucky and they put me in some Special Services unit to entertain the troops, I took along my violin.

When I walked into the induction center with my violin case under my arm, the sergeant in charge looked at it and then down at my feet and said, "What's that? An extra pair of shoes? Check it with your other stuff. We supply shoes." They gave me a very hard time. I was everything they didn't like down there, mainly a wisecracking Yankee from Brooklyn. They'd seen too many of those Army comedies in which the kid from Brooklyn is always making jokes and gets shot just before the picture ends. I was the type they wanted shot.

They gave me a very fast tongue-out, bend-over, breathe-in, breathe-out, read-this, O-kay, A-1 "You're in the Army."

"Well, I finally made it," I said, "I'm the only guy whose mother raised her boy to be a soldier."

"Don't be funny," he said, "or you'll get KP before you even take your oath."

I said, "There's one thing I'd like to ask you, Doc. Why is it that when I bend over, I get this sharp pain in my back that makes me nauseated?"

He said, "Bend over."

I did. I was so scared I threw up.

He said, "Let's take another look." Then he examined my back very carefully, and in a few seconds he said, "You're out of the Army. You have lumbar arthritis."

I told him I felt terrible that I'd have to go back and admit to my wife and kids that I wasn't fit to be in the Army of the United States. He just smiled and said I couldn't imagine how awful the Army felt about it. Then I asked how long it would take before I could go back to my family and my job. He said about three days was what it took to process the papers.

"Do you have a leave coming up?" I asked him.

"This weekend. Why?"

"I thought you and any friends you might want to bring along might like to make a little trip down to Lou Walter's Latin Quarter in Miami. Lots of gals and gags and, of course, you'd be a guest of the house."

I was cleared to go home in two hours. I ran to catch the bus so fast I almost forgot my fiddle, just caught the last bus, and stood all the way from Jacksonville to Miami. I stood there with a big grin on my face, a standing joke. I'm sure Sadie and the kids were happier to see me than any drill instructor would have been.

Later, after the war ended, I was doing a routine of how different things were everywhere. "No food stamps. No clothing stamps. No rationing. No black market. No more war pictures." And I happened to ad-lib the line "Whatever became of Sessue Hayakawa?" It was one of those things. The right line at the right time in the right place. It went over big. So I kept it in. Sometimes it worked. Sometimes it lay there. But when it worked, it worked so big that it became a sort of running gag.

Then came the night that *The Bridge on the River Kwai* opened on Broadway. During intermission I was standing in the lobby of the theater listening to people rave about what they had already seen when a man came up to me and said, "Well, here I am." It was Sessue Hayakawa.

As I'm writing this, a piece of news has shaken show biz around New York. The famous Copacabana is going to close this summer for the first time. This not only means that a lot of tourists won't have a really posh nightclub to go to, but means a lot of singers, dancers, chorus girls, and comedians won't have a spot to work in in New York.

To play the Copa in New York was like playing the Palace in the old days. So when you played the spot for the first time, it was important that you went over big. You had to be better than just all right.

The first time I walked out onto the floor at the Copa, who do I see sitting at a ringside table but my old boss Billy Rose and his wife Eleanor Holm, the Olympic swimmer? Billy at that time was writing a very popular newspaper column. What he said about you could make you or break you. I liked Billy, and I knew he liked me, personally, but I knew he was too sophisticated a gent to go for the kind of lappy jokes I tell.

Maybe I'd better explain the word "lappy." Milton Berle made it up. It means easy to understand. Right in the audience's lap. Nothing subtle.

I couldn't wait to see how Billy treated me in his column. Here's how:

A funnyman named Youngman is entertaining at the Copacabana. This patter-chatter gent has been around Broadway almost as long as the stores that sell souvenir turtles. I first caught his act 20 years ago in something called the Kentucky Club. I thought Youngman had talent but I didn't care very much for his jokes.

Unfortunately, I'm not a good audience for joke tellers. Most of their wheezes were old to me before Captain Billie printed them in his "Whiz Bang." You see, I bunked with Ralph Spence twenty-five years ago when this movie title writer was assembling the first comprehensive gag file in America. I sat around for years at the old Friars Club when Georgie Cohan and Willie Collier were swapping comic punches. I listened to Wilson Mizner ad lib for a couple of hundred nights and I was around when the old Palace had its pick of 200 great next-to-closing acts.

And so I was a little sorry for Youngman when they planted me at a ringside table the night he opened. "At least try to look interested," Eleanor said, "Henny has a wife and kids."

But a minute after the comic got going I found myself laughing—laughing like I haven't laughed on Broadway for a long time.

Thanks to the inspired pencil of Danny Shapiro, Youngman has a new routine—glib, giddy, topical and hep. [It was "hep" in those days, not "hip."]

The bistro bosses around the country who are going snow blind looking at white table cloths could do a lot worse than hitch onto Henny.

It must have made Billy very happy to learn that the bistro bosses read him and took his advice. It made me very happy. It made Sadie and Marilyn and Gary happy, too.

Billy Rose was the last man in the world you ever thought of as spreading happiness.

But I guess everybody spreads some, whether he means to or not. Seeing my name in print is all it takes to make me happy. I agree with Barnum . . . just spell it right. Who cares what you say? People get it wrong anyway. It's the name that gets remembered.

This deep thinking was inspired by looking into today's newspaper, the comic section, of course, where men like Al Capp spread around a lot. There, before my tired eyes, was Capp's *Li'l Abner* strip with my name in it in large letters . . . spelled right. That's pretty good for Capp.

There are a lot of signs along the path to the open-front office of Capp's character Available Jones. The first sign says: "If yo' has cash Ah is yore friend." The next one is his professional shingle, "AVAILABLE (Ah'll do anything fo' a price) JONES." The third is: "Babies Minded—Dry Babies 10¢ . . . Other Types 25¢." Then there's a sign saying: "Finest grade advice given at lowest grade prices." Finally there's the big important sign: "Wanta be well known as a wit? Ah'll laff at yore jokes. 5¢ a joke. . . . to Henny Youngman, 10¢!"

Ah'll be danged! Mah jokes is twict as comical.

In the barbershop of the Palmer House in Chicago I said to the manicurist, "How about a date?" She said, "I'm married." I said, "Tell your husband you have a date with a girlfriend." She said, "Tell him yourself. He's shaving you."

22

That Toddling Town

OCCASIONALLY the Raleigh cigarette show that I took over from Skelton went to Chicago. Why did a radio show that was produced in New York go to Chicago? Maybe a sales meeting or a convention of some sort. In those days radio shows traveled around as much as President Nixon. Any place the agency wanted the show to go, it went.

You see, radio shows were produced by advertising agencies. The bigger the show, the bigger the agency. The Raleigh show was produced by Foote, Cone and Belding. Anyway, that's the name I remember. Maybe Foote, Cone and Belding did some other show I was on. They all had funny names like Scuffle Scramble and Grabbe or Penny Weiss & Ponfullish.

But the funniest thing about advertising agencies is that they all seem to be run by the same people. No matter what agency ran the

show I was on, the same guy always was in charge. He had a
different face and a different name. But he was the same guy.

Ralph Camargo was the announcer on the show. I remember him
clearly because of one awful night he gave me. After the broadcast
he asked if I liked Mexican food. I told him I liked Lupe Velez, why
not?

The whole experience is as clear in my mind as if it were
yesterday. It could have been the inspiration for those two great
Alka-Seltzer commercials that were such smash hits. I mean the
ones that started so many jokes. Remember "Try it! You'll like
it! . . . I tried it! Thought I was going to die!" And the other one:
"I can't believe I ate the whole thing!"

Both of those were enacted, in the order mentioned, by me. First
in the Mexican restaurant Ralph took me to and later in the Croyden
Hotel. I really did think I was going to die. Ralph kept ordering new
dishes for me to try. The inside of my mouth became numb. I lost
my sense of taste. I thought the horseradish at Seder on Passover
was hot. It was like fudge compared to the stuff Ralph was feeding
me.

By the time I got back to the hotel not only my mouth but the
whole inside of me was on fire. Wisps of blue smoke were coming
out of my mouth. I drank a glass of water and there was a hiss of
steam. I remembered hearing that as a result of the Great Fire
Chicago had the best fire department in the country. With a hazard
like that Mexican restaurant in town they needed it.

On this trip to Chicago I stayed at the Croyden, which was where
I always stayed on my earlier, less affluent visits. I did it for old
times' sake. The Croyden wasn't the Blackstone by a long windy
walk, but I told myself I stayed there for convenience sake. It was
nearer where I worked. It was also nearer what I could afford. It
wasn't only that I didn't get a lot; I had to send home a lot of what I
got. So going back there brought back a lot of sentimental
memories. And saved a few bucks.

In the old days all of us who stayed at the Croyden—mostly
vaudeville and nightclub acts—saved as much as we could, any way
we could. Money was so tight we wished we all could have stayed in
the same room. There was really a community of poverty.

I might have died of malnutrition if it weren't for an act called the
Cerillo Brothers. I have no idea what they did. I guess I just took it
for granted they were acrobats. But whether they were high-wire
walkers or jugglers, they sure could cook. Cooking was about the
only activity that was against the rules in the Croyden. But nobody
ever heard of the rules.

The Cerillo Brothers' big specialty was spaghetti and meat balls. We'd each chip in a quarter or so, and one of the brothers would go out and buy a ton or so of spaghetti and a few pounds of ground meat—that's how prices were in those days—and they'd make enough spaghetti with meat balls to feed the whole hotel.

Two of the regulars at the Croyden were a vaudeville act that called themselves the Stroud Twins. They not only looked exactly alike, they thought exactly alike . . . always about girls. Knowing it was almost impossible to tell them apart, they developed a terrific system for making one girl do a night's work for two . . . and I do mean work.

The Strouds would take a suite of two rooms with a connecting bath. They could afford this because of the money it saved them.

Their names were Claude and Clarence. If Claude could induce a broad to come up to his room to see his collection of rubber goods, he'd pass the word to Clarence, and they were both set for the night.

Claude would take his make up to his room, and when he'd gone farther than they ever went in Kansas City, he'd get out of bed and go into the bathroom. In a few minutes, refreshed from washing, a renewed Claude would appear . . . but it was Clarence. Claude rested in the other room. You get the picture? This went on all night. I always wondered how they figured who would pay the girl the most, whether they just split her fee down the middle or paid her on a piecework basis.

I finally played the big downtown presentation house in Chicago, the Chicago Theater. Before that I'd always been booked into houses in the outlying sections, Hyde Park, Englewood, Garfield Park. And when I played these dates I'd double at a nightclub downtown. One of these spots was called the Yacht Club, no relation to the Yacht Club on Fifty-second Street in New York. Also on the bill with me was a gal named Faith Bacon who once made the headlines by being caught at an Earl Carroll backstage party skinny dipping in a bathtub full of champagne.

This spot was run by "one of the boys," named Nick Dean. His girl worked the cigar and cigarette concession. She also sold candy and little novelties, like stuffed toys and perfume, that a big spender could give his girl to remember him by. It was all pretty crummy merchandise, but the price was high. To make it easy on what Texas Guinan used to call "the suckers," they could play the 26 Game with Nick's girlfriend.

It's a simple little game in which you play against the house by trying to get closer to the number 26 in the fewest rolls of six dice. Most of the time the customer lost. I don't know why. Because most

of the time I won. It made Nick's girl mad because when I won, I
took the cash and beat it. Most of the customers took merchandise
that was worth only a fraction of what they'd won. I'd just pick up
my money, walk away, and say, "That's life." The line bugged
her.

Dean booked a comic by the name of Willie Sharr into the club to
follow me. I was playing at a theater in Englewood and came into
the club every night after the show for a few laughs.

Willie was a guy who thought he was the second coming of
Casanova. Women just couldn't resist him, he told everybody. One
night Nick and I were having coffee and discussing whether Willie
was really the Don Juan he said he was or whether he was just
another joke to whom the gals said, "Don' wanna!" We couldn't
make up our minds.

A few nights later, one of the most stunning-looking high society
broads I ever saw walked in. She looked so familiar to me that if she
didn't show so much real class, I'd have thought I knew her. I
figured I must have seen her picture in the rotogravure section of the
Sunday paper or something. It was a sure bet I didn't see her in *The
Police Gazette*. She was a real knockout all done up in furs and
jewels . . . and all alone.

She ordered champagne, laughed it up big for Willie, applauded
loudly, and then left. Naturally Willie had spied her, and when she
walked out, he followed and got a good look at the mile-long
limousine that was waiting for her. The chauffeur jumped out, ran
around, and opened the door. She got in and drove off. Willie's
mouth began to water.

The following night she was back, different outfit, different furs,
same table. When Willie finished, she left, as she had the night
before. But this time as she brushed against Willie who was crowd-
ing her way out, she said, "I enjoyed your act very much. Thank
you." Willie nearly fainted.

Her visits continued for three or four days more. Each night, as
she left, she told Willie how good he was. Willie was getting so hot
you could fry eggs on him. Then came Saturday night. There was a
big crowd, and she was at her usual table. And a note arrived at his
dressing room, courtesy of a waiter, asking him to join her at her
table when he finished his act.

I think he only did about half his routine he was so anxious to get
it over and meet her. She introduced herself as Mrs. Nellie Condone, the widow of a wealthy cattleman, and asked if he'd like to
come out to her home, after the second show, for a nightcap. I doubt
if Willie wore nightcaps, but he was sure willing to try. If he hadn't

caught a glimpse of Nick standing by the door, he would have skipped the second show and tried on the nightcap a little earlier. But he said he'd be delighted to join her for anything she had in mind. She said, "Naughty! Naughty!" and swept out of the club and into her waiting limo.

Willie came over to our table. "What have I done?" he moaned. "Why did I have to start up with her right away? I made my move too soon. I killed the whole thing. Now she'll think I'm just another horny comedian."

"Ain't you?" asked Nick.

I asked, "Did you say horny or corny?"

"I'll never see her again," Willie went on crying. "Why couldn't I have waited a little while? Me and my big mouth."

"Forget it," said Nick. "That dame was class. You couldn't have laid a glove on her."

"Oh, no," said Willie. "I know women. I've had plenty of them. The bigger they come, the harder they fall. Play your cards right and you can have any broad in the world for . . . for . . . for a well . . . for a song."

"Right," I said. "'The Wedding March.'"

"Would that be bad?" asked Willie.

"Only for her," said Nick, and we both got up and left the table.

The second show that night could have been the worst show Willie ever gave anywhere. His heart just wasn't in it. He couldn't get over berating himself for blowing what was clearly a wonderful chance with a rich dame. But when he and I walked out of the club to go back to the Croyden, there was her chauffeur standing by the limousine waiting for him.

"Mr. Sharr?" he asked.

"Yeah. That's me. I'm Sharr," said Willie in a voice a couple of tones higher than usual.

"I was told to pick you up and take you out to the house."

"Okay. Thanks. Let's go!" By this time Willie was almost inarticulate with excitement as the driver opened the door and Willie leaped in.

Still holding the door, the chauffeur said, "Can I drop you anywhere, sir?"

Before I could answer, Willie said, "He'll walk. He needs the exercise. It's only a few blocks."

I said, "He's right. I need the exercise."

"Very good, sir," said the chauffeur, closed the door, and away went Willie to his merry widow.

The rest of the story I picked up piece by piece later.

They drove out along the Gold Coast on the North Shore to a magnificent mansion with a lot of land around it and a great big iron fence to keep it from spilling into the city. The driver pressed a button; the gates opened; they drove up to a big paneled door; the chauffeur rang the bell and then disappeared. A uniformed butler opened the door and led Willie into a huge drawing room, told him to make himself comfortable, and left. He returned in a moment with a bottle of champagne in an ice bucket and a tray of caviar with lemon, chopped onion, chopped parsley, and thin toast.

When the butler had arranged everything and left, Willie's target for the night walked in wearing about a million dollars' worth of negligee and ostrich feathers. "I'm so glad you could come," she said, holding out her hand. "Tonight is the servants' night off, and I hate to be left alone in this enormous barn of a house."

They talked a little about the club and Willie's work, and I'm sure he bragged a lot about where he'd been and what he'd done. While this was going on, they drank the champagne and enjoyed the fish eggs, and before long the lights were lowered, and so were their voices.

Willie moved over beside her and slipped his arm around her. She didn't object. He came closer and closer and finally got up enough nerve to kiss her. She kissed back very hard, and from then on he knew he was home free. Before long she took him by the hand and said, "Come."

Willie was ready.

She led him up the winding marble staircase to her bedroom. She slipped out of her expensive negligee and helped Willie out of his forty-five-dollar Maurice Rothschild suit. Before long they were scrambling around on the bed, making weird noises and having every kind of fun with each other that a man can have with a woman and vice versa, with the accent on the vice. Finally, Willie got tired. After all, he'd done two shows that night. He sighed and lay back quietly on the bed. And then a funny thing happened.

The sliding doors at one end of the room opened, and there were about twenty guys. They'd all been watching through holes in the doors. Willie had done three shows that night. Each guy had paid Nick twenty-five dollars, and he'd set up the whole deal.

It wasn't until after I'd found out all this that I realized why the Mrs. Condone I'd seen at the club looked so familiar. It was the same girl I beat at the 26 Game. Nick's girl. Only she was so gussied up I didn't recognize her. An Eskimo makes a friend welcome in his house by offering the guest his wife. It was the first time I knew Nick was an Eskimo.

Not long after Willie's little affair, I heard the girl had been burned to death. How it happened I don't know. But things like that happen to girls who run around with "the boys." That's life.

Something happened during one run I had at the Chicago Theater that I'll never forget. I'd been doing some club dates in California, which I'll come to later. Al Jolson was living at the Beverly Hills Hotel. Jerry Lester and I used to go out to his bungalow there and hang around the pool with him to cheer him up. His career was in a slump, and everyone was saying that Jolson was all washed up. The excitement of his first talkie—*the* first talkie—*The Jazz Singer*, was long gone. The excitement of having his own radio show was over. And Jolie couldn't get himself arrested. What a situation like that did to an ego like Al's is unbelievable.

I kept telling him not to worry, that everybody had hills and valleys, and that if he'd had as many valleys as I had, his name would be Rudy. "Things have got to get better," I kept telling him.

"Why didn't they ever get any better for you?" he asked, which I thought was a lousy joke. But when a man's bitter, he doesn't think what he's saying.

What happened for Jolie was a little guy named Sidney Skolsky. He ran a gossip column in the Hollywood *Citizen-News*, and I think it was later syndicated nationally. Skolsky got an idea that he managed to sell to Harry Cohn, who was head of Columbia Pictures. The idea was to do a picture called *The Jolson Story* with an actor playing Al but using Jolson's voice for the dialogue and the songs.

Now back in Chicago. I'm starring at the Chicago Theater. I haven't seen Al since those afternoons at the Beverly Hills Hotel. Across the street from the Chicago is the Oriental Theater where the feature is the Chicago premiere of *The Jolson Story*. And just to make it tougher, George Jessel is on stage, in person. It didn't help our business a bit.

To top it off, Jolie flew into Chicago for a personal appearance at the premiere. The streets around the theater were jammed with people. Cars couldn't get through. I could hardly get through to *my* theater. I almost gave up. I figured, what for?

When I walked out onto the stage and saw an audience I was amazed. I couldn't believe the manager had that many friends. I just looked at them and said, "What happened? You're in the wrong theater. There's two Al Jolsons playing across the street, one of them named Larry Parks, and you're here with only one Henny Youngman? But I'll tell you what you can do. When I'm finished, get a door pass. Go across the street. Hire a kid to stand in line for you. Then come back and see this show three times, new jokes every show, and by then the kid on line may be close enough to the door of the Oriental so that you can get in." The way people laughed, I think that's what a lot of them had done.

After the first show I was sitting in my dressing room wondering if I could get out of the theater to get to Henrici's for something to eat when two Chicago cops walked in. "You Youngman?" one of them asked. I said, "Don't hit me. I'll confess."

"Come with us," the other cop said and took me by the arm.

"What's the charge?" I asked as they started to take me out of the room. All of a sudden it began to look serious.

"Wait a minute," I said. "What *is* this? What have I done? I know I left my car double parked, but that was in New York. Can they extradite me for that?"

The cops just said, "Come along."

I'll never forget the expression on the manager's face when he saw the star of his show being dragged out the stage door of the theater by two policemen. "You can't do this to me," he screamed.

"Want to bet?" said one of the officers, and out he went.

"Wait! I'm coming with you," he hollered after us. But my two escorts weren't waiting for anyone. In a minute we were pushing through the crowd around the Oriental Theater and heading for the stage door.

"Okay," said one of the cops, finally. "You asked for it. Now I'll tell you what this is all about. Al Jolson asked us to come and get you and bring you to his dressing room."

When I stepped through the door, Jolie grabbed me and hugged me, and I said, "See. I told you this would happen. You're a fantastic hit again."

"Thass right, Henny. You tol' me an' I believed ya. 'Cause deep down here in my heart I kep' sayin' to myself, 'There ain't nothin' that can keep Jolie down. Nothing'!'"

Jolson was more humble than I'd ever seen him be.

He'd sent the fuzz for me because the show was going on and he knew if he phoned me I wouldn't be able to get across the street and through the crowd in time.

I walked down to the wings with Al. Georgie Jessel walked on from the other side and started a whole long introduction to Jolson that began to sound like one of his eulogies. Al couldn't stand to wait for Georgie's finish. He wanted to get in front of that audience.

So he walked onstage, saying, "Okay, Georgie! That's enough. Nobody has to introduce Jolie. Everybody knows who I am, don't you folks?'' Terrific applause. ''And listen, folks, you ain't heard nothing' yet.'' Then he sang.

And he was right.

In spite of Jolie, I did so well at the Chicago that I was booked into the swanky Empire Room at the Palmer House. I was to follow Hildegarde. Some change of pace. From the strapless, long-gowned, long-gloved ''chanteusy'' of the piano from Milwaukee to the gag bag fiddler from Flatbush.

The Empire Room had a regular clientele, and I knew I had to do something besides just walk on with my fiddle in my hand or they'd think they were in for another musical act. I finally hit on what to do.

For my entrance I wore a pair of long white gloves. If I'd been Berle, I'd have worn one of Hildy's dresses.

I went to see a Beverly Hills analyst. He said, "Lie down and tell me everything." I did. And now he's doing my act.

23

Hooray for Hollywood

AS this is being written, I'm flying West. That means that this book has not only been written on the ocean but in the sky. No wonder it leaves you all at sea on some things and up in the air about others. Some of the writing has even been done with both feet on the ground. But you could never tell.

Most of the work so far has been done in New York, Florida, California, Illinois, Michigan, Pennsylvania, and North Carolina. That makes eight states. If you only count seven it means you've skipped the state of confusion. That's where I vote.

The point I'm getting to is that I travel a lot, mostly by air, and I just don't understand why people are always complaining to me that the airlines lose their baggage. I say, "Don't complain to me! Tell *them!*"

In the last twenty-five years I've flown millions of miles between New York and London, New York and Paris, New York and California, New York and Chicago, New York and Florida, New York and Newark and to innumerable little cities you never heard of all over the country. I've flown to some places that are so small that when they get word I'm booked there, they build an airport. I've often thought of flying my own plane. One thing frightens me. I've never seen a Shell station in the sky. I'd hate to run out of gas and get stuck up there forever. Parachutes don't appeal to me. I never go in for anything where you don't get a second chance.

What I'm getting at is, in all the flying I've done the airlines have never lost my baggage. It always arrives right on time. Of course, occasionally, they've lost me. I walked on a plane the other day and asked a man, "Does this go to Kansas City?" He said, "Don't ask me. I'm not the hijacker."

I don't think there's another comedian today who operates the way I do . . . by choice. I've been offered my own television show, but I don't want to be pinned down. For the ones I've been offered I could get shot down.

The problem started way back in radio. Three guys named Joe Stein, Marty Glickman, and Herb Moss came to me with a great idea. It was a show that featured acts like a man who played *Rigoletto* on his skull with two spoons. A fellow who made music on a bicycle pump and a crosscut saw at the same time. A woman who made sound effects with her mouth. The name they had for the show was *Going Nowhere*. I told them the only thing right about the show was the name. A show called *Going Nowhere* could take me with it.

Incidentally, Joe Stein, under the nom de plume of Joseph Stein wrote the libretto for *Fiddler on the Roof*. That he didn't offer me. If he had, I probably would have turned it down. Who cares about a bunch of poor Jews in Russia?

The boys finally made *Going Nowhere* with Jim Backus. He closed each show by saying, "Good night, Henny." I thought he was being sarcastic. Henny is his wife's name. But the show didn't last. The title proved prophetic. I don't like titles that give critics an automatic opening laugh. They can't resist it. They're only human. It's hard to believe, but it's true. I know some of them. They eat and breathe and do a couple of other things just like the rest of us. Some of them have tried walking on the water, but they've disappeared from sight. Even the Coast Guard couldn't find them.

I remain visible. You should walk down the street with me someday. People reach out to me on all sides. But I grab them by the hand before they can mug me. The reason? I've done shows for so many different groups in so many different places that if I decided to run for President of the United States, I'd have a ready-made network of workers, a nationwide bunch of clubs and societies that would go to bat for me . . . or go for me with a bat. You know,

Elks, Lions, Moose. I'm great at zoos. I only had one bad time. The Woodmen of the World. They chopped me down.

It's true that my name is a household word, even in the big houses . . . Sing Sing, San Quentin, Atlanta. The last time I did a show in Dannemora they loved me so they didn't want to let me go. They kept shouting, "Lock him up! Lock him up!" The governor pardoned me.

Playing club dates is a world of its own. Organizations even get in touch with me direct. Sometimes they go through an agent. Sometimes it's an agent I don't even know.

The phone will ring, and a voice will say, "Hello, Henny baby, you've made it at last!"

"I'm glad I waited. Who is this?"

"Dave."

"Oh? Dave." I wait to hear Dave who.

"Listen, Henny, a fellow from the AMSSS just phoned me to ask if I could get you to MC the wind-up dinner of their annual convention."

"Chicago or Miami?"

"Butte."

"Where's that?"

"The heart of the mustard seed country."

"Hot, mild, English, French, Dijon, or Bahamian?"

"It's in Montana. There'll be over a thousand members and friends."

"Do they know the price?"

"Okay. Plus all expenses."

"I'll be there. When?"

"Tomorrow."

"Easy. But what is the AMSSS?"

"The American Mustard Seed Sorters Society."

"What do they do?"

"It's some trick name for the association of mustard growers."

"In Butte, Montana?"

"They tell me it's the heart of the mustard country."

"I thought the heart of the mustard country was either Yankee Stadium or the Stage Delicatessen."

The point of this little bit of dialogue is to emphasize the way the world and my life is today. Nothing is too remote. I can go anywhere, play any date for any kind of people at the drop of an offer. And that's what I like to do. I'm not exposed to blasé critics who think they're smarter and funnier than I am and try to prove it at my expense. I'm only invited by people who like me. The result is an almost endless succession of successful appearances. It's great for the ego. Some of my friends call me Henny the Hawk because I fly more than Pan Am and American put together. And maybe if they were put together, they might not be going broke separately. Now go back and read how a chance meeting with a drunk on a plane gave me the idea for this book.

Flying into Los Angeles, I can't get over how it's changed. Now there's nothing but high-rise buildings and banks. When I first saw it, there was nothing but orange groves and bungalow courts. Now the bungalow courts have all moved out to where the orange groves used to be, they're owned by the banks, and they're called Leisure Land or Sunset Haven. They're wonderful. I spent a week in one of those places one day. Every morning the people choose up sides and play a game called symptoms. It's the only game where the ones who do the worst do the best.

Last year I had to spend a little time in L.A. while I was shooting for *Laugh-In*. I asked a friend to find a small furnished apartment for us, one with a small kitchen. The reason the small kitchen was important was that every evening Sadie could say, "This kitchen's too small to cook in. Let's go out to dinner."

We never found an apartment. There's a shortage. Almost all the land is occupied by banks. My friend got us a large box in the vault of the Bank of California. We didn't like it. They lock up the place too early.

It's not very interesting living in a bank. But I guess we didn't stay long enough. If you're in the bank for two years or more, the interest increases.

Only one unusual thing happened while we were living in the bank. A robber dropped in, and I recognized him. He was a guy who used to be an agent. I said, "Aren't you working for William Morris anymore?"

"No," he said. "I wanted to get married, so I decided to go straight."

Well, so much for fantasy. The first time I went to Hollywood the big thing for types like me was Sunday night at the Trocadero. The Troc was on "the Strip" on the south side of Sunset diagonally across from where La Rue's Restaurant used to be. Now it's run by Nicky Blair. It had a big parking lot in back with a great view of the lights of the city spread out below you. Now it's all parking lot. People who thought New York's skyline was sensational also got a kick out of Los Angeles' ground line, a carpet of lights from the windows of homes, streetlamps, and neon signs. In those days there was no smog, and it really was impressive. It was so sensational that if the people at the Troc didn't like the show inside, they went out to the parking lot and applauded the city. Later on, a spot called Mocambo opened with the same view, but it put in huge picture windows so you didn't have to go out to see the lights. The people could sit right at their tables and ignore the show.

Playing the Troc was my big plan for getting into pictures. I'd work the Trocadero. All the studio heads, Jack Warner, Darryl F. Zanuck, Harry Cohn, Louis B. Mayer (I had a special "in" with him), and all the top directors and writers would be there Sunday night. They'd see me, tall, handsome, thin, funny, and with a nose like the anchor on the *Leviathan*, and immediately start grappling with each other to be the first to sign me to a long-term contract. Clearly it was the beginning of my movie career.

The big night came. Everybody who was supposed to be there was there. The setup was exactly like the setup in every nightclub since Eve ate the apple and took Adam out on the town. Dance floor with band, in front of which the comedian did his stuff.

If you were Joe E. Lewis or someone like that, you could tell the band to take five or ten or twenty or as long as you figured you could hold them. But I needed the music for my finish when I played the fiddle. So this is what happened. The minute I came on and started my routine the band began to jabber like a bunch of bargain hunters in Macy's basement. It threw my timing off completely, and it's possible the audience couldn't hear me. I didn't know what happened. Normally musicians don't behave like that. Especially those who work in nightclubs.

Later I found out what happened. A comic by the name of Archie Robbins had told the men that I had a big reputation in New York as a fast ad libber who could handle hecklers, so they needn't bother about keeping quiet. They could just go ahead and say anything they wanted to and I'd handle it. That's a great rep to have, but it was a rough rap to take. It might even have turned out all right if they'd thrown their cracks at me, but what they did was talk among themselves like a group of gossipy chorus girls.

Clearly that was the end of my picture career.

But a piece of historic significance about my first trip to Hollywood appeared in James Bacon's "Hollywood Hotline" column early in 1972. Bacon wrote:

Merv Griffin taped a bunch of us the other night for his 'Hollywood—Today and Yesterday.' But Merv didn't have enough time to ask me questions about wild Hollywood parties so the television audience will not hear a great one about Henny Youngman.

Back in the '30s Youngman came to do a movie. It was his first visit to Hollywood so, like many an Easterner, he kept bugging his friends about going to wild Hollywood parties with naked starlets and such.

All of them told him it was all a myth—that people in Hollywood were hard working and didn't have time for that kind of hanky-panky.

But Youngman persisted, especially with Harry Crane who is now head writer for Dean Martin.

Finally one day Crane called Youngman and said, "Henny, you're in luck. I got you an invitation to the Starlets Nudist Association Annual Party."

Harry gave Henny a Bel Air address and told him to show up at 8 P.M. When Henny got there a butler Crane had hired from Central Casting greeted Henny and said, "You may take off your clothes in here." The butler indicated an ante-room off the hallway.

In a matter of minutes Henny was stark naked except for a cigar. The butler directed him to the dining room and then left.

Henny walked in and found himself naked at a black tie sit down dinner of some of Hollywood's biggest executives and their wives, none of whom were in on the gag except his host, Crane and the Central Casting butler. Of course Henny will deny the story. If he didn't his wife, Sadie, would kill him.

As for denying the story, Sadie's had lots better reasons for killing me in the past forty-five years. I don't know why she hasn't except that she can't stand the sight of blood.

As for nudity, years before *Cosmopolitan* had the idea and Burt Reynolds had the body and the guts to be the first male nude centerfold, I wrote Hugh Heffner and suggested that I'd be willing to be the first boy Playmate. I figured what did I have to hide that everybody didn't know about? Besides, a guy who plays the violin, like one who plays a guitar or banjo (mandolins are too small), doesn't have to worry about clothes. He can go anywhere in the nude as long as he brings along his instrument.

I got even with Crane. When Sid Piermont, Marvin Schenck, Louis Sidney, and some of Louis B. Mayer's friends in New York heard I was going to Hollywood, they each pitched in a few bucks to send him a gift they knew he'd enjoy—sturgeon. At the time there was a law in California against selling sturgeon. I think it was lobbied through by the West Coast salmon industry.

When I got on the 20th Century, I had the dining-car steward put the fish on ice for me. At Chicago I transferred the fish to the refrigerator on the Chief. Mr. Mayer had been told that this fish he liked so much would arrive with me. When I got off the train at Pasadena—that was the chic thing to do; you never rode all the way into L.A.—there was an MGM limousine waiting to take me to my hotel and take the fish to Mr. Mayer.

For a while I didn't hear from him. Then one day I got a call that he'd like me to come to his office. I was on the lot to make a screen test, so I walked over to see Mr. Mayer.

This happened to be just about a week after Crane had played his naked joke on me. Crane was then a writer on the MGM lot and did a lot of showing off in front of me.

Mr. Mayer told me how much he appreciated getting the stuff from his friends in New York and wanted to thank me personally for going through the bother of escorting the fish across the country. I said it was no bother. It was the richest fish I'd ever traveled with. Then he asked if there was anything he could do for me. Instead of saying, "You can see that when the people look at my screen test, they'll like it and sign me," all I could think of was getting even with Harry Crane. So I told Mr. Mayer about the gag Harry had pulled on me and asked if I could borrow his office for a few minutes.

Mayer was sore because he hadn't been invited to the dinner and immediately said, "Sure. Is that all you want?"

I said, "Have someone call Harry Crane and tell him to come to your office right away. Then you take a walk and let me sit behind your desk till he arrives."

Even if it cost me the chance to be put under contract to MGM, the gag was worth it. When Crane walked in and saw me at Mr. Mayer's desk, he turned eight different colors. If there had been a hole in the floor, he would have gone through it. Headfirst! Lots of times you can work out a joke on someone but aren't able to be there for the payoff. When you can be there, it's worth any amount of trouble you go to.

Today I find Hollywood a very pleasant place to visit. I know a lot of people out there, and I have a lifetime permit from the police to walk in Beverly Hills. When I first went out there by train, I used to worry if I'd make it in Hollywood. Now when I fly, I worry if the plane will make it. Nobody knows where he's going anymore when he travels by air. I heard about a man who boarded a plane in Los

Angeles. As soon as it was airborne, he put a gun to a stewardess's head and said, "Tell the pilot to take me to San Francisco."

The girl said, "That's where we're supposed to go."

He said, "I know, but I want to be sure I get there."

But seriously, folks, as Milton Berle would say, we people who fly a lot worry a lot about hijacking. Several innocent travelers have been killed or wounded. I hope by the time this book is printed something effective has been done to curb air piracy.

Not long after Slapsie Maxie's opened on Wilshire Boulevard, I went out to headline a bill with Evelyn Knight. When I showed up for rehearsal, they had my name up in lights, but it was under another name, Benny Fields. Fields was an old vaudevillian who always claimed he sang through a megaphone before Rudy Vallee used one. He also claimed he boo-boo-boo-booed before Bing. Big deal! Do you hear me going around claiming that while Bing was boo-boo-boo-booing for audiences, *they* were boo-boo-boo-booing for me?

I went storming in to find out what was wrong with my billing. They told me Evelyn Knight had been forced to cancel, and the only singing person they could get on short notice was Benny Fields. They said he wouldn't work unless he got top billing.

I said, "Supposing I won't work unless I get top billing?"

They told me, "Then we'll have to get a man with a ladder to climb up and change the name in lights to whoever we get to replace you." Then they got very nice and gave me a little more loot and told me all the things they'd do for me if I'd just go along with things the way they were. That would have been all right. But when Fields heard me rehearsing a Mammy medley of Jolson tunes I'd had specially arranged, he screamed his head off. He was closing with an imitation of Jolson, and my medley would kill his finish.

We fought about that for a while, and I suggested that they take both our names down and put up Jolson, who seemed to be the star of the show.

Fields said if I felt that way, why didn't I cut my medley? I said I wasn't imitating Jolie; I was just playing some of the songs he sang. I said I thought any singer who had to imitate another singer to "get off" needed a lot of help. So I cut my medley and closed with a violin solo that would have made Isaac Stern cry. It would have made any good violinist cry. Jim Bishop once wrote that I played the violin as if I had something personal against it.

The funny thing about that fight I had with Benny Fields was that while it was going on, he was ordering a birthday cake for himself. He explained exactly what size it should be, how he wanted it decorated, and that he wanted it to say "Many More Happy Birthdays Benny!"

That night as he finished his Jolson medley, Eddie Cantor, who was in the audience, stood up and said, "Ladies and gentlemen, I want you all to join me in wishing happy birthday and many more of them to a friend of mine and a great guy, Benny Fields." Then a waiter marched in carrying the cake with enough candles on it to light the room . . . and heat it. Eddie was surprised. But no one acted more surprised than Benny. I came on and congratulated him and said I thought we both should wish happy birthday to Al Jolson.

Benny and I had known each other for years. The first time we met was during my two-year run as house MC at the Flatbush Theater in Brooklyn. Benny was on the bill one week.

At that time we lived in Brooklyn not very far from the theater, and one Friday night I wanted to get home for dinner with the family. I told Benny what I had in mind and asked him if he'd help me by cutting his act a little for the supper show, which would shorten the show and get me out a little earlier. He said he would.

But he didn't. He even added a few songs, and I didn't have enough time for the home dinner I'd been looking forward to.

At the end of his act at that time, Benny did a patriotic number that would start a war. He was backed up by a film of our boys marching, flags flying and more Yankee Doodle hoopla than even George M. Cohan would have dared put on a stage.

I was so sore at him I had to do something to get even. I found an old Uncle Sam hat backstage, left by some passing kiddie revue. And I remembered a little dry goods store near the theater that had a red, white, and blue bathrobe in the window. I ran down the street and bought it.

When Benny's big finish was over and he was taking bows, I walked onstage wearing the red, white, and blue bathrobe and the Uncle Sam hat, stood in front of Benny, and said, "Wave me."

Without realizing what he was doing, he did. You can imagine the audience's reaction. But nobody could possibly imagine Benny's reaction. He and his wife, Blossom Seeley, who was also a great singer and working with him at the time, came storming into my dressing room screaming that they'd see to it that I never worked anywhere again.

Another example of how my sense of the ridiculous or my short temper, or both, kept getting me into fights with people. And to make things worse, my friend Jan Murray happened to be in the audience. He'd just had a nose job, and he laughed so hard he tore open a couple of stitches. I'd heard of putting people in stitches, but

I'd never heard of getting them out.

I signed to work for Earl Carroll right after he opened his theater restaurant on Sunset Boulevard diagonally across the street from the Palladium. One of the conditions Carroll had in the contract was that if I got a movie deal while I was working for him, he'd get 50 percent of my take. I was so crazy to get to California again I signed the contract. My agent, Miles Ingals, was so crazy for the 10 percent he let me. Carroll must have been a little crazy, too, because he had in the contract that I was not allowed to work any place else in the area, like, for instance, one of the vaudeville houses in downtown Los Angeles, where I might be seen. About the end of my third week with Carroll, Eddie Cantor invited me to appear at a Warner Brothers benefit.

I said to Eddie, "If things are so bad with the Warner Brothers that you have to run a benefit for them, I'll do what I can." Actually it was an affair Warner Brothers was sponsoring for the B'nai B'rith or the United Jewish Appeal. Naturally, Cantor was the MC.

No one could collect money from a houseful of Jews like Eddie. He'd embarrass the hell out of people. He'd take a handful of pledge cards and go through them like this: "I see Harry Cohn has pledged five thousand dollars. Are you in the room, Harry?" Proudly Harry would stand up. Then Eddie would say, "Harry, I happen to know how much you won in that poker game at Connie Bennett's house last Friday, Saturday, and Sunday. So I think you should give at least half of that, which I figure comes to twelve thousand dollars."

Cantor's knowledge of all the old jokes in David Freedman's file helped him, too. David was the much-written-about creator of the first radio joke factory. He wrote almost all of Eddie's radio routines, as well as for Block and Sully, Lou Holtz and Fanny Brice, for whom, they say, he created Baby Snooks.

There was a man named Benny Holzman who was very close to Eddie, and they'd play a trick at benefits. Benny would stand up and pledge a thousand dollars. Eddie would pretend not to hear, "Did you say seven hundred and fifty?"

"A thousand!" Benny would shout.

"How much?" Eddie would ask, cupping his ear.

Benny would scream even louder, "A thousand dollars!"

By this time the whole audience was getting impatient and two or three people would shout, "A thousand! A thousand!"

"Thank you all very much," Eddie would say, pointing to each person who'd said a thousand and calling him by name. Then he'd tell the ushers to take a pledge card to each of them.

Which reminds me of the bank in Tel Aviv that had on its

window: "Cash on hand—$5,000,000—Surplus $50,000,000 in pledges."

Naturally I accepted Eddie's invitation because I'm naturally charitable and because I figured it would be a great place to be discovered. So Carroll canceled me. My contribution was one job.

I made one trip to Hollywood just to play a private party that was being given for Darryl F. Zanuck. They brought out Raymond Scott and his Quintet, and a couple of the others on the program were the Ritz Brothers and Edgar Bergen and Charlie McCarthy.

I'd heard stories about how ventriloquists get a little confused about which one is the dummy. It wasn't until that night at the Zanuck party that I saw any sign of it. I was standing in the wings when Edgar came off carrying Charlie and saying, "Well, Charlie, I guess we did all right, didn't we?"

Charlie said, "I don't know about you, Bergen, but I killed 'em, so help me, I mowed 'em down!"

Talking with Dorothy Lamour, who was on the Chase and Sanborn radio show for a long time with Bergen, I told her about this. It didn't surprise her. She said it was always as if Charlie were the boss and Bergen the helper. She said that at rehearsals Bergen fluffed all over the place, but Charlie never went up in his lines. So, in that way, Bergen was different from all other ventriloquists. He wasn't jealous of the dummy. He was like a father to it. Dottie said that once Charlie told Edgar, "Stop moving your lips, Bergen, or people will think it's you talking instead of me."

I did everything all wrong every time I went to Hollywood. Out there you're not supposed to walk. If you can't drive a Cadillac, you stay home and wait until your agent calls. Well, I was taking a walk one Sunday morning along Sunset Boulevard out near the Beverly Hills Hotel. A sports car drove up beside me, and a voice said, "Hello, Henny."

It was Dick Powell. I'd played the Palace Theater in Cleveland when Dick was the house MC, and we got along great. He never tried to tell jokes, and I never tried to sing tenor. We hadn't seen each other in a long time, so we talked awhile and then he told me to call him in the morning because he thought he could get me a part in a picture he was making.

I called him, and he did. The picture was *You Can't Run Away from It* starring Jack Lemmon and June Allyson. It was a remake of *It Happened One Night*.

Want to know a funny thing? Hollywood producers go very highbrow if they catch a comic switching an old joke that takes thirty seconds to tell. But they go on switching old movie plots to make pictures that take eight or nine months to shoot.

The part Dick had for me was the bus driver. I told Momma I was the most driving personality in the picture. They all said I was pretty good, and I agreed. But I would have been twice as good if half of my part didn't wind up on the cutting room floor. My face is on so many cutting room floors some people think it's linoleum. I never could understand why.

Harry Cohn, of Columbia Pictures, which was the studio that made *You Can't Run Away from It*, saw me working in Las Vegas a few months after the picture was released. He came backstage and said, "You know, Henny, I liked you in that picture. I'm sorry we had to cut your part. The whole film was running too long. But I'll see that we use you again." Not long after that he died. It was bad luck for me. Worse for him.

Abbott and Costello were so grateful to me for getting them on the *Kate Smith Show*, where they were discovered for films, that they got me a part in one of their movies called *A Wave, A Wac and a Marine*. I thought the story would turn out to be about a marine who waved at a girl and got a whack.

I was cast as a gob. Later the casting director apologized to me. He said he read the script wrong. He thought it said slob.

But the most embarrassing moment of my whole motion-picture career was when Jerry Lewis gave me a part in *The Bellboy*. When I finished working, everybody on the set applauded. So I talked to Momma on the phone and told her how good I was and to be sure to see the picture when it opened in New York. Before that happened, I was cut out of the picture. She went around telling all her friends, "My son, Henny, has made his greatest movie appearance."

She took a party to see the picture, and when she didn't see me, she, naturally, asked what happened.

I told her, "You misunderstood me, Momma. I said it was my greatest *dis*appearance."

One of the screwiest screwings I ever got in Hollywood was when I was supposed to be billed as "The first talking clown working in the center ring of a circus." It sounded like a good idea. And to this day I don't know what went wrong. Posters were printed and everything. They had a big picture of me in tramp-clown makeup, playing the fiddle. The copy said:

Dobritch International Circus
Presents in the Center Ring
Henny "Emmett" Youngman
King of the one Lion-ers

> With nothing but a chair and his bare
> violin and a handful of jokes.
> April 3, 1968—Sports Arena Los Angeles,
> California.

We never played the date, but it's still a good idea. Are you listenin', Mr. Ringling?

Benny fiddles while Youngman burns. Possibly 1969.

Zinn Arthur photo

With Bob Hope and Jimmy Durante. What a bouquet of noses!

Zinn Arthur photo

Trying to steal a picture from
Tiny Tim in the year 1970.
Bill Mark photo

With Phyllis Diller and Ward Donovan before
she had her nose fixed. Must be about 1971.
Metro News photo

I know why Charlton Heston's laughing—
but why am I? Could be around 1970.

Telling Nancy Sinatra to "watch the birdie."
The year must be about 1969.

The young Youngman with Ted Collins, Kate Smith,
and Franchot Tone. 1936.

A rare picture of Milton Berle in men's clothing.
Doesn't he look cute in glasses? 1972.

Ed Sullivan said, "I don't like the hat."

I said, "How do you like this one?"
(I also changed my tie.)
Circa 1963

With Mayor Lindsay laughing at
Fun City. 1967.

With Zsa Zsa Gabor and Don Rickles in
"Beauty and the Beast"...but which one is he?
Maybe 1965. *Jules Davis photo*

King of the one-liners with the Earl of Wilson
and the Arthur of Godfrey.

Circa 1969. *Photo/Ross & Weiss Inc.*

Backstage with Groucho Marx and Marty
Rudnick, "but who knows when or where."

I'm scared because Joey Bishop's worried.
This must be 1970.
Zinn Arthur photo

**Walking onto the dance floor at El Morocco
with Fred Astaire. About 1967.**
Bigelow photo

Telling my troubles to Johnny Carson,
who was too young at the time to appreciate them.
1962.

Showing Max Asnas of the famous Stage Delicatessen
how to build a sandwich.

When he said he was Hayakawa,
I thought he was kidding and I said, "Sessue?" 1959.
United Press International

Was Jerry Lewis that funny back in 1963?
Jerry Lewis Prods. Inc. Photo

Sadie being very happy with Jimmy Stewart
and Dean Martin. But what am I laughing at?
Must be about 1965.

This picture of Carol Lawrence.
Robert Goulet, Danny Thomas, and me,
taken by the funniest-looking
photographer you ever saw. 1966.
Jules Davis Photo

The portrait of Dorian Youngman. Las Vegas. 1955.
Air Force Photo by Nellis Air Force Base, Nevada

A nice bed and breakfast place, but no vacancy.
London *Circa* 1955.
Or, you've heard of Lincoln's Gettysburg Address.
This is Winston Churchill's London address.

With Bing Crosby and Ray Bolger, and what's funny is that Bing's wearing the tie. Must be about 1950.

With Tony Martin and a fellow named
Cyd Charisse, and the year's about 1951.

Explaining to Morton Downey how a friend of mine
became a tenor. Must have been about 1930.
Photo/Ray Fisher

This picture's so old even Eddie Cantor looks
young in it. I'd say about 1930.

Holding hands across the table with
William Holden. About 1952.

With Ed Sullivan, opera star Risë Stevens, and the
Alfred Hitchcock profile after one of Ed's really
great shows.

With Momma when she used to smash baggage
for the Florida East Coast Railway. About 1946.

This is Miss Peggy Lee when she was very young.
But why don't I look young? 1943.

The two teams are Abbott and Costello and Henry and Sadie.
The umpire is Pat O'Brien. The year about 1939.

Steve Lawrence, Red Buttons, Alan King, Bishop Sheen, Milton Berle, the biggest nose in the crowd, Jack Benny, and Jan Murray. At the Friars, 1971.

J. Peter Happel photo

With Jolson and Jessel
in a jolly mood. At last
Jolson's jolly. 1944.

Philip J. Weinstein—Lawrence-Philip Studios

Sherlock Youngman, Hildegarde,
and Basil Rathbone. This shot's so
old the shoes are back in style.

Philip J. Weinstein—
Lawrence-Philip Studios

Jack Benny listens while George Burns takes a
nap and George Jessel lends an ear.
Circa 1964 *Jules Davis photo*

Eddie Fisher, Elizabeth Taylor, Mike Todd, Jr.,
and me with my mouth closed. She's the one
with the Old-Fashioned. 1954.

Trying to make Robert
Taylor laugh while he's
cheating to the camera.
Must be about 1949.

Sinatra, Tommy Dorsey, and Henny in
"The Music Lesson or Teaching Frankie
to Move His Vowels." 1937.

Matching teeth with Don Ameche, Frances
Langford, and (out of the money) Jack Carter.
1949.

Gary Youngman out-mugging Frank Sinatra,
Jerry Lester, and his old man. 1947.

Showing Charles Laughton how a young
comedian looks with his hands on his hips. 1939.

Vaudeville was killed by radio. Radio was killed by television. Now television is being killed by television.

24

Entertainment by the Tube

I'VE always been a television fan. I'm either watching it or on it. Sometimes both, watching me being on it.

To me the greatest invention in the world was videotape. It made it possible for me to go home and watch myself and see what I did wrong. I get pretty sick of *that!* But I'll never stop watching. It's so much fun to see when I do something right.

The Sunday after Lee Harvey Oswald shot President John F. Kennedy, Sadie and I, like almost everybody else in the country, were watching TV's wonderful coverage of the continuing story of the President's tragic visit to Dallas. The police were transferring Oswald to a "safer" jail. Suddenly, right before our eyes, a guy jumps out and shoots him. I don't have to describe the scene. It was shown over and over again, and I hope it will continue to be shown from time to time for years to come. The shooting of Governor Wallace looked a little like a rerun of it.

It was the first time television had ever shown a murder . . . live. And it was also the first real live murder (live murder?) I'd ever seen in which the bad guy was someone I knew.

Whenever I was in Dallas, I'd drop in on Jack Ruby's crummy little dive to see what was doing and catch up on the latest Texas scandal. If you knew Jack at all, you had to know there was something nutty about him.

One evening between shows one of the girls of the line came and sat at my table. She kept talking about Jack. She sounded afraid of him. "He's a lunatic," she said. "They're going to have to put him away someday or something." I asked her why.

"Ever since I've been dancing here, he's been trying to make me," the girl said.

"He'd be crazy not to," I said.

"Sure. Sure."—she half laughed—"but I don't like him. I don't like the way he talks. I can't stand to have him touch me. I don't like the way he looks. But he keeps coming on real strong. A couple of nights ago he beat up a guy just to try to make an impression on me."

When Jack shot Oswald, I really think he got the one thing he wanted. He cemented his name in history.

After TV got one on-camera murder, you'd think they'd have had about everything. Then along came what happened to Bobby Kennedy and another on-camera shooting of George Wallace. Pretty soon to get life insurance you'll have to promise to stay out of politics. I wonder if there's any record of what Wallace said the first time he saw the videotape of his own shooting.

What a country this is! There's a whole reel of videotape showing clearly that Bremer jumped out of the crowd, aimed a gun at Wallace, and shot him down. Then Bremer came into court and pleaded "not guilty." They should have immediately brought charges of perjury against him.

Anyway, that's the part TV plays in the history of the United States. I'm proud I've been on it so many times in so many different shows that everybody knows the name (oh, *that*) Henny Youngman. It's as familiar to everyone with a TV set as Arrid Extra Dry—which is a champagne—or Pampers—which is where the gauchos in the Argentine raise their cattle.

As TV went into the seventies, the craziness of the country was emphasized by the fact that it was a mark of distinction to be on a blueprint for lunacy called *Laugh-In*. It was supposed to show your humanity to allow yourself to be made fun of. Even President Nixon fell for the gag. I guess the only person that *Laugh-In* never tried to show the human side of was Don Rickles. The camera doesn't lie.

But before *Laugh-In*—for years before *Laugh-In*—the big prestige show for a comedian to appear on was Ed Sullivan's, which started out as *The Toast of the Town*. For years people made fun of "no-talent Sullivan," while a lot of talented people came onto the TV scene and disappeared. Like "Ol' Man River," Sullivan kept "right on rollin' along" and was just about as funny.

Unlike Milton Berle, when he was Uncle Miltie, Ed in his TV show, which set the pattern for almost all variety shows that followed, never tried to get into anybody's act. Berle got into everybody's act. And right here I want to say that it's not true that he rented all his old dresses to Flip Wilson. He sold them outright and made a nice capital gain.

Just the opposite from trying to get into your act, Sullivan tried to get stuff out of it. He didn't like anything to run very long. So if you did eight minutes in rehearsal, Ed would tell you to cut two of them. This was made worse by the fact that he insisted on telling you what to cut.

There's an old vaudeville saying, "The best ad libs are the ones you write down the night before." This is true. Woody Allen, who is as different from me as it's possible to be, and I each know exactly what we're going to do. Mess around with our routine, and you louse us up. Allen seems to be making everything up as he goes along. Not so. I seem wondering what my next joke is and can't think of it. So I say whatever comes into my head. Not so.

Well, the first time I played the *Ed Sullivan Show* I had two problems. The first was to get some new material. The second was to be allowed to deliver it the way I thought it ought to go. I'll take the two problems in order.

I had about four days to get new material. All the writers I knew I could depend on for jokes were now working in Hollywood on various shows. There were about twenty of them. I sent this same wire to each: "Going on with Ed Sullivan next Sunday. Please wire one good joke. Fast. Love. Henny."

Two days later I heard from every one of them. Each did just what I asked. Each sent me one good joke. The trouble is they'd all checked with each other and sent me the same joke.

Now the second problem. When I put the joke in my routine, Sullivan didn't like it. After the show I sent them each another wire, "Thanks for the joke. Now send me one good Sullivan."

What happened was, Ed insisted on certain cuts, certain jokes. It threw my timing way off. I bombed from coast to coast, and I knew it wasn't my fault. I didn't have the nerve to question Ed's decisions before we went on the air for fear he'd say, "Okay, if you don't want to do it my way, you're off the show." After the show I wished I had been.

I was so mad I got into a fight with Ed and didn't play the *Sullivan Show* again for five years. Another example of how tactful I always am. But after those five years were up and my salary was up several hundred percent, I played the show eight or ten times every year. Just doing the *Ed Sullivan Show* would have been a nice living.

I think Sadie and I had the first television set in Brooklyn. It must have been. Everybody in Brooklyn was in our living room looking at it. I invited all the neighbors in to see the Louis-Firpo fight. We took in more than a hundred and seventeen dollars. That includes seat cushions, beer, popcorn, hot dogs, and the price of the seat. I say "we" took in. Actually we only got 10 percent. Jack Benny had the concession.

We knew that after the fight was over, the problem would be to get everybody to go home. Jack solved that. He and I played a duet on the violin. It was mine. He didn't bring his.

In those days it was a mark of distinction to have TV. The set we had was a Hallicrafter. The screen was about the size of a paper napkin, and the picture made it look like a used paper napkin. We'd watch anything. There were a lot of hockey games. Watching hockey on that little screen was like those commercials we see now showing how some spray "kills bugs dead." I'm sure if they could think of another way to kill them, they would.

When I think of how much hockey I watched and how little I knew about the game, it reminds me of the horse player who put win, place, and show bets on every horse in every race every day and never cashed a ticket. When he called the bookie on Sunday, he was told the track wasn't open, but he could get a bet down on a hockey game. The guy said, "What do I know about hockey?"

I've already told you about the guys who came around selling imitation TV antennas that you could put on your roof to make people think you had a set. The price was two dollars. If someone came in to see a show, you told them the set was in the shop. This was generally true about people who actually had sets.

The place most people went to watch TV was in bars. The saloons had them first because at first they were too expensive. I have two or three friends who became television fans in those days, but they're all right now. They joined AA.

In those days when Berle was king of the tube, I was often on his show. I played the man. He used to run his show like a czar. He directed everything. He even told the electricians how to put in the light bulbs. Why not? To get them to work you screwed them.

Rehearsals were at Nola Studios at Fifty-third and Broadway, upstairs from Lindy's. It was great. You could send down for either a waiter to bring up some food or a comedian to bring up some jokes. Berle walked around the studio in a bathrobe with a towel around his neck like a fighter waiting to enter the ring. When he was in a scene, he'd slip off his bathrobe and put on a dress. His first marriage broke up because his wife could never go out. He was always wearing her clothes.

He wore a whistle around his neck, like a referee, and blew it to get attention. Once he came into the place, and there was no one there but me, reading a newspaper. He blew the whistle. I got up and went and sat in the penalty box.

Later, when Jackie Gleason, my old neighbor in Brooklyn, began to hit it big on the tube, I used to sit around with him in Toots Shor's with Mel Brooks or, sometimes, Bob Considine. I used to give him gags.

Not long ago on the *Larry King Show* in Miami, friends down there tell me Jackie was asked who he thought was the funniest comedian. He said, "Henny Youngman breaks me up." That was one of the gags I gave him.

Once in California I was scheduled to do a show with a cowboy fiddler named Spade Cooley. He was the only man in the world who played the violin worse than I do. The show originated in a dance hall in Long Beach and went out over KTLA. At that time KTLA was owned by Paramount Pictures and had studios right across from their main gate on Marathon Avenue. Everyone who was on the Spade Cooley show was supposed to go there to rehearse and get made up.

My brother Lester was visiting me in California at the time so I took him with me to KTLA. I rehearsed what I had to do and the floor manager said, "Everybody back here at ten P.M. for makeup. The bus leaves at eleven." There was lots of time, so Lester and I went over to the Brown Derby to get a cup of coffee. Talking to people there, we heard that Sinatra and Durante were doing a show at CBS. So we left our coffee and walked over to see Frank and Jimmy.

When we got to CBS, the crew told us they'd gone to the makeup room. So we went up there to find them. When we walked in the makeup man said, "Sit down," and motioned to two barber chairs. Before we could stop them he and his assistant began to slap pancake makeup on our faces. I decided not to stop him. I didn't want to embarrass him. Besides, I needed the makeup for the midnight show in Long Beach anyway. It was Lester's first experience.

We never did find Frank and Jimmy, but I went on KTLA

wearing CBS makeup. Lester was so proud he wouldn't take his off until he almost got picked up a week later in the New York subway. He's all right now.

If you've been paying attention so far, I don't have to tell you I'll do anything. To prove it I'd like to quote from a piece by Frank Judge of the Detroit *News*.

Henny Youngman, undisputed King of the One Liners for more than a quarter of a century, is going straight. But he has to go crooked to do it.

After 40 years in show business the 55 year old comedian plays a straight dramatic role for the first time in his life. "And for the Theater Guild, no less," Youngman says with obvious pride. "Last March the Persian Room in The Plaza in New York and now this. The kid from Brooklyn is getting there."

We interrupt this article by Frank Judge to explain the reference to the Persian Room at the Plaza. I was the first comedian to ever play that room. They'd always had classy singers, generally girls, with fancy wardrobes that the Park Avenue trade liked to look at. When the singer was a man, he wore white tie and tails. I'd never tried low comedy in a high comedy outfit like that, but I was game to have a go at it. But I wanted the best. I didn't want anybody looking at the way my coat didn't fit instead of paying attention to the jokes. So I went to one of the best tailors in New York and ordered a complete white tie outfit.

Every day I went for a fitting. He pulled a piece off here, stuck a piece on there, made marks all over the cloth, and told me to come back the next day. Day after day this went on. Finally I told him I positively had to have the suit the next afternoon for the Persian Room opening. "I wouldn't let you open without it," he said. "It'll fit like you grew up in it. Like it was made for you."

"It *was* made for me," I said.

"See," he said, "would I lie to you?"

The next day when I went to get the suit, there were a lot of people and trucks in front of the building his shop was in. Most of the people had on rubber coats. Most of the trucks were red with flashing lights. "What's burning?" I asked one of the firemen.

"A tailor shop on the third floor. They were out to lunch."

"Was there much damage?"

"Everything."

Suddenly I realized I didn't have a suit to wear that night at the

Plaza, or if I did, it would be the first charcoal gray swallowtail in town. First I didn't know what to do. Then I did the only thing I could do. I called Brooks Costume Company, gave my name and asked if I could rent a set of tails. The wise guy on the line asked if I wanted a set to match the one I had.

I wasn't in the mood for amateur jokes, so I hung up and looked in the Yellow Pages for a place that rented formal outfits to wedding parties and things like that. They told me to come right over, and in about four hours the suit was ready for me.

The next morning the reviews were not only complimentary to me, but one reviewer said I was wearing the best-looking, best-fitting full-dress suit he'd ever seen. So I bought it and wore it for the whole Persian Room run. Then a terrible thing happened. I got fat.

Now back to Frank Judge's piece. It goes on to say:

Youngman stars in a U.S. Steel Hour drama, "The Golden Thirty." The other stars in the Theater Guild production are Nancy Kovak and Bibi Osterwald. Larry Cohen, the man who wrote the original tv play describes it as a tragedy not a comedy. [I want to throw in here that he said that *before* he saw my performance!]

"It's about a borscht belt comedian who's been a flop for 25 years," Youngman explained. "He hasn't got an act and he doesn't know how to get one. He struggles to make a buck in the Catskills by insulting the very people who pay to see him. You can only insult people for so long. So he finally steals the act of a young comedian—all 30 minutes of it—and becomes a sensation."

Youngman has no qualms about playing such a heel. He says he plays it with soul. "It's a challenge, really," Youngman says with a one syllable laugh.

"Look, comedians have been stealing my material for years. Maybe it's about time I struck back."

Youngman has a simple explanation for everything that's ever happened to him in his life and that includes his delay in going dramatic. "Nobody ever asked me before."

Personally, I hope Henny sticks to his one liners. "I've got a Texas friend so rich he bought his dog a boy." Sometimes Henny switches it. "I've got a Texas friend so rich he bought his kid a chemistry set . . . DuPont."

It's doubtful if, as the thieving comedian in the Steel Hour, he'll be able to steal material that good.

"You never know," Youngman cracks. "After all it's the Steel Hour."

I don't mind saying, I was great on the show. Momma used to say, "Self-praise is no praise." But I figure if you're getting no praise anyway, you might as well throw in something of your own.

Since then, I've played a lot of legitimate roles on the stage. I played Itchy, the social director in *Wish You Were Here*. It's a musical comedy about the Mountains and could have been the story of my life.

I played the psychologist father in *The Impossible Years* in Chicago.

George Gobel, Dagmar (who makes Raquel Welch look like Twiggy), and I did *A Funny Thing Happened on the Way to the Forum*. I even played in the *James Thurber Carnival*.

I love working in a show that has a story. I even had an idea for a play to be called *Take My Wife, Please!* It wasn't anything like this book.

The hero was a guy like me. (Who else would I write it for?) He's married to a very young girl with very hot pants who demands more of him than he can deliver.

Actually it was to be a sort of three-act version of the joke about the guy who was having an affair with a nymphomaniac whose husband was on the road. They're in bed one afternoon when she hears a key in the door and says, "My God! There's my husband!"

The guy says, "Thank God he got my wire!"

In my show this comedian, in his early sixties and married to this sharp chick, likes to take her out and be seen around town in all the spots with her but . . . well . . . he has a mistress he likes to spend most of his time with. She's a nice lady a little bit younger than he is. When he comes to see her, she gives him chicken soup and home-cooked meals. They talk. They play gin. They watch TV. In other words his mistress is wifelike, and his wife behaves like a mistress. With this sort of setup his problem is getting guys to "baby-sit" with his wife, so she'll leave him alone when he comes home.

There's also a gimmick which could use different guest stars every night by having scenes in the grill room of the Friars Club where the comedian is having lunch, talking to writers and making dates for them to meet him at his apartment. He doesn't expect to keep these dates and knows that his wife will be parading around in a transparent negligee and he knows what will happen. But it doesn't.

The people he sets up for her won't go for the wife because the comic is their friend or they work for him and don't want to louse up a business connection.

Finally, one guy really falls in love with the wife, and she falls in love with something he has, and she asks for a divorce. It works out great. The kid who falls in love with the wife is the son of the comedian's mistress. Happy ending.

I even wrote the first few lines of the first act. And here they are:

ACT ONE—SCENE ONE

The living room of Danny Dilman's apartment. There's a piano with a violin case on it. All kinds of stuff are scattered all over: newspapers, scrapbooks, mail, and eight-by-ten glossies. There are some autographed pictures of stars on the piano.

As the curtain rises, the phone is ringing. When it starts to ring for the third time, Flora Dilman enters. She's a beautiful young blonde with long, straight hair, and that's all she's wearing. She rushes across stage and picks up the phone. Without waiting to hear who's calling, she speaks.

FLORA

I'm in the bath. I'll call you back.
She hangs up and runs back to the bedroom, leaving the door open. The phone starts to ring again. The front door of the apartment opens, and Danny Dilman comes in. As he takes off his coat and hat and hangs them up, he speaks to the phone.

DANNY

Aw . . . shut up!!!!!
The phone continues to ring. Danny finally goes over and picks it up. He listens a minute before he answers.

DANNY

No. It's not Flora.
He puts the phone down and wanders toward the violin, picking up some peanuts or popcorn, which he throws in

the air and tries to catch with his mouth but misses. He
leaves it on the floor, shrugs, and speaks half aloud to
himself.

DANNY

Man, would I have been a lousy juggler.

FLORA (*offstage*)

Is anyone out there?
Danny looks toward the door and nods his head to mean
yes.

FLORA (*off*)

Did someone come in?
Danny nods again more vigorously, annoyed that she did
not "hear" him the first time.

FLORA (*offstage*)

Is that you, Danny?
Now Danny is very annoyed and nods "yes" so vigorously
it could give him a headache. Maybe his toupee slips
forward. He picks up the fiddle, sits in a comfortable
chair, and starts to play, badly, for a few bars.

FLORA (*offstage*)

Are you out there, Danny?

DANNY (*as he plays*)

No. It's the fiddling burglar.
After a short pause as Danny plays.

FLORA (*offstage*)

I'm in the bath. Come on in.

DANNY

Too crowded. It's different with the Japanese. They're littler.
Danny takes some papers out of his pocket, unfolds them,

props them on the music rack of the piano, sits down at the bench, and starts to play a few bars of any sentimental standard. Then he stops, looks at paper, and reads.

DANNY

Show me a very tall African who bites his nails and I'll show you a Masai worrier.
As Danny is doing this and puzzling over the "joke," Flora enters wearing a bikini and a bra that's not hooked in back.

FLORA

Who's a worrier?

DANNY

Mr. "Masai Worrier." The kind of jokes these kids give you. It's ridiculous. Who knows what a Masai is.

FLORA

Who doesn't? You go to him for a massage.
She starts to walk around Danny in a provocative manner. He's too provoked by the material he's been handed to notice her.

DANNY

Whatever happened to jokes people can understand? "I'll show you a Masai worrier." What is that!

FLORA

I told you. A man who gives you a rub.
Flora backs up to Danny.

FLORA

Hook me, huh?
Danny has been totally unmoved by her effort to interest him. But he tries to oblige her by hooking up her bras-

siere with his chin holding his fiddle and the bow in his other hand. The bow touches her behind the ear.

FLORA (*giggling*)

Danny . . . stop . . .

DANNY

A man could make a fortune just by inventing a turtleneck bra.

FLORA

That's cute.
Danny puts down fiddle and bow and finishes hooking up the bra.

DANNY

Okay. There.

FLORA

You're supposed to pat me on the fanny when you're finished.

DANNY

Okay.
He picks up fiddle and pats her on the fanny with it.

FLORA

Ooooh . . . what big hands you have.

DANNY

Next time I'll use the bow.
He demonstrates how he'll use it as a rapier. She turns, and he starts to play the fiddle hastily.

FLORA

That was some audition you sent me to today.

DANNY

Did they ask you to read?

FLORA

They didn't even ask me to take my blouse off.

DANNY

Who needs it? If you've seen two, you've seen them all.

FLORA

Well, it's insulting. A girl goes to all the trouble to show up, and they don't even look at her.

DANNY

Flora, there's a certain kind of play where the author's lines are more important than yours. Now go back and finish your bath . . . or start a new one.
    Flora exits, and Danny picks up the phone and dials.

That's as far as I got with the play. But reading it over, I've seen successful situation comedies on TV made out of less than that. Or even a movie. I wonder what Goldie Hawn's doing?

A man goes to the racetrack and wins. He calls it luck. He goes to the track and he loses. He calls it fate. He stays home. He calls it marriage.

25

And in Conclusion

I'VE played between thirty-five and forty-five TV variety, game, and talk shows a year for as long as I can remember, which is as far back as the day before yesterday. And that doesn't include commercials. On almost every show some mention is made of how long I've been in the business. And I'm asked the number of different kinds of dates I've played. The list runs from social dances and joints to theater MC'ing, hotels, nightclubs, vaudeville, radio, motion pictures, musical comedy, summer stock, and, of course, Bar Mitzvahs.

I don't even mention that I've worked talking slot machines because who but me ever heard of a talking slot machine?

In case you think I'm kidding, here are some quotes from a news story that appeared in the Anaheim California *Bulletin* on January 19, 1971. The headline is: "New Machine Vends One-Liners." It goes on to say,

". . . your dime soon will get you more out of a certain vending machine than mere candy . . . Henny Youngman . . . he won't be wrapped in cellophane but his voice will give you a quick one-line joke along with your snack.

"Thanks for the dime, buddy," Henny intones from the vending machine innards. "My mother-in-law got a mud pack. For two days she looked great. Then the mud fell off!"

If you have forty dimes and an appetite you can eat through all of Youngman's jokes in each machine.

If you're lucky you might hit the jackpot and get these two jokes for the price of one candy bar: "I wish my brother-in-law would go to trade school so I'd know what kind of work he's out of. He tells people he's a diamond cutter. He mows the lawn at Yankee Stadium."

There's lots more to the story. For instance, now I'm trying to find a machine I can put a dime in and get in touch with the people who got me to record for their broken-down machine. It never worked properly, and another good idea is still waiting for someone to get it right. I've even lectured at colleges, which is about the same as Bar Mitzvahs except that the kids are older.

Then, of course, there are all the things I have to do for free because I have so many friends. Funny thing. For friends you do things for nothing. If they were friends, they'd pay you.

The Friars and the Lambs, two actors' clubs, are always having dinners honoring people by insulting them. There are the Friars Roastmaster Dinners and the Lambs Lambasts. The last one I did, which was last night, was a Lambast in honor of that hero of Lee Miles commercials, Rocky Graziano.

I had a gimmick for those things, but a lot of people didn't dig it. I let all the other comics on the dais make insulting cracks about the guest of honor. When I came on, I ignored him completely. Didn't look at him, didn't mention his name. What could be more of an insult? But a lot of people thought I'd missed the whole idea. They thought I was stupid. Who am I to argue? I dropped the gimmick.

Anyway, the biggest laugh at the Graziano affair was when I was talking about how sentimental Rocky is. I said, "The club just gave him a gold medal. He was so proud he had it bronzed." It was the only clean joke of the evening. That's the trouble with most of those actor club affairs. They're stag, and the stuff you have to do is so blue you can't use the jokes in public . . . only in pictures.

As I'm writing this I have the TV turned on—I have to have something to take my mind off my thoughts—and all of a sudden I come on, talking to me. That always shocks me like when you get into a car, turn on the radio, and hear yourself. Right at this moment I'm listening to one of the ten-second spots I did for Hoffman Beverages: "I just got two cases of Hoffman's for my wife . . . good deal, eh?" I'd quote some more of the Hoffman jokes, but they won't give me a ten-second plug for this book.

Then there's the Allen Funt picture *Money Talks*. If you saw it, your name must be Funt.

Allen called me a couple of months ago and said he was doing this film about the barter system . . . about eliminating money . . . even credit cards. I said, "I can see how you can get rid of money, but how can you ever get rid of credit cards?"

"That's what I want to explain," he said. "It would work like this: You go into a restaurant, eat a meal, and when the check comes, instead of paying in cash you tell jokes."

"Do I also tell jokes to pay my bail?"

He said, "Don't worry. I'll get you out if it takes a lifetime."

"Yours or mine?"

He asked if I'd do the picture. I said I didn't think it would work. But it *was* work, so I took the job. You know, a fella just starting out tries everything. So do I. Why should the young have all the fun?

Allen said he'd call me. Just for kicks I spent a day going around trying his idea. I stopped at three hot dog stands. At each I ordered the specialty of the house, bit into it, and then told them I didn't have any money but I made a lot of dough telling jokes, so I'd pay for the hot dog in jokes.

The first place the lady laughed and asked, "Are you Jewish?" I said, "I was born an atheist but converted when I found out they didn't have any holidays." She laughed again and let me walk away.

The next hot dog vendor was a man. I did the same thing and said, with my mouth full of his sausage, "I get over a thousand a night for telling jokes. At those prices this hot dog's not even worth a straight line, but I'll overpay you . . . 'I know the latest dope on Wall Street. My son!'"

The guy just waved his arm in disgust and started to push his cart away.

When I did this routine for the third hot dog vendor, he grabbed the half-eaten dog out of my hand, threw it in the street, and said, "Are you crazy or something? I ought to have you locked up!"

I said, "I'll have you locked up for dog littering."

After a few weeks I called Funt to ask him when we were going to start shooting the picture. He said, "We've already shot it."

"Without me?"

"With you. We followed you around. Didn't you ever hear of the Candid Camera?"

"Great," I said, "when do I get my check?"

"No check," he said, "we pay off in candid film."

The picture's playing right now over on Eighth Avenue, which now looks like a cross between the Reeperbahn in Berlin and Pigalle in Paris. One of the street's bewigged and bebooted vestibule Venuses walked up to the box office and asked the man if the picture, *Money Talks,* was the one about doing away with money. The guy said, "Yes. You pay for what you get with what you *have* or what you *do.*"

"Great," she said. "Let me in and let's do it."

But I really haven't time for nonsense like that. I have to get this book finished before I leave for Hollywood next week. Rowan and Martin are bringing me out there for a *Laugh-In* bit they're calling *High Noon* shoot-out. It'll be comedians meeting on a Western street to shoot gags at each other. That's why I have to finish this book before I leave. "One of them varmints may git me."

When I told Sadie about it, she said, "Do you want to do it?"

I said, "Nope."

She said, "Are you going to do it?"

I said, "Yup!"

She pleaded with me not to. I said, "A man's got to do what he's got to do." I'm ready for the next Gary Cooper part that comes along. I know all those one-syllable words. That's all I know.

But, as I was saying about interview shows, they always ask me if, among all the shows I've done, there was ever a job I was really sorry I took.

The answer is always "Yes!"

I had a booking to play a one-nighter in Rochester, New York. I was undecided whether to cancel the date or keep it. My father, who was seventy-three years old, was very sick. But the doctor assured me there was no need to cancel. "You'll be up there and back in less than twelve hours," he said. "Everything will be all right. Go and don't worry." Again I found out that doctors can be wrong.

A man can die in twelve hours. If I'd listened to my heart instead of the doctor, I might have been with Poppa at the end.

This question is also asked, sometimes, "What do you consider the most important date you ever played?"

That's easy. It was a day in May, 1928. If I remembered the exact date, Sadie would faint. She and I went to the office of James J.

Walker, New York's playboy mayor. If he weren't such a playboy, I would never have known him.

During the time that Walker was mayor, there probably wasn't a theater or spot of any kind in town that didn't get a friendly visit from His Honor. It was while I was playing in one of these places that we met and he liked me. He called me over to his table and said, "I have to make a lot of speeches. If you ever think of anything funny that I might be able to use, call me and leave your number. I'll call you back." He always did. I don't know if he ever used any of my stuff because I didn't exactly run around with him. Except one night.

We met in the lobby of the Hotel Astor. He said, "Hello, kid. Where you going?" (He always called me "kid" because that's what I was.)

I told him I was there to play a charity dinner. He said, "So am I. Come on with me."

So I followed him as a bellboy led the way to a ballroom on the second floor. There seemed to be a little unusual excitement when we walked in, but I figured this always happened when the mayor showed up. Then we were seated on the dais. It was my first time.

As soon as the speeches began, the mayor leaned over to me and said, "Kid, I think we're in the wrong room."

I had that idea from the moment a minister gave an invocation and then asked "Our Lord Jesus Christ to bless the food and all those who will partake of it."

"I was headed for a B'nai B'rith affair," I said.

"So was I," said His Honor. "Sneak out and find a phone. Tell them I'll be a little late and you'll be with me."

People who noticed me leave the table and come back in a few minutes must have figured I just couldn't control myself.

And that's the story of how Mayor James J. Walker, "Gentleman Jimmy," the man who wrote the lyric for the song "Will You Love Me in December as You Do in May?," and I played two benefits, one of them unscheduled, at the Astor one night.

Which explains how Sadie and I happened to be married in his office. His song worked for us.

Of course, as soon as Sadie's folks heard about our marriage, they insisted that we get married again by a rabbi. That was a problem. What rabbi?

There's a story that when the meanest man in town died, they couldn't find a rabbi to say a few words for him. They finally went to the next town where the man had a brother. There they found a rabbi who agreed to say a few words. He said, "His brother was worse!"

Friends of a younger generation have asked, why a rabbi? Well, the reason is slight but important. If you're married by a rabbi, you have to fast on Yom Kippur. If you're married by the mayor, you're not allowed to double park. For years Sadie and I didn't own a car on account of that. Then I figured out how to get a parking space. I bought a parked car.

Finally I've come to the time when I can enjoy the fruits of my years of hustling . . . the fruits and the nuts. The former is my family, the latter my friends.

I'm getting to know and appreciate my two children, now grown-up, and I'm trying to make it up to them for years of neglect, years when instead of reading nursery rhymes, I was reading timetables. I still think the timetables are funnier and easier to understand. Who wants to read to his kids about a girl who gets herself mixed up with seven weird midgets?

The trouble was when Marilyn and Gary were little, I had to choose between getting to know them and feeding and clothing them. So, naturally, for a long time, my kids and I didn't understand each other at all. But then, did *my* father understand *me?*

Gary is now a successful film maker, doing what he wants to do and I'm proud of him. Marilyn's in the advertising business, and she and I love each other very much. And her son, my grandson, Larry Kelly, and I are real pals: I think he wants to follow in my footsteps, so I do what I can to explain show business to him. He explains everything else to me. He wants to be a critic. My *own* grandson!

By the time you read this Sadie and I will have been married more than forty-five years. None of them were easy for her. My father's nickname for my mother was Glicka. It means lucky. He meant she was lucky to have married him. Sadie should call me Glicka for the same reason.

Many times, I'm sure, she's said to herself, "Take my husband . . . please!" And now it's worse than ever because she sees more and more of me because I'm home more often.

Where is home? What do you like? We have a place in New York City. We have a place in Miami Beach. We have a place in Woodstock, New York, and we have a place in Palm Desert, California. I could do a tour of one-night stands just going home.

How else would you want it for a man whose father had itching feet which he inherited from *his* father? Now I have them. We haven't had a new pair of feet in the family for three generations.

Now I'm doing what I know I like to do best. TV guest shots, one-nighters, and short engagements that don't keep me away from home too long. Any home.

For a while I thought I'd like to make movies. I did it. It's monotonous. You sit around a lot. It's all right for men like Dean Martin. He drinks. I don't. Poppa used to say I had no *sitzfleisch*. He was right. Getting up every morning and driving the same route to the same studio to see the same people on the same job month after month would bore me stiff. I suppose it could also make me rich. But money isn't everything. There are also stocks, bonds, insurance policies.

Once I thought I'd like to be a legitimate actor on Broadway, a funny one. And those who have seen my acting say it's pretty funny. But it's just like making movies, only worse. You have to make the same thing happen over and over again six nights a week and two matinees. That's like reading a roller towel.

I started out in show business playing the violin and saying whatever came into my head. And that's what it turns out I still like to do best. The only thing I haven't tried is having my own TV show. I might like that if it could be done so it wouldn't tie me down to one place too long. As it is, I do more TV shows than most of those who have their own and only do twenty-six or thirty-nine shows a year.

To sum up, how many men can walk down almost any street in almost any city and have people holler after them, "Hey, Henny!"? How many men are there named Henny?

How many men have achieved this kind of recognition and remained as sweet, natural, and lovable as me?

And in the end, how many men can wind up a life having fun doing exactly what they like to do best and be well paid for doing it?

If you know how many, count me in.

Call me Glicka.